Global Pension Crisis

Global Pension Crisis

Unfunded Liabilities and How We Can Fill the Gap

RICHARD A. MARIN

To Russ,
Thanks for
listening
Rich

WILEY

Published by John Wiley & Sons, Inc., Hoboken, New Jersey.
Published simultaneously in Canada.

For general information on our other products and services or for technical support, please contact our Customer Care Department within the United States at (800) 762-2974, outside the United States at (317) 572-3993 or fax (317) 572-4002.

Wiley publishes in a variety of print and electronic formats and by print-on-demand. Some material included with standard print versions of this book may not be included in e-books or in print-on-demand. If this book refers to media such as a CD or DVD that is not included in the version you purchased, you may download this material at http://booksupport.wiley.com. For more information about Wiley products, visit www.wiley.com.

Library of Congress Cataloging-in-Publication Data

Marin, Richard A., 1954-
    Global pension crisis : unfunded liabilities and how we can fill the gap / Richard A. Marin.
        pages cm. – (Wiley finance series)
    Includes bibliographical references and index.
    ISBN 978-1-118-58236-7 (cloth); ISBN 978-1-118-58249-7 (ebk); ISBN 978-1-118-58247-3 (ebk)
1. Pensions.   2. Pension trusts.   3. Individual retirement accounts.   I. Title.
    HD7091.M2347 2013
    331.25'2–dc23

                                                                          2013014089

Printed in the United States of America

10 9 8 7 6 5 4 3 2 1

*This book is dedicated to the memory of Jerry Haas,
one of my mentors at Johnson at Cornell University,
who always encourages me to keep getting up when I fall
and who wrote and taught with enthusiasm
for the love of knowledge.*

Contents

Foreword

Rich Marin's *Global Pension Crisis* is a lively, entertaining, yet terrifying book. Before you read very far into it, you'll realize that looming Boomer retirements are a ticking time bomb that threatens even those who have saved prudently for most of their lives. That's because many millions of others will enter retirement with virtually no private savings. The second group, which is far larger than the first, will face unmet needs that governments will find politically impossible to ignore. And to meet those needs, we'll need lots of additional tax revenue, which can only come from those in a position to provide it. As Willie Sutton replied when asked why he robbed banks, "that's where the money is."

So no matter whether you have planned carefully for your retirement or you haven't, there's some tough sledding ahead. For most of us, private pension plans, Social Security payments, and other assets will combine to generate a flow of monthly income that's much smaller than what we had grown accustomed to spending during our working lives. As people in scores of other countries demonstrate every day, it's possible to live comfortably on even only a small fraction of the average American retiree's Social Security check. So it might seem that future retirees could get along well enough simply by tightening their belts. But it would be a mistake to think that cutting back would be simple or painless.

Retirees can and will tighten their belts, but that won't be enough, because what we feel we need depends so strongly on the social environment. As a young man just out of college, I lived for two years as a Peace Corps volunteer in a village in Nepal. My house there had two rooms; it had no electricity or plumbing, and its grass roof leaked when it rained heavily. At no time did that house ever strike me as unsatisfactory, since it was in fact considerably nicer than the houses of the other teachers in the school where I taught. But it's one thing to live in a hut in a place where huts are the norm, and quite another to live in one when most others live in mansions. In any American community, if you lived in a house like the one I lived in in Nepal, your children would be ashamed to invite their friends over. Context plays a similarly powerful role in retirees' evaluations of their living standards. Those who are forced to tighten their belts will endure some painful adjustments.

People typically employ two different frames of reference when they reflect on a question like "How are things going?" One is interpersonal: "How am I doing compared to others around me?" And the other is intrapersonal: "How am I doing now compared to how I was doing before?" *Global Pension Crisis* suggests that tens of millions of American retirees are poised to take big hits on both fronts.

Although struggling retirees may take comfort that many others are in the same boat, they'll also see that millions of other retirees are continuing to prosper. Unlike the three decades right after World War II, when incomes grew at almost 3 percent a year for families up and down the income scale, most income growth during the ensuing four decades has been heavily concentrated among those who earned the most to begin with. Those who prospered during those decades will thus continue to be able to afford the amenities that support health and vitality in retirement, whereas those who retire without adequate savings will not. For the latter group, the contrast is bound to be painful.

Their discomfort will be reinforced by the contrast between their preretirement and post-retirement standards of living. People who retire with little savings and are forced to get by on Social Security alone will typically be able to spend less than half of what they spent before retirement. Again, there are many people around the globe who seem to live comfortably while spending even less than that in absolute terms. But even for those people, having to abandon an accustomed standard of living can be extremely unsettling.

The current deficit in retirement savings took a long time to develop, and the resulting problems will require an equally long time to solve. But the important point is that these are soluble problems. The United States is still a very rich country. Growth rates have slowed in recent years, but technology and growing prosperity in emerging markets promise renewed robust growth going forward. If we act quickly, intelligent financial planning can enable us to meet the current challenge.

But we're unlikely to respond forcefully to that challenge unless it becomes more broadly recognized. And that's the main reason to celebrate the publication of *Global Pension Crisis*.

ROBERT H. FRANK

Preface

This book is a direct result of six years of teaching the practicum in asset management at Cornell University's Johnson Graduate School of Management. In 2007, when the markets dealt Bear Stearns Asset Management (BSAM), via two of its hedge funds, a deathblow, we spent 11 days in June in the top three news items in the *Wall Street Journal*. In case you were out of the country that month, it all ended abruptly for me as the Chairman and CEO of BSAM. In the first few days that followed I took a call from my old professor Joe Thomas, who was then the dean of Johnson. He called to suggest that if I wanted a break from Wall Street for an indefinite time, the school had a place for me teaching the practicum.

When I accepted the offer for a part-time position, Dean Thomas told me to spend a semester helping with the asset management curriculum and students and find topics to teach that were needed and inspired me. What I found was a hunger for a course about hedge funds, with which I clearly had *too much* recent experience. What I found was an absence of teaching about securities finance and securities lending (I actually found very few courses in any business school on the topic). I had recently revitalized my involvement in that arcane arena. And finally, what I also found was a desperate need for more education about pension funds and the impact they would have on the world of finance that students would be facing. I had spent a lot of time in the past 20 years doing a lot in the pension and insurance arenas.

Pensions and their kissing cousin, insurance, are very specialized fields in finance and, unless your school has gathered a faculty in that specific space, the chances are your students get no exposure to the subject. I found this the case at Johnson.

So I crafted a course series that I call the Alpha Series, starting with a review of hedge funds, moving up to securities finance and securities lending, and then culminating with a pension course. This would logically emphasize the intersection of pensions and hedge funds. It has become a very popular course series at Johnson. I believe it is popular because it is relevant and I bring to it my 36 years of experience from every corner of Wall Street, anecdotes and all.

Along the way I have had some great students each year. Many stay in touch with me and feed my thirst for data and knowledge from the front lines in their chosen arenas.. One student in particular, Ari Weber, went on to become my teaching assistant, my associate (at a hedge fund we launched), and now, on this project, my researcher and sometimes first draft writer. It is particularly valuable when a member of the Baby Boom generation writes about the Privilege Gap and impending generational warfare to have a co-conspirator from Generation X to keep you honest. It's nice to think that young people like Ari and his Gen X brethren might be able to fix some of the mistakes we Boomers are leaving behind.

Let me be clear—I am not an academic, I am not a researcher, and I am not a pension expert. I have a great respect for primary research and the work that flows from it, but that is not what I do. There is no primary research in this book, just secondary research building on the work of those with the patience and rigor to do it. I actually do testify as an expert witness on hedge funds and securities finance (and even touch on pensions in that capacity), and I have been around pensions from every direction, but it is such a complex topic I hesitate saying I am an expert. Luckily I know a few who do qualify as experts in the field. What I am is an aggregator of data, an integrator of knowledge, a translator of complexity and, more than anything, a storyteller.

The hedge fund story is easy to tell. What student doesn't want to learn how to make $1 billion per annum? Securities finance is an arcane and misunderstood jaw-dropper for finance geeks, so that's fun and rewarding. But never have I found a better, more compelling story than the story of the impending pension crisis that stalks us. This is a story that grabs everybody I speak to about it, whether they are academics, students, practitioners, or just common folk. It is an interesting blend of economics, behavioral finance, actuarial science, demographics, economic anthropology, geopolitical strategy, and plain old common sense. The story hangs together. It is big, it is logical, and it needs to be heard, so here goes.

Acknowledgments

There are many people I must thank for encouraging me to write this book. To Kim, my lovely and caring wife, thank you for trying to be a good listener as I read my latest chapters to you in bed (very romantic). To my three kids, Roger, Carolyn, and Thomas, for giving me the fountain of youth by forcing me to keep working. To David Taggart, my friend and agent, who goaded me into seeking a book deal and then getting one for me faster than I could imagine. To Hal Bierman for teaching me finance even though I knew no accounting. To Bob Frank who inspired me to think that economics ideas could be made inspiring. To my contributors, Peter Freund (SynFunds), Steve Keating (PRT), and Scott Molnar (The Yale Model), thank you for your insights and help. And finally, to my "Boyo" Michael Walsh for constantly reminding me that we're "a long time dead."

About the Author

Rich Marin, after a long career on Wall Street, now serves as President and CEO of the New York Wheel, a major project being built on New York Harbor at the "Gateway to America." He also teaches finance and asset management at The Johnson Graduate School of Management at Cornell University where he is a Clinical Professor of Asset Management. He has worked as a senior finance professional and management committee member for three major firms (Bankers Trust, Deutsche Bank, and Bear Stearns), ran a $3 billion distressed property company (AFI-USA), and launched both a successful venture capital fund (Beehive Ventures) and a distressed mortgage hedge fund (Ironwood Global). He has recently taken on expert witness work in securities litigation representing mostly pension funds in their hedge fund and securities finance activities. He is also an advisor to several specialized consulting firms including RogersCasey and Penbridge Advisors, a leading Pension Risk Transfer firm.

As a senior Wall Street executive, entrepreneur, and teacher of the investment practicum, he writes for several professional publications, the *Cornell Business Journal, Cornell Alumni Magazine,* and contributes as a columnist for *COO Connect,* a professional hedge fund peer network website. Rich began writing in the 1980s for pleasure, and in 1998 wrote a story that was selected from 3,000 entrants by HBO and was subsequently made into the top-rated (by *The New York Times* and *Daily News*) *Subway Stories,* starring Jerry Stiller and Steve Zahn. He also loves and reviews movies regularly when not riding his motorcycles somewhere in the world.

CHAPTER 1

Your Worst Nightmare

It's 2050 and you are surprised to still be alive. You actually feel pretty good and the combination of a new titanium hip and your daily regimen of a customized Corrective Cocktail of diuretic, beta-blocker, statin, and a few new nanobots seems to keep you on a pretty even keel. You worked longer than many and both did well professionally and saved regularly, but at 96 you have been formally retired for one-quarter of your life. Your children are hoping to set a time frame soon for retirement and your grandchildren are in the peak of their careers, starting to focus on the cost of putting your great grandchildren through college.

You are one of the lucky ones. Your savings have lasted and you live comfortably. Many of your friends are still around, though mostly those who could afford the Corrective Cocktail market since Medicare and many private health insurers simply could not afford the preventative regimen. You sleep reasonably well thanks to increasing doses of soporifics in the Cocktail, but you wake thinking about all the others and what will become of them.

Your old high school buddy Rob, who was a fireman for 30 years, was just on the news. It seems he was accosted at the supermarket by young blue-collar workers who took offense at his buying steak and beer. Illegal websites highlighting state pensioners drawing pensions over certain amounts have proliferated, and groundswell movements of overtaxed and put-upon young workers are banding in community pension vigilante groups. This particular group underestimated Rob's belief that he deserved every ounce of red meat and beer. For their righteous trouble, they got doused in Michelob Light by one ornery ex-fireman.

THE FAMILY

Linda and Barbara

In 2050, you have one sibling left, an older sister, Linda, who is 98 and lives on the outskirts of Las Vegas. She moved there in 2015 when the real estate oversupply caused home sales to go begging and banks were so tired of carrying foreclosed properties in bulk that they sold entire tracts of too-long-vacant homes to hedge funds positioning to make a killing on distressed property. Those hedge funds were funded by large pension funds and sovereign wealth funds. When the markets simply did not recover in certain areas, the pension funds attacked in a manner akin only to what *Wild Kingdom* would describe as the antelope taking down the lion. Pension funds have been forced to take on more aggressive tactics just to try to keep up with the massive cash demands on their dwindling resources.

Nowhere was this more notable than in the gambling capital of the world, since gambling had become a ubiquitous revenue generator for all but the most puritanical of states, and you could get better slot machine odds on the West Side of Manhattan than you could in Las Vegas. The hedge funds had to suspend distributions and finally distributed assets in kind . . . causing the sovereign wealth funds to dump their allocation of single-family homes into the hands of the pension funds. The pension funds cut a deal with an insurance company that was shifting its business model into retirement community management. Today some stronger pension funds seem to have moved to the top of the food chain while the more wounded ones are ruthlessly and sometimes foolishly forced to be active risk-takers.

Linda likes Las Vegas, but due to the heat she seldom leaves the house, except to go to the outdoor pool in the townhouse complex. She has her daughter, Barbara, nearby to watch over her. Barbara does the bookkeeping for her son's garage door business and several of his friends' local support service businesses. Linda has enough to survive, but there is an interesting dynamic underway. Barbara juggles Linda's lifestyle (certainly providing the necessities), but tries to preserve what little capital is left since she is the logical inheritor . . . and she does have people who depend on her. The condo gets properly maintained since that is a preserving asset, but the slot machine allowance has clearly suffered . . . as have gambling stocks in general.

Barbara is brilliant. She found an old used video poker machine for $100 and put it in Linda's living room. Linda plays it all day, but regularly asks Barbara why, when she wins, it doesn't pay out so many coins. Barbara hasn't figured out how to explain that it is set to continuously recycle the 50 quarters she puts in it, and only that. It's not clear Linda would grasp the economics of the situation anyway, but Barbara figures it saves $500 per month in gambling losses. Given that Linda needs a cane to walk now, saving her from the long casino treks that are no longer broken up by high-end retail shops, seems like a blessing . . . at least to Barbara.

Dave and Sharon

Your older brother, Dave, who never went on for graduate work like you did, never really left your old hometown. He worked for years for the municipal zoning department and retired at 62 with a decent pension, supplemented by his Social Security and his wife of many years' teacher's pension. He moved to the west coast of Florida 38 years ago, in 2012, to take advantage of the soft real estate market. He rode his sedentary lifestyle to the age of 85, but died in 2035, and was survived by his second wife, Sharon, who lived out her life until 2040 going for her daily pilgrimage to the Nordstrom in Sarasota. His pension survivorship benefits made that possible and Sharon, who always said in the last 20 years of their life together that she would wear a red dress to his funeral, did just that . . . and it was bought at Nordstrom. When you arranged for her funeral a few years ago, you had her buried in that red dress.

Michael and Beth

Dave's son, Michael, followed in Dad's footsteps and joined the local municipality after college. The difference was that where Dave had gone to a state school that was virtually tuition-free, the government could no longer afford to offer state and federal tuition subsidies. So, even though Michael attended the same state school as his father, he graduated with $180,000 of student loans accruing at 3.4 percent. Free higher education is not over with altogether; you just have to achieve it via defaulting on your student loans, killing your credit rating for seven years, and then hoping Congress doesn't legislate bigger penalties, which has been a regular op/ed topic in more militant newspapers. It has occurred to you that Michael may soon suffer the same fate as Rob if these anti-pensioner groups proliferate.

Michael's municipal salary level is enough to live a decent local lifestyle and pay interest on the loans, but he is unsure how he will ever pay off the principal. Michael always joked about how he hoped Dave would remember him in his will. By the time Dave died, "remember" was about all he was able to do for Michael since there was not much else left.

Michael is now staring at an inability to service his old student debt, an inability to fund anything for his own children's education . . . and then there is his own retirement to worry about. Years ago, the municipal workers' union was forced to trade off future employee pension benefits just to retain job levels and living wage salaries. The Faustian bargain they struck was about preserving Dave's cost of living adjustments and spousal survival and Michael's wage levels in exchange for dramatically reduced funding obligations into a 457 Plan [the municipal version of 401(k)]. The whole concept of a defined benefit plan like Dave had gotten was taken completely off the table, but when Michael was 25 that seemed okay, since his plan was to save enough in his 457 to make up for it.

That was a nice concept, and Michael did save, but he kept putting his funding allocation into whatever funds did well last year. You've heard that called "cocktail party investing," and things never seemed to work out very well with his choices. He once tried to calculate what would have happened if he had just picked the low money fund option. When he realized his return rate was almost 6 percent below that (yes, that meant he had actually *lost* money), he decided to stop calculating and just put all his allocation in money funds even though they never seemed to provide much appreciation at all.

Well, at least he had his wife Beth's defined benefit plan to lean on, or so he thought. She has worked for years as a flight attendant for a major airline . . . until it went bankrupt and they got a notice that her pension was being taken over by the Pension Benefit Guaranty Corporation in Washington, DC. That notice said that the **PBGC was a "quasi-governmental" entity that did not carry the full faith and credit of the United States Government** (emphasis added into the letter). Michael did not know what that ultimately meant, but he did note that the PBGC had turned down one merger proposal from another airline and each monthly statement now showed funded and unfunded amounts. There was an asterisk next to the unfunded portion and a disclaimer at the bottom of the page. This did not make Michael feel better when he went to sleep at night after clocking out of his second job as a security guard.

Kim

Your wife, Kim, is five years your junior, and has had dementia for the better part of a decade. She is as sweet and beautiful as ever and you love her dearly, but her joints gave out due to her years as a musical theater dancer. After two knee replacements and continuous bone degeneration from a combination of osteoporosis and rheumatoid arthritis, the surgeon said it was best that she simply use a wheelchair. The insidious thing is that while every athlete knows that the legs and knees go first, they do not necessarily realize that without the legs the exercise level and reduced ability for aerobic exercise takes its toll on reduced blood flow to the brain to ward off the demon dementia for as long as possible. The slippery slope of aging has everything to do with staying active, and anything that reduces that ability increases the risk of dementia.

You keep playing and replaying that old movie, *The Notebook*, for her (or maybe for you) and you realize that Nicholas Sparks, the author, was onto something that was very prescient. You also find yourself replaying the song from *The Highlander* in your head: Who wants . . . to live . . . forever. . . .

Pete and Geoffrey

Your kids (Pete, age 68, and Nancy, age 64) have their own issues to worry about. Pete kicked around in his twenties and finally got a job with benefits, but only a 401(k) plan without company match. It was not until he was almost 40 that he began even thinking about retirement savings. But the retirement income issue gets lost behind the health-care cost issue for Pete. Pete is gay and he and his partner Geoffrey have wended their way through the domestic partnership liberalization trend of this century. They feel they have that mostly worked out, but there's the whole retiree medical benefit issue. The good news is that they have a level playing field with heterosexual couples. The not-so-good news is that health-care costs have continued to skyrocket over the past 50 years.

This has had a strange double whammy for the Generation X crowd like Pete. Not only does he have to suffer rising health-care costs, but he also has a lot less coverage than you had! He also has been paying the Health Care Surcharge that started 40 years ago during the Obama administration at 3.8 percent of virtually all income . . . even capital gains and dividends. That surcharge has had to gradually rise to 8.5 percent to support the combination of rising health-care costs and "deteriorating" demographics, with fewer wage earners supporting more retirees on Medicaid. The dynamics of pension costs and health-care costs turn out to be pretty similar.

As for retirement income security, Pete and Geoffrey have pretty much decided that their only solution is to simply not retire. Pete sat down with a retirement specialist when he turned 60 (pretty much when everyone starts to wonder what their retirement picture looks like). The advisor did the math on a retirement calculator program and was just rude enough to state quite bluntly that, like the motorist asking for directions in the little Maine coastal town, "You can't get there from here." The rub was that Pete had simply started saving for retirement too late. He was saving the right amount. He was allocating his investments well. He was not fiddling and trying to time the market only to be chasing his tail. But he had started too late.

For the past 100 years, business school students have lost this bet to learn about the time value of money: "Would you rather have $1 million or $0.01 (a penny) doubled every day for 30 days? How about doubled for

27 days?" The answer has not changed in 100 years (or, actually, since the time of the Phoenicians). That is, that a penny doubled for 30 days is worth over $5.37 million, but a penny doubled for just 27 days is only worth $671,000. What is the point of this age-old example? Well, for retirement purposes, the benefit of compounding has always been the Holy Grail. If you started soon enough, if you saved enough, and if you have been able to compound (invest) at a decent rate, you could have multiplied your retirement nest egg to a size that could have indeed lasted you for your natural life span and could have left your other savings for their intended purposes (gifting, wealth transfer, health care, etc.). While all these things were necessary ingredients for a good retirement outcome, the *key* element has always been the retirement cycle of 40-plus years. That was the power that needed to be harnessed for retirement planning to work whether at the personal, institutional, or national level.

Nancy and Anthony

Daughter, Nancy, and her first and only husband, Anthony, are in a very different place. They fell out of love many years ago, but have stayed together out of economic necessity. They are both conservative and fiscally responsible sorts who are frugal and oriented toward planning. Nancy is no financial wizard, but she instinctively knew that starting to save while young was sensible. Ask her to answer the B-School time value of money question and she would tell you to go away, but in her gut she understands the importance of time and the accumulation of savings.

Nancy runs a retail store for a large chain and gets full benefits. Anthony is a local trust and estates attorney who makes a decent living, but the overabundance of lawyers has clearly brought the hourly rate down to minimal levels and the combination of Internet virtual lawyering and less wealth transfer to worry about has made his practice the modern-day equivalent of the ambulance chaser. In fact, he thinks of himself as sort of a mall scooter chaser. But he does understand money, investments, and the perils of retirement.

Nonetheless, they have enough for retirement even now, if they choose a frugal spot like the Blue Ridge area of North Carolina, an area they are both fond of for its hiking trails and laid-back way.

Neither Nancy nor Anthony is bound to their area of suburban Baltimore. They figure they can transfer their work to wherever they choose to live in retirement, but they are drawn to staying in the area mostly to help their kids out as much as possible. They have a boy, Jesse, and a girl, Valene, who are both married and have kids of their own.

Jesse and Sofia

As your oldest grandchild, Jesse has been the apple of your eye. He and Sofia met in Brazil, where Sofia is from. Jesse is an engineer who got a scholarship to Carnegie Mellon and chose to focus on structural engineering. He graduated in 2017 and, during an internship with Cargill, he went to Brazil to work on a series of high-tech and massive grain elevators.

Brazil has spent its oil and natural resource wealth wisely by reinvesting it in developing its vast agricultural lands in the south where the climate is more like the Pampas of Argentina than the jungles of the Amazon. While the jungle topsoil of the north is denuded of nutrients and makes productive agriculture challenging, the southern area of Brazil provides the potential to feed the world. Major commodities companies like Cargill are the new GMs of the world. The old adage, "As goes GM, so goes the nation," can be updated to "As goes Cargill, so goes the world."

Sofia comes from an old, Portuguese rubber baron family that migrated to Porto Alegre 150 years ago and still has holdings in the hundreds of thousands of acres of fertile farmland. They are on the list of Brazilian billionaires, but only modestly so, given that 40 of the top 100 billionaires of the world are now of Brazilian descent. Nevertheless, like many families of great wealth, they live modestly and focus locally, so Sofia's decision to return to the United States with her *marido* was frowned upon, but eventually accepted.

Jesse and Sofia both work in Washington, DC. He is rising in the engineering department of Cargill and doing quite well, and Sofia focuses her attention on international human rights work. It is interesting to her that her family controls the lives of perhaps 300,000 local families in southern Brazil and here she is working to make sure they all have a voice in their destiny. Her father doesn't understand her thinking and keeps saying that one needs to be firm but fair with the workers. He provides retirement plans for his workers exactly as is minimally required by the Brazilian government. Every worker has post-retirement health-care benefits, a guaranteed and fully funded defined benefit plan with spousal survival, and even a small wealth transfer bucket. Sofia feels it is not sufficient.

Meanwhile, Jesse is working hard to save enough from his salary and bonuses for their only child's education. He is determined to pre-fund all of Thomas's college and graduate school costs and refuses to discuss taking money from Sofia's trust for that purpose. Cargill has a 401(k) plan with a generous match and Jesse was smart enough to put 20 percent of it in Cargill phantom equity (Cargill remains a very large private company), but too conservative to put more than that in one stock . . . too bad since Cargill has gone 11X over the 10 years Jesse has worked there.

Valene

Valene is your granddaughter, and you never thought you would be faced with a family rift over prosperity or lack thereof. In the movie *The Man in the Iron Mask*, Leonardo DiCaprio plays both the prince and the pauper, who was his twin brother destined for no reason other than lack of birthright to a dreadful life in an iron mask. If Jesse is the family's prince, Valene is living in the stifling mask of insufficiency. She is a college graduate working as a programmer for PayPal Bank and Trust as a consultant. Her husband, Zack, is a freelance production assistant for Facebook Reality Entertainment.

Google and Pay Pal are now the biggest consumer banking companies and Mark Zuckerberg is now the Samuel Goldwyn of modern reality programming. Despite working for such prosperous firms, neither Valene nor Zack enjoys benefits of any kind. This gap is compliments of the post-Obama Republican administration when Congress passed, and the new president signed, the Mobile Workers Self-Determination Act. This act makes it unnecessary for big tech companies (especially those threatening to redomesticate to New Zealand, the tax haven of choice since 2025) to provide any benefits to the newly expanded 1099 (independent tax contractor status) consultants.

Valene and Zack can barely scrape together their quarterly tax payable bills, much less fund their IRA and IHC (Individual Health Care) accounts. Those linger in the $60,000 range in total . . . just enough for six months of Corrective Cocktail when they need it.

So let's review the family tree:

- **Linda and Barbara:** One living sibling and her daughter, making do, hoping to save some inheritance money.
- **Dave and Michael:** One deceased sibling and his son, barely scraping by with a big hole to dig out of and no hope for a decent retirement.
- **Kim:** An ailing spouse (let's not even discuss occasional sorties from ex-wives) and a dwindling savings account.
- **Pete and Geoffrey:** A gay son and his partner who are playing retirement catch-up.
- **Nancy and Anthony:** A daughter and her estranged husband staying together by need and reasonably well set for a fair retirement.
- **Jesse:** A grandson who was lucky enough to marry well into an emerging markets family.
- **Valene:** A granddaughter devoid of any sort of retirement security.
- **Thomas:** A great-grandson who may have enough money for his education . . . and let's not even ask about his pension.

THE WORK

You worked almost until your 70th birthday (and found it invigorating). Unfortunately, you are the global exception in many regards. You spent the time with your retirement calculator and made sure you had enough retirement income to keep you going 20 percent past your life expectancy, which at 70 was 88 years old. That meant you budgeted for your savings to last you until you were . . . 93. Oops. But luckily, you are a pretty good investor and planner, and you adjusted as you went so you and your spouse are still good for another three or four years without a problem.

Of course, that won't help your kids since you've pretty well eaten up whatever inheritance you or they were hoping for. You're not sure it would matter much anyway since the government was forced decades ago to reverse itself on the wealth transfer rules, and inheritance tax rates have risen by necessity to almost 90 percent, a trend that has been followed in Europe, where the age-old tradition of inherited wealth has completely gone away. The world is gripped by the need to finance this retirement shortfall, and anything that looks discretionary or is not nailed down is heavily taxed to fill the gap.

What were paternalistic companies in the twentieth century have turned into outsourcing way stations for employees as they literally, but mostly virtually, carry their toolkits with them from situation to situation. In the post–World War II world, employers had just lived through the war years where shortage of raw materials was only eclipsed by shortages of trained labor. The worldwide cultural shift to broaden the workforce to include both men and women was a necessity. Rosie the Riveter proved that women could do the work and the postwar education emphasis, compliments of the G.I. Bill and a peacetime mentality, began preparing women for more and more workplace responsibility. That was a good thing because child labor was becoming increasingly frowned upon, depending on the degree of development of each country.

This all made the growing American corporation an "enlightened" employer of choice long before the term was ever coined. At the top of the list of demands from this bedraggled lot of veterans was the right to a peaceful and prosperous retirement. Security was the goal and now that national and global security was restored, retirement security was a priority. This spawned the proliferation of defined benefit plans that cradled employees in the bosom of the mother corporation. This same security blanket turned out to be the demon spawn for the corporate CFO.

By the end of the 1960s, the Baby Boomers were out of the womb, and it was time to get those growing pensions regulated so that everyone played by the rules . . . peace, love, and happiness for the working man meant being sure that his pension was being properly looked after. By now the paternalistic enlightened corporation was "The Man," and you had to WATCH him every second or he would steal your soul . . . and your pension. So enter ERISA. No, that is not the name of some IBM supercomputer. It stands for the Employee Retirement Income Security Act, and it was promulgated in 1974 and is perhaps the most arcane and devious tool of corporate torture ever invented (though Sarbanes-Oxley would give it a run for its money in 30 years). It would make Torquemada blush, and it was all about making sure Baby Boomers had a new pair of shoes to wear on the shuffleboard court.

The Investment Arena

I need to digress for a moment because it is important to note that the advent of ERISA had many unintended and good consequences besides the pain and suffering it caused CFOs. You have to start by buying into my assumption that, regardless of your politics or your religion, when it comes to retirement income, Pearl Bailey was right. She said something like, "I've been rich and I've been poor, and believe me, rich is better." So to get more retirement income, you need better investment results.

Better investment results do not just happen, and they do not just happen all across the retirement management spectrum. It took years for what is called Modern Portfolio Theory to take root and for investment professionals to shift from banks doing balanced fund management (60 percent "nifty-fifty" stocks and 40 percent government and corporate bonds) to boutique investment firms specializing in everything from small cap equities to high yield debt, and then on to alternative investments that broke the bonds of constrained investing in search of what was commonly called alpha (outperformance).

The road wars in *Mad Max* were child's play in contrast to the road wars in the search for alpha after the Great Recession. Hedge funds and private equity firms morphed, grew, and expanded to the point where they were the dominant financial houses of the twenty-first century. Their hunting grounds became the big game of pension fund management. Pension funds were forced to run as they always had in herds like wildebeests with the predators on their heels. They were so underfunded by that time that they simply had to throw the "Hail Mary" pass every play to have any hope of meeting their obligations. The predators produced modest returns, which had only trace elements of alpha as investment outperformance became the unicorn of the investment veld, but management and incentive fees just kept rolling in.

Pete and Geoffrey's penny is worth a whole lot more in 30 days than it is in 27 days. And if we weren't doubling it (100 percent return) each day, but increasing it by 50 percent, well then, instead of over $5 million in 30 days, you would have only $1,278. It's a lot tougher to retire on that, right? Let's get a little more real than our penny trick. A professional money manager can generally outperform a regular nonprofessional investor by 3 percent (and that assumes you are being fairly intelligent about your investing and *not* trying to time the market). So if a pro can do 8 percent, you can do 5 percent on average. If you put away $10,000 per year for 40 years, that's an absolute total of $400,000 of savings. The professional would turn that into $2,590,565, while the amateur would end up with $1,207,998. The power of compounding has given you a 6.5x multiplier on your money if done professionally and a 3x multiplier if done at home. This should tell you two important things:

1. That the retirement life cycle of 40 years works nicely to magnify your savings.
2. That what you earn on your money makes a whole lot of difference over that 40 years.

Pension Math

I guess the time value of money lessons we discussed with the penny eluded the postwar managers. Let's take a simple look at pension math (stay with me, it's actually VERY simple):

- Calculate how much you will owe employees when they retire.
  - Figure out when those payments start and how long they will last (how long they will live).
  - Add in any spousal survival period.
  - Discount that by a reasonable rate to reflect inflation and investment returns.
    - That equals how much you will need to fund that promise.
- Now, figure how much you must put in the pot every year and how well your investments will perform.
- Now, just be sure those two balance.

This seems easy, but it is actually very hard. It's hard to know what rate to discount the future obligations at and it's hard to estimate how long people will draw benefits, when they will retire, and when they will die. It's also hard to know how much to fund each year since so much depends on the investment returns you achieve over 40 years.

Here's a pernicious example to show you how pension math can bite you. In the second decade of the century, following the Great Recession (some would say *because* of it), interest rates went down to record low levels. This was due to risk perceptions and the flight of capital to the lowest risk investments investors could find. It was also due to pension funds moving out of equities into bonds for both risk and volatility reasons. Bonds are simply safer and less volatile and that seemed like a better fit for many pension managers. Of course, bonds underperform equities over time, and the one thing we know about pensions is that they have very long time horizons. So imagine more money flowing into bonds, driving up the price, and lowering the yield they earn. This was consistent with the slow economic cycle, but guess what else it did?

Remember how we calculate pension obligations by discounting them? Well, the lower the bond yields, the lower the discount, and the *higher* those pension obligations in today's dollars. Then, at the same time, due to the slowing economy and the lower rates, we have had to lower our expectations on investment returns. This is sort of like being hit on both sides of your head with the same stick . . . and somewhat by your own hand!

Remember those predators we left on the savannah? Well, I don't know what sound a wildebeest makes when it senses danger, but whatever it is would be the appropriate sound to make right now. When funding levels deteriorate (as they do when rates drop as low as they did from 2010 to 2020) and the return pools have dried up, the wildebeest finds itself asking the predator for directions to the nearest watering hole.

I am reminded of a great Anderson Consulting ad (remember them?). These wildebeests conquer the lions by getting ATVs (undoubtedly suggested by McKinsey). After getting left in the dust, the lions go to see Anderson, and in the final scene, you see the lions lounging around the gas pump. The moral: There's a consulting solution for every problem if you have the fees to pay for it. And the pension funds paid the fees to get the investment outperformance they desperately needed to get their heads back above water. If only they had done so earlier and if only a pension consultant could make performance happen and . . . if only pigs could fly (other than in insurance commercials).

The States

You and your third wife (you've been together since 2007) were living in a gated community in San Diego until California imposed both a retirement surcharge for anyone with retirement income more than 120 percent of the newly reduced Social Security maximum payment and a wealth transfer surcharge (some hard-hit states like California, Florida, and Illinois are now tacking on a 15 percent surcharge to the federal inheritance tax).

It has been fascinating to see how the states have fared so differently across the country in this century. In the nineteenth century, the sea changed from agrarian to industrialized, and we saw the southern states bow to the might of the northern states. In the twentieth century, we saw the Midwest Rust Belt get smacked due to foreign labor and outsourcing and the Sun Belt boom with the Baby Boom. But the twenty-first century has not been about agriculture, manufacturing, or even home building. This century has been about whether those states have been ants or grasshoppers in the fabled sense of being good savers or spendthrifts. Did they provide for the retirement and postretirement medical needs of their workers and general population? If they did, then their tax rates are low and they have attracted more and more retirement industry business. If they did not, then they have had the double whammy again of having to charge higher tax rates to catch up and cutting services and benefits to state and municipal workers such that overall service and morale levels have made those states disaster zones from a public works and services standpoint.

Here are the losers: Arkansas (unless Walmart hires everyone), Connecticut (Greenwich declares its independence and arms the Stamford and Portchester walls), California (take the 405 to the 10 to the 15 and drive until you get to Utah), Hawaii (in merger talks with Alaska), Illinois (18 governors, mayors, and congressmen now incarcerated), Louisiana (suing both FEMA and the National Weather Service for Katrina), Mississippi (cotton and catfish aren't enough), Montana (Big Sky spectrum slices on sale), New Hampshire (motto changed to *Live Poor and Die*), New Jersey (the Gardener State, since everyone can no longer afford landscapers), New Mexico (nuclear testing and waste disposal now open for business), and Rhode Island (too little to notice . . . annexed accidentally by Massachusetts).

By contrast, the winners are: Delaware (the post office box state), Idaho (Sun Valley is the new home of the Dalai Lama), North Carolina (home of the Blue Ridge condo explosion), Oregon (weather or not), Utah (Mormons now do all their mission work in California via private charter flights . . . and have made a hostile takeover of South Park Studios), Vermont (now more poodles than cows), and Wisconsin (10-year proof of residency required for state citizenship due to overfunding of pension and health care programs).

You've now moved to Southern Utah because, in an effort to attract people to its relatively unpopulated southern areas, Utah has decided to become a retirement Mecca by eliminating retirement and inheritance surcharges. Some say this was driven by the Mormon Church and its strong preference for Republican thinking, which accompanies beleaguered retirement-age folks. The community is also gated and is a Kendal Continuing Care Retirement Village, a wholly owned subsidiary of the Prudential Retirement Corporation. The walls were recently raised from 8 to 12 feet to keep coyotes from getting in and snatching local pets . . . particularly poodles.

The Country

The society in the United States has shifted dramatically over the past 50 years. As a country, we used to be segregated into the haves and have-nots with a large quotient of wannabes in the middle, many of whom were from the immigrant populations. We didn't think in terms of demographics and retirement life cycles. Longer life spans were simply a good thing. There were always "generations" throughout the twentieth century. Gertrude Stein got it started with the Lost Generation, who fought in "The War to End All Wars," World War I, as labeled by H. G. Wells. And then Tom Brokaw tagged the Greatest Generation as those who survived the Great Depression and fought in World War II. Those born in the crucible of the Depression and the Total War of the war years became known as The Silent Generation because they were awed by the gravitas of the moment and generally silenced by events such as the Holocaust and Nuclear Winter. And from this has sprung the Baby Boomers, who are the demographic tipping point of human kind.

That's a big contention. Are the Baby Boomers, just by virtue of their sheer bulk size, the agents of societal change that some purport? Yes, Baby Boomers represent a disproportionately large 26 percent of the population and almost 40 percent of the work force. This would be even larger were it not for the growth of the size of the subsequent generations. Generation X was not quite as large as the Boomers, but the Gen Y/Millennials represent almost 28 percent of the U.S. population. And now the "Always On" Generation may grow even larger still (health care and falling early death rates being big contributors to the natural mathematics of population growth). But it has much less to do with absolute size than it does with extended longevity. This health trend intersects with the "privileged" nature of the Baby Boomer culture and their belief in earlier retirement, such that the post-retirement span has grown and is still growing exponentially.

This "Privilege Gap" is the essence of the financial crisis that has gripped the world for most of the twenty-first century. Under normal demographic cycles, a generation lasts about 20 years. Take a larger generational cohort or pool and extend its life span more significantly than ever before, while allowing it to retire from the productive workforce sooner than ever before, and you now have a 40-year problem. The world has long since stopped thinking that the financial crisis of 2008 was really about Lehman Brothers, AIG, or even Fannie Mae. It is now widely acknowledged that what happened in the crisis was really the first wave of the Baby Boom "shockwave," as it was felt on the housing market in particular. In fact, the 2050 Nobel Prize for demographic gerontology (a new category this year) is going to Dr. Kenneth Dychtwald for his groundbreaking work on the Age Wave theories, which spawned new academic disciplines in gerontological economics and age-related behavioral finance.

The World

You've stopped reading the "paper" (delivered wirelessly and electronically on a simulated paper reader) because the news just gets worse and you have less and less ability to do anything about it. Europe was such a nice place to visit for years, but now what were unified countries have become so xeno-phobic that it's harder than ever to pass from one to another. Debt abrogation has become the norm. The infrastructure there has all but collapsed and any semblance of eco-consciousness has faded by necessity. Europe is creeping into disrepair and immigration requests for passage to Brazil and even some Central African nations are at an all-time high. The United States is still the most desirable immigrant destination, but the flow is controlled to optimize the economic age-supporting equilibrium. Young is better and young and edu-cable is ideal. Older people in Europe are not faring well with a marked de-cline in life expectancy due to inadequate restorative pharma supplies.

The "good" news is that Brazil, Canada, Russia, Indonesia, and pockets of Africa are doing quite well. Their biggest problem is producing enough to meet the competing and quite corrupt yaw of China and India, who have imposed long-dated mandatory financing requirements on the net commod-ity exporters. Military actions are few, but economic bullying and brutality are at record levels. No one bullies better than China and few can resist since India has taken graft to an art form.

WHERE DOES THAT LEAVE *YOU*?

So by now you have woken up from your nightmare in a cold sweat. If you are smart you have realized that, indeed, you can't build your walls high enough to avoid this problem: no matter how wealthy you are, no matter how smart you are, no matter where you live or what you do for a living. Clearly, there are ways to position yourself better for this Anschluss, but can you really outrun or outclimb a tidal wave?

Another favorite joke of mine is the one about the priest (you can sub-stitute pastor, rabbi, or mullah here) who is stuck on the roof of his church as the flood waters rise. A boater comes by and asks him if he wants to be saved . . . he says, "my Lord will save me." An hour later another boat comes by as the waters rise and asks him again, to which he answers, "my Lord will save me." Then as the raging waters are about to engulf the house, a third boat offers and he again simply says, "my Lord will save me." When the poor priest gets to heaven, he seeks out his maker and asks why such a humble and loyal servant as he was not saved. The Lord says, "Well, I sent three boats to save you. . . ."

So salvation may lie in the obvious and not in prayer. We didn't get here quickly, so it's not a quick fix, but the first step in any case of overindulgence and addiction is recognition and acceptance. And make no mistake about it: This is an addiction. It is the addiction of prosperity. Maybe *Star Trek* (or, more specifically, Mr. Spock) misled us when he said, "Live long and prosper." What he should have said is, "Save, live long, and then you might prosper if your investment program works."

Since we didn't go the route of the ant when we could, what does the world do now to fix this problem? Does ignoring the grasshopper pounding on the door looking for a handout solve the problem? Have you ever noticed how much bigger a grasshopper is than an ant? I rest my case.

We tend to like to think that technology and general progress will bail us out of all our global issues. That is simply not the case here. There is no technology fix needed, but there is a redistribution fix desperately needed. Since people with wealth are generally not in the habit of liking the sound of words like redistribution, the trick may be to find ways to make the pie seem bigger for all and with some, but not too much, recutting of the pie.

That probably sounds like alchemy, but let me remind you that lead and gold are not so very different elements. If we alloy a little gold with the lead, we might be able to get through this crisis. Put simply, the five steps toward a possible solution could be:

- **Step #1:** Fill the widening gap in the pension world. This is an asset problem. Find some spare assets, give them to those with the wealth, and use the wealth to plug the hole.
- **Step # 2:** Then, make sure the wealth does not leak out to those in the middle, as always seems to happen, even more so in the less scrupulous places like Russia, China, India, and Illinois.
- **Step #3:** Devise a system to distribute the wealth to the existing elderly. Subsidize retirement villages and medical care and make sure, whatever we do, that we do not sell our souls for the sake of a few dollars. There is no money that can compensate for a lost or shortened life.
- **Step #4:** And then make sure you devise a system for the younger population, which gives the hope that their lives in retirement will be as prosperous as or better than their parents' lives. If you cannot do this successfully, you will never get the buy-in needed for Step #3.
- **Step #5:** Repeat for subsequent generations.

CHAPTER 2

Dimensioning the Problem

If you read the paper, watch the news, or even if your sole source of current events is derived from snippets captured on late night political satire, you have probably heard of or read stories warning of the "pension crisis," "pension underfunding," or "pension tsunami." However, unless the story directly affects your firm's pension, or your state's pension, it may seem irrelevant to you.

For instance, why should a person from New York care that;

The Illinois credit rating [has been] downgraded after pension reform failure.[1]

The near-bankrupt San Bernardino votes to default on debt.[2]

Retirees wrestle with a pension buyout from General Motors.[3]

French President François Hollande cuts the national retirement age (to 59).[4]

These are all pieces of a much larger puzzle. In this chapter, we tell the pension story, because in order to understand why every single American will be affected by the pension crisis, we need to dimension the crisis and quantify each of the components. Broadly characterized, every issue

---

[1] http://articles.chicagotribune.com/2012-08-30/news/ct-met-quinn-credit-rating-20120830_1_pension-reform-pat-quinn-credit-woes.

[2] www.reuters.com/article/2012/07/25/sanbernardino-bankruptcy-idUSL2E8IOBZZ20120725.

[3] www.nytimes.com/2012/07/19/business/retirees-wrestle-with-pension-buyout-from-general-motors.html?pagewanted=all.

[4] http://telegraph.co.uk/finance/French-president-Francois-Hollande-cuts-retirement-age.html.

will come back to managing four things: people, wealth, obligations, and expectations.

In this chapter, we attack the following questions:

- What is a pension?
- What is the pension crisis?
- How much of the world's wealth is committed to retirement?
- How wealthy is the world?
- How will demographic trends affect the way we look at a four-generation world?
- Will developed nations maintain their statuses as world leaders?
- And, most importantly, how will the crisis affect you?

The answers to these questions help explain why everyone across the globe, whether very wealthy or less affluent, will have to prepare for the imminent pension crisis.

CALCULATING THE SUFFICIENCY OF SAVINGS

When talking about pensions, one is mostly concerned about sufficiency of the wealth set aside for retirement. If we start with the simple premise that one of the main reasons to save is to provide for the "winter" of our lives, when we are not productive for the most part and must decumulate (defined as the spend-down of assets in retirement) our assets to live upon, then we can go about calculating the sufficiency of our savings to perform such a function.

The things we must understand in order to properly assess that sufficiency include answering the following five questions:

1. What is the stock of retirement assets available and how does that relate to global wealth and global GDP?
2. How many people will be in retirement as we march forward? (Note that this is more about the aging of the population and less about the population growth trend.)
3. How long will they be in retirement and, therefore, drawing on the pool of funds? (This is defined as the span between retirement age and life expectancy.)
4. How much can they reasonably earn on their assets during decumulation? (This is the decumulation earnings rate.)
5. How much will they need to live on annually (generally expressed as a percentage of current income)?

Most of these are factual and not projection-based estimates. There is, of course, some longevity estimation, but if we simply use the current retirement age and national longevity averages, we get a fair estimate of the full average retirement period.

As for the number of people in the retirement pool, this is a constantly changing and, unfortunately, constantly growing number that has a great deal of impact on the retirement burden.

As for the retirement earnings rate, it is said that the impact of the earnings rate on retirement funds during the decumulation stage (that is, after retirement has commenced) impacts the total amount available for retiree income to the tune of 50 to 60 percent. This is logical based on the scale of funds to be invested at that point in the cycle and the overall compounding impact in the later years of any investment cycle.

Probably the easiest estimate to make of all is retirement need percentage, which has proven fairly steady and universal at 60 percent of final income. What is perhaps less clear is whether this absolute number must rise to match average national income numbers for the higher growth countries in question. Luckily, the "problem" situations are generally lower-growth countries, so it should present less of an issue. Inflation indexation of pensions is a politically charged issue and is particularly so in European countries, where this has become the norm. This probably lines up with many other entitlement issues, which are likely to be thrown into serious challenge as the full extent of the pension crisis problems unfolds.

We delve into these five areas in the remainder of this chapter.

Worldwide Wealth and Retirement Assets

We should start gathering information by estimating the amount of wealth that exists in the world and what proportions of it are dedicated or set aside specifically to fund the retirement of existing and future pensioners. That alone is already a challenging concept because it is unclear exactly how to measure wealth and then delineate its intended use.

We can certainly start by understanding several key generic "buckets" of wealth:

- Private wealth
- Pension funds
- Mutual funds
- Insurance companies
- Sovereign wealth funds

I believe this list captures the bulk of the world's recorded wealth with minimal overlap. One might argue that private wealth encompasses mutual funds, since most of those assets are, indeed, held in private hands, but the category has become so big as to justify its own bucket, and it is uniquely important as the vehicle of choice for the past 30 years for housing the bulk of the defined contribution pension obligations.

New, alternative buckets such as hedge funds, private equity funds, and real estate funds do not seem to make this list. Why is that? Well, to begin with, they are all pretty much imbedded in the other categories. They all began as high-net-worth investment vehicles and have now gravitated more and more toward being institutional investment vehicles, which means they can be found as parts of private wealth (also encompassing endowments and foundations), pension funds, insurance funds, and sovereign wealth funds. Despite being thus subsumed, they will be very important to delineate eventually since they drive a disproportionate amount of the activity and price movement of the major and most emerging markets (especially due to the extraordinary use of leverage that acts as a multiplier effect, not to mention their high turnover, which also magnifies their impact).

Let us also remember that there are substantial natural and even intangible resources that constitute "wealth" that is not being captured by this approach to tallying assets. A perfect example I always use in the United States is Yosemite National Park. Nowhere does its value, either as a unique natural wonder or simply as a big chunk of valuable real estate, appear on a balance sheet with a value assigned to it. Some have tried to postulate a balance sheet for the United States (usually to make some balancing argument or assessment of the impact of our national debt levels), but nowhere is the full value of our resources officially or formally captured in terms of the fullest complement of wealth. And then there are even more challenging asset valuations like satellite spectrum. We now certainly understand the value of satellite spectrum for global telecommunications. Not too long ago someone might ignore the small pie slices of the sky as embodying value, but today, private companies pay a great deal for spectrum as a scarce resource, which enables current technology to operate and gives these companies an ability to charge for the voice and data that flow through satellites. Once the value of such a resource is recognized and paid for, it constitutes an asset on company balance sheets that gets reflected in our buckets above in any number of places. However, nowhere do we capture the vast natural resources that constitute the perhaps unknown or certainly unrecorded patrimony of the world's nations or, for that matter, for the universe as a whole. If we add to those resources the vast amount of human and intellectual capital that exists in the mind of man (whether we consider the historically accumulated wisdom, the current intellectual property, or the future brainwaves of countless generations), we can easily conclude that, although this value is actually quite real, it is infinite and therefore not able to be captured. But what can be captured are the existing recorded assets that constitute the balance sheet of the world as we know it, and that is what concerns us for now.

So if we go back to our generic buckets, our best estimate of the sizes of those asset buckets today (that is, global recorded wealth) are as follows:

Private wealth	$ 43,600,000,000
Pension funds	$ 30,000,000,000
Mutual funds	$ 23,800,000,000
Insurance companies	$ 24,600,000,000
Sovereign wealth funds	$ 12,000,000,000
Total	$132,000,000,000

I am therefore prepared to estimate the recorded wealth of the world to be $132 trillion. Is that a lot of money? Not really. Put it into perspective, according to global gross domestic product, which is approximately $70 trillion. That means that we produce a recorded amount of wealth around the world every year of $70 trillion. If we think of this in more personal terms, the world "earns" $70 trillion in salary per year, spends much of it to live, and then saves some portion that has accumulated into a pot of about 1.89x the amount of its annual income. So if you earn $70,000 per year, it would be like saying that you have a net worth of $132,000 without taking into consideration your future earnings and savings or whatever greatness and wealth you aspire to accumulate. Having a stock of wealth that is only a tad under twice the amount we produce each year is better than a poke in the eye with a sharp stick, but it is hardly an abundant honeypot. This is especially so when we consider what that stock of wealth is dedicated to and whose hands it resides in.

Let's consider private wealth as a category. We have all heard statistics that decry the disproportionate distribution of global wealth and make the point that most (85 percent) of the world's recorded wealth is in the hands of 1 percent or less of the population. This turns out to be very true and, furthermore, most of that wealth does not specifically exist to pay for retirement obligations. One of the things that private bankers figure out very early on is that rich people do not worry about retirement income security. They worry about wealth accumulation and preservation, but they rarely, if ever, focus on their pensions. The relevance of that factoid is that the private wealth category holds very little in retirement assets. In fact, since I now want to start tallying those retirement assets, it would be very generous to assume 1 percent of private wealth can be categorized as retirement assets.

Pension funds, by definition, are entirely retirement assets. What isn't clear without substantial analysis is what portion of those assets is set aside for currently retired people versus to-be-retired people. I will argue for this purpose that such a distinction is irrelevant since we are assessing the current or static sufficiency of retirement assets and will tell a sufficiently dramatic story of shortfall without further minimizing the pool of assets designated as available for retirement. So, for this exercise, let us use 100 percent of pension fund assets as calculable retirement assets.

Mutual funds serve two purposes: They are general savings vehicles (undesignated by individual savers, but probably somewhat expected to be used in retirement) and specifically retirement savings vehicles used principally by defined contribution programs such as the 401(k) programs in the United States. If we do some quick math, we find that according to global pension consultancy Towers Watson, defined contribution assets as a percentage of retirement assets are now at about 45 percent. Since it estimates global retirement assets to be at about $30 trillion, that means that $13.5 trillion of that is housed in defined contribution pools. Those pools are most often held in mutual funds (that is certainly the case in the United States and other big defined contribution countries like Australia and Switzerland). That implies that fully 50 percent of mutual fund assets are retirement assets . . . an entirely logical conclusion.

Now insurance companies are much more complex beasts, but it is approximately accurate to split this pool in half: one-half representing property and casualty insurance, which is patently not about retirement, and the other half representing life insurance. Life insurance is used for many purposes well beyond simple intergenerational wealth transfer. A good deal of life insurance is actually about tax efficient accumulation of savings for retirement. The best estimate I can make is to suggest that 50 percent is effectively comprised of retirement assets. This then says that about 25 percent of insurance company assets are set aside as retirement assets.

That leaves sovereign wealth funds. This bucket needs to be split into FX reserves, which total about $7.5 trillion at last estimate, leaving about $4.5 trillion in the actual funds themselves. Of that amount, most is simply in accumulation vehicles for national wealth without specific designation for retirement. The exception may be the largest sovereign wealth fund, Norway, which is really a national retirement fund. If we liberally assume $1.5 trillion of these funds are specifically set aside for retirement funding, that would be more than fair.

Thus, if we add all the retirement assets up, we can estimate them (the portion of global wealth allocated as retirement assets) as follows:

Private wealth	$ 427,000,000
Pension funds	$30,000,000,000
Mutual funds	$12,350,000,000
Insurance companies	$ 6,150,000,000
Sovereign wealth funds	$ 1,500,000,000
Total	$50,427,000,000

At $50.4 trillion in retirement assets, that represents 38 percent of the global wealth stockpile as recorded. Furthermore, this amount represents about 72 percent of global GDP. This calculation is entirely justifiable and jives quite nicely with calculations of retirement asset coverage for developed nations made by Towers Watson at approximately 72 percent of GDP. It is reasonably easy to argue that the global number is somewhat lower than the Towers Watson number since Towers Watson calculates its number based on those countries that have significant recorded retirement programs. While the rest of the world is a rather *de minimis* portion of the global economy and adds only a bit to global GDP, it is also fair to acknowledge that these countries tend to set aside little or no resources for retirement. Thus, we will stand by these percentages:

- Retirement assets at $50.4 trillion represent 38 percent of global wealth ($132 trillion).
- Retirement assets at $50.4 trillion represent 72 percent of global GDP ($70 trillion).

National Retirement Asset Sufficiency

When we examine these sufficiency numbers at a national level of detail, we discover the beginnings of great disparities that become primary themes of this book. Towers Watson has, for years, been compiling and publishing its Global Pension Asset Study. One of the first charts it publishes shows the percentage of GDP that each major country has in funded pension assets. This is a fairly simple calculation that relies on accurate GDP numbers published by the OECD (the Organisation of Economic Co-operation and Development), the UN (United Nations), the IMF (International Monetary Fund), and even the CIA (Central Intelligence Agency). Towers Watson then has internal mechanisms for calculating the amount of funded assets held in public and private defined benefit and defined contribution pension plans as well as other retirement accounts (such as independent retirement account [IRA] vehicles). Whenever I show the statistics to my students, there are regularly asked questions about what gets captured as a retirement asset, but over the years, I have come to respect the integrity of these numbers as highly indicative of total funded retirement assets.

The primary countries shake out as follows in Exhibit 2.1.

Does anything jump out at you on this chart? It should. What I always note for students is the amazingly low percentage of GDP in funded retirement assets held by the two pillar countries of the European Union, Germany, and France. These are actually astounding numbers at 15 and 7 percent, respectively. What is even more astounding is the way the adjustments to these numbers (for retirement period, population age, and old age dependency) will make these numbers even more starkly adverse. I will not go into too much detail on the ramifications of this for the European Union and the Euro, but will instead leave it to the reader to ponder for several more chapters the rhetorical question of how likely the pillars of the European Union will be to prop up their weaker southern partners with this pension debacle staring them in the face.

EXHIBIT 2.1   Country Pension Assets versus GDP

Country	Total Pension Assets 2012 (USD Billions)	% GDP	2012 GDP
France	$ 168	7%	$ 2,580
Germany	$ 498	15%	$ 3,367
Ireland	$ 113	55%	$ 205
Switzerland	$ 732	118%	$ 623
Netherlands	$ 1,199	156%	$ 770
Brazil	$ 340	14%	$ 2,425
China	$ 1,300	18%	$ 8,250
Chile	$ 153	61%	$ 248
South Africa	$ 252	64%	$ 391
Japan	$ 3,721	62%	$ 5,984
Canada	$ 1,483	84%	$ 1,770
Australia	$ 1,555	101%	$ 1,542
United Kingdom	$ 2,736	112%	$ 2,434
United States	$16,851	108%	$15,653
14 Countries	$31,101	67%	$46,242
World	$40,000	58%	$69,135

Pension Assets and %GDP from Towers Watson.
GDP Numbers from IMF Data.
World Pension Assets, speculative estimate.

Source: Based on Towers Watson, *Global Pension Assets Study 2013.*

The other takeaways from this chart should be that the small conservative European neighbors like Switzerland and the Netherlands and the Anglophone countries in general have at least worked hard to prepare for retirement of the Baby Boom generation. It's hard to tell what's up at this stage with the emerging markets, but China is certainly looking weaker than expected and Japan looks to be momentarily and slightly better than its historic Axis partner Germany (I mention this only to remind us that much of this problem is rooted in the decades directly following World War II and to provide some foreshadowing of where this analysis is heading).

I hope that this chart has raised more questions for you than it has answered. One of the biggest questions it should raise is: What percentage of GDP should a country aspire to maintain in retirement assets, even as a rough rule of thumb? The only clue I will give at this time is to mention that the most recently produced Melbourne Mercer Global Pension Index, which rates national pension schemes on the dimensions of adequacy, sustainability, and integrity, gives no countries an "A" and only manages a "B+" for The Netherlands with its 156 percent of GDP funding level.

Retirement Age and Longevity

The key tenet of sufficiency is how much one needs. In retirement income security, need is a function of duration more than anything else. This actually has two specific dimensions to it; one that works to increase the need and another that serves to mitigate the need.

Clearly, needing income for a longer period of time increases the need and sets the sufficiency hurdle higher. The other is that the retirement period also serves to lengthen the decumulation period and therefore the earning potential of whatever corpus of assets are available to the retiree at retirement. While, as previously mentioned, decumulation earnings can be quite significant in the whole scheme of retirement planning, I am choosing to ignore them in this calculation because we are working with gross global numbers and it is far more important to calculate the retirement obligation as accurately as possible. To do this, we discount the retirement income need over the retirement period to compare it to the current stock of retirement assets. We assume a fair discount rate (I've used 5 percent) and recognize that the decumulation earnings rate could exceed or fall short of that rate. Historically, pension actuaries have agreed with pension managers that this discount rate should be less than the earnings rate (both of which have tended to approximate 7.5 to 8 percent), but recent experience makes that assumption highly suspect in our changing pension landscape. It may, in fact, be that during a period of secular decumulation (which we will show you as we go that the world is clearly moving into), the earnings rate will struggle to match the liability discount rate. This is, definitionally by pension economics standards, a period of deflation. In any case, we choose to focus on the all-important retirement period calculation and ignore the decumulation earnings rate at this point.

The retirement period is a simple calculation of the difference between the mostly administered and sometimes voluntary retirement age and the life expectancy of the average retiree. Both numbers are pretty easily accessible on a national level with some variation in retirement age for gender and oc-cupation. Longevity statistics are equally available by gender and profession, but I think for this type of exercise, it is fine to use national averages for both that cut across gender and profession. The important point to note is that retirement age is generally an administered age while longevity is a natural phenomenon, which is clearly influenced by national health policies, but suf-ficiently unmanaged as to be a natural age. Thus, the difference between the two represents the operable retirement period and this certainly does vary by country and may very well modify over time based on policies and science.

Before delving into country-specific figures, let us acknowledge that in general people are living longer and theoretically can work longer. If a prehis-toric man lived to age 40, the chances are that he worked until age 40, or 100 percent of his productive life (retirement period = 0 years). Several hundred years ago, man's life expectancy may have risen to age 60 and chances are he worked until age 55 or, assuming he started work at 15, for 89 percent of his life (retirement period = 5 years). Today, average life expectancy is age 78 while retirement age averages age 64 for a work life of about 44 years, imply-ing man works for 76 percent of his life (retirement period = 14 years). In fact, the range of retirement period in the countries observed was from a high of 22 years (as you could probably guess, in France) to a low of –16 years (yes, you read that correctly—in South Africa the average life expectancy is 49 while the mandatory retirement age is 65). What we therefore can say with a rea-sonable degree of assurance is that, as prosperity and science have extended human longevity, they have also induced a disproportionate and noticeable reduction in retirement age. This is actually not that hard to comprehend since progress by most peoples' personal standards would be to work less and have more time for leisure. Clearly this has happened during the twentieth century and may have been even more exacerbated in the postwar psychology that returning veterans "deserved" some rest in their later life. However, as we roll along into the twenty-first century, there is a reckoning to be had, and go-ing forward, there will need to be a much better correlation between longevity and retirement age. This phenomenon has had the effect of greatly lengthen-ing the retirement period and most certainly increasing the retirement burden and the risk to the sufficiency of retirement income. There are only two ways to address this in the future:

1. Workers will have to save at a higher rate to enjoy a longer retirement period.
2. Retirement age will have to continue to advance as longevity advances.

What is particularly important is to examine these numbers country by country since half the equation is administered by national labor policies and the other half is impacted by level of national development and perhaps national health-care policies. Let's look at the same array of countries in Exhibit 2.2 and see how their retirement periods differ.

What jumps out from these numbers is that they tend to reinforce the funding level numbers. That is, all of the European Union countries have higher retirement periods due mostly to higher longevity, but also, especially in the case of France and Germany (the two highest retirement periods), due

EXHIBIT 2.2   Country Retirement Period

Country	Average Retirement Age	Life Expectancy	Retirement Period
France	59	81	22
Germany	61	80	19
Ireland	64	80	16
Switzerland	65	81	16
Netherlands	62	81	19
Brazil	60	73	13
China	65	75	10
Chile	67	78	11
South Africa	65	49	−16
Japan	68	84	16
Canada	63	81	18
Australia	64	82	18
United Kingdom	63	80	17
United States	65	78	13
14 Countries	63.6	77.4	13.7

Average Retirement Age data from OECD Pensions at a Glance (www.oecd.org/els/social/pensions/PAG).
Life Expectancy data from (CIA World Fact Book) https://www.cia.gov/library/publications/the-world-factbook/rankorder/2102rank.html.
14 Country and World data is population-weighted, based on CIA World Factbook Population data.

to relatively young retirement ages. The non-U.S. Anglo countries and Japan suffer from higher retirement periods, whereas the United States looks more like an emerging market country with its lower average life expectancy (presumably partially driven by much higher levels of immigrant populations that have not yet had the opportunity to benefit from better health care). Leaving South Africa out of the mix due to its aberrant life expectancy level and what is obviously a bimodal population, the emerging markets simply have a lower retirement period burden to bear during this critical Baby Boom generational cycle.

The most noteworthy news from this actuarial data is that the countries with the lowest funding levels look to have the highest retirement burdens. This is not a good thing.

GDP Projections and Demographics

GDP growth is a logical solution to many economic ills and it can certainly make the difference in pension funding. The problem is that there are tectonic shifts in growth underway, and they simply do not favor the developed nations that are most behind the eight ball on their pension funding problems. In fact, the primary reasons behind this slowing in growth may well be attributable to the very same problem that will likely present one of the most pernicious problems to developed countries . . . a dramatic slowing or reversal in population growth.

Look at Exhibit 2.3, the World Bank chart on Japan showing its past 50 years and the seemingly direct correlation between population decline and decline in growth.

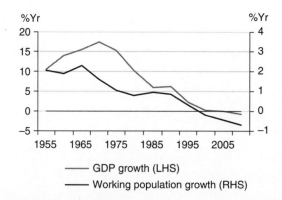

EXHIBIT 2.3   Japan Economic Malaise
Data source: Based on HSBC Global Research, "The World in 2050," January 2012.

This draws a pretty clear picture that should act as a strong cautionary tale for other developed countries as they move forward into their next cyclical stage. It seems clear that the natural postwar demographics combined with the urban crowding and naturally xenophobic cultural tendencies of the Japanese have left the country in both a weakened economic state (we have all certainly observed their demise in the past 20 years) and a weakened pension funding state. This is particularly curious given the Japanese conservatism (Japanese pensions are the highest proportion of defined benefit plans *and* have the highest allocation to bonds, both indicators of cautious investing practices) and national savings rate, and that speaks even louder to the power of demographics in driving growth and the concomitant impact on pension funding and, indeed, the overall pension burden on the population.

Growth is a critically important issue for pension management for many reasons, not the least of which is that it is the primary driver for equity valuation and bond yields:

> *The longer-term assessments for GDP growth are turning decidedly lower than the long-term 3 percent we saw over the last century . . . whether your favorite economist foresees 2, 1, or 0 percent long-term growth, the outcome for returns is similar in direction: the impact will lie somewhere between bad and worse.*[5]

And of course the complications with low growth are considerable, especially to the equity markets:

> *For more than a century, stock-market investors have endured secular stock-market cycles driven by the inflation-rate cycle. But there is a second variable that determines stock-market valuation. Until recently, that variable could be ignored because it was accepted as a constant. The second variable impacting stock-market value is the growth rate of earnings. It is especially relevant now that the constant of economic growth is uncertain.*[6]

It has become virtually common wisdom that global growth is shifting decidedly toward favoring the emerging markets with the developed world

---

[5] John Mauldin, "Somewhere Over the Rainbow," December 31, 2012. www .mauldineconomics.com.

[6] Ibid.

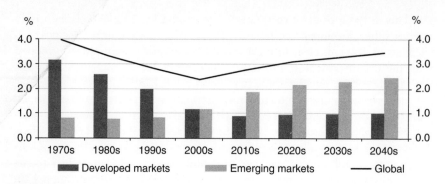

EXHIBIT 2.4   Global Growth Contributions
Data source: Based on HSBC Global Research, "The World in 2050," January 2012.

stagnating or at best flattening. In their 2050 prognostication, HSBC published this vision of the future shown in Exhibit 2.4.

What we see are developed countries flattening to contribute growth of 1 percent or so (much as Japan has done over the past 15 years) to worldwide advancement while emerging markets contribute 2 percent or more. This is

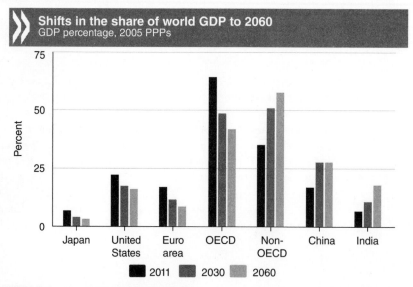

EXHIBIT 2.5   Future Global GDP Share
Source: "OECD Economic Research Paper, No. 3," 23, at www.oecd-ilibrary.org/
docserver/download/5k8zxpjsggf0.pdf?expires=1364154521&id=id&accname=gu
est&checksum=0E5BB9305CFBEEE9EBA4D7C2AA789E5B.

even more skewed when you remember that OECD contribution to GDP is about 65 percent at this point.

Naturally, that will shift over time and several other hidden truths become self-evident as well, as shown in Exhibit 2.5.

The march of the emerging markets and the fading of the OECD dominance is the obvious theme in Exhibit 2.5. The more dramatic demise of the European Union in this picture is not as surprising as the apparent flattening that appears headed for China as the impact of its dramatically altered demographics kicks into full swing.

These demographics overlaid on the global growth projections produce some interesting per capita numbers, which might even throw the GDP projections that drive the numbers into some serious doubt as shown in Exhibit 2.6.

I have no problem accepting the strong growth in per capita income in the emerging markets as GDP growth outstrips population growth (note

EXHIBIT 2.6   Country GDP/Capita Projections

Country	GDP/Capita 2010	GDP/Capita 2050	Multiple
France	$23,831	$40,643	1.7
Germany	$25,083	$52,683	2.1
Ireland	$27,965	$61,363	2.2
Switzerland	$38,739	$83,559	2.2
Netherlands	$26,376	$45,839	1.7
Brazil	$ 4,711	$13,547	2.9
China	$ 2,579	$17,759	6.9
Chile	$ 6,083	$29,513	4.9
South Africa	$ 3,710	$ 9,308	2.5
Japan	$39,435	$63,244	1.6
Canada	$26,335	$51,485	2.0
Australia	$26,224	$51,485	2.0
United Kingdom	$27,646	$49,412	1.8
United States	$36,354	$55,134	1.5
14 Countries	$19,728	$28,535	1.4
World	$ 9,773	$20,831	2.1

Source: Based on HSBC Global Research, "The World in 2050," January 2012.

the particularly dramatic rise in China as population growth slows). And the Anglo countries and Japan, with their lower growth levels seem appropriate given their growth prospects. But look at the European Union numbers. I sense there is a serious disconnect that may well reflect the "Japan" phenomenon where growth rates are even more seriously curtailed as population growth halts and recedes. I actually believe that the pension crisis itself will severely curtail growth in that region even more and that per capita income growth will be severely impacted.

The *New York Times* has just reported on the situation in France where young, educated Frenchmen are facing dismal prospects for employment, and that this may well be a structural problem for the economy that will not go away with the normal turning of the cycle. These youth are in the midst of 22 percent unemployment, "who cannot find a permanent job that gets them on the path to the taxpaying, property-owning French ideal that seemed the norm for decades." The *New York Times* calls them a "floating generation" whose trials and tribulations are made worse by the overall euro crisis, the impact of which is an "inability to find good jobs (which) damages tax receipts, pension programs and the property market. France and other countries in Western Europe risk losing a generation, further damaging prospects for sustainable economic growth."[7]

If we agree and believe in the negative impact of slowing population growth on the prospects or overall national economic growth, we need to examine the population trend expectations regionally in greater detail as shown in Exhibit 2.7 from HSBC's and the UN's 2050 population predictions:

The charts in Exhibit 2.7 are ordered by level of growth from lowest to highest and there are few surprises. I surmise that population growth in the United States, Canada, and Australia is all about open immigration policies. Shrinkage in other European Union countries, as well as in Japan, China, Singapore, and South Korea, are more or less predictable at this point. The slowing population growth in places like Brazil, Mexico, and Indonesia, especially when compared with India, Pakistan, and the Philippines, auger some interesting shifts. And, of course, the Islamic world and sub-Saharan Africa speak volumes about where economic activity is likely headed in the absence of extreme external influences.

Old Age Dependency Ratios

At this point, we get down to some crucial statistics that focus on the most important demographic data relating to the pension crisis. This is a statistic that has been defined by the EC,[8] and it specifically highlights what

---

[7] Steven Erlanger, "Young, Educated and Jobless in France," *New York Times*, December 3, 2012.

[8] Data published in 2012: http://epp.eurostat.ec.europa.eu/tgm/table.do.

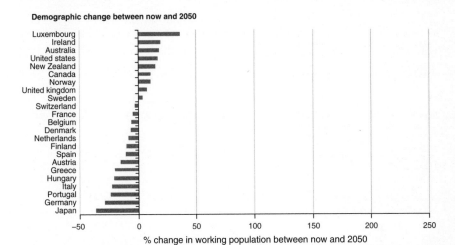

MODEL PROJECTIONS FOR TOTAL GDP

	2010–2020	2020–2030	2030–2040	2040–2050
Developed world				
Australia	2.4%	2.3%	2.5%	2.6%
Austria	2.7%	1.9%	1.9%	2.1%
Belgium	1.0%	1.2%	1.7%	2.1%
Canada	2.3%	2.1%	2.6%	2.5%
Denmark	0.5%	0.8%	1.1%	2.0%
Finland	1.1%	1.4%	1.9%	1.9%
France	1.1%	1.4%	1.6%	2.1%
Germany	1.7%	1.1%	1.4%	1.7%
Greece	2.9%	2.6%	2.2%	2.1%
Ireland	2.8%	2.8%	2.2%	1.9%
Italy	1.4%	1.9%	1.5%	2.1%
Japan	0.4%	0.9%	0.5%	0.8%
Luxembourg	2.8%	2.2%	2.3%	2.5%
Netherlands	1.1%	1.2%	1.5%	2.2%
New Zealand	3.4%	3.0%	2.9%	2.9%
Norway	0.9%	1.3%	1.5%	2.1%
Portugal	3.0%	2.6%	2.3%	2.2%
Spain	2.8%	2.9%	2.3%	2.2%
Sweden	0.4%	1.3%	1.7%	2.1%
Switzerland	2.6%	2.0%	2.0%	2.3%
United Kingdom	1.6%	1.7%	1.9%	2.2%
United States	1.1%	1.4%	1.9%	2.1%
Developed world average	**1.8%**	**1.8%**	**1.9%**	**2.1%**

EXHIBIT 2.7 Global Population Projections
Source: Based on HSBC Global Research, "The World in 2050," January 2012.

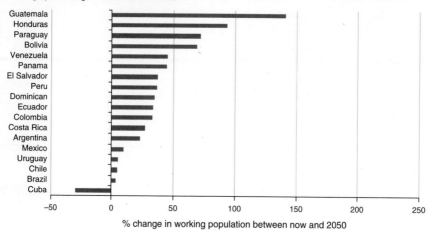

% change in working population between now and 2050

MODEL PROJECTIONS FOR TOTAL GDP

	2010–2020	2020–2030	2030–2040	2040–2050
Central and South America				
Argentina	3.4%	3.3%	3.1%	2.7%
Bolivia	7.9%	6.9%	5.9%	5.2%
Brazil	3.3%	2.9%	2.9%	2.8%
Chile	5.9%	4.6%	4.0%	3.4%
Colombia	4.5%	4.2%	4.1%	4.0%
Costa Rica	5.1%	4.3%	4.1%	3.6%
Cuba	2.0%	2.2%	2.0%	2.9%
Dominican Republic	5.1%	4.6%	4.2%	3.9%
Ecuador	6.5%	5.7%	5.2%	4.6%
El Salvador	5.1%	5.0%	4.8%	4.5%
Guatemala	4.3%	4.5%	4.6%	4.6%
Honduras	5.6%	5.4%	5.3%	5.0%
Mexico	3.3%	4.4%	3.5%	3.1%
Panama	5.3%	4.6%	4.0%	3.7%
Paraguay	7.0%	6.4%	6.0%	5.2%
Peru	6.9%	6.0%	5.0%	4.2%
Uruguay	3.0%	2.9%	2.9%	2.8%
Venezuela	3.1%	3.2%	3.3%	3.3%
Central and South American average	**4.9%**	**4.5%**	**4.1%**	**3.9%**

EXHIBIT 2.7   (*Continued*)

Demographic change between now and 2050

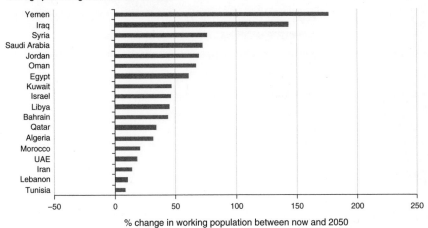

% change in working population between now and 2050

MODEL PROJECTIONS FOR TOTAL GDP

	2010–2020	2020–2030	2030–2040	2040–2050
MENA				
Algeria	5.6%	5.4%	4.9%	4.1%
Bahrain	5.7%	4.2%	3.0%	2.7%
Egypt	4.7%	5.6%	5.2%	4.8%
Iran	4.5%	4.4%	3.8%	2.8%
Iraq	3.4%	3.7%	4.2%	5.2%
Israel	1.1%	2.5%	2.5%	2.7%
Jordan	5.9%	5.8%	4.8%	4.2%
Kuwait	5.4%	4.4%	3.1%	2.6%
Lebanon	5.7%	4.5%	4.0%	3.3%
Libya	5.3%	4.3%	3.4%	2.7%
Morocco	4.2%	3.9%	4.0%	3.9%
Oman	4.8%	4.1%	3.7%	3.0%
Qatar	2.1%	2.1%	1.8%	1.3%
Saudi Arabia	4.5%	3.9%	3.5%	3.2%
Syria	4.3%	5.3%	4.8%	4.6%
Tunisia	4.9%	4.6%	4.3%	3.6%
United Arab Emirates	4.7%	3.5%	2.2%	0.9%
Yemen	1.4%	2.5%	3.7%	4.8%
MENA average	**4.2%**	**4.0%**	**3.6%**	**3.3%**

EXHIBIT 2.7 (*Continued*)

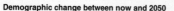

Demographic change between now and 2050

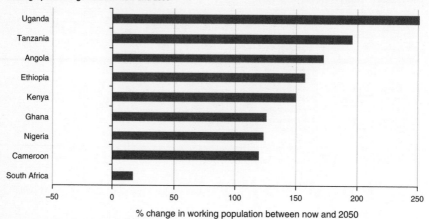

% change in working population between now and 2050

MODEL PROJECTIONS FOR TOTAL GDP

	2010–2020	2020–2030	2030–2040	2040–2050
Africa				
Angola	3.3%	4.0%	4.8%	5.3%
Cameroon	3.3%	4.4%	4.9%	5.4%
Ethiopia	5.5%	6.3%	6.7%	7.0%
Ghana	5.9%	6.5%	6.6%	6.8%
Kenya	4.6%	5.8%	6.0%	6.3%
Nigeria	3.8%	4.8%	5.2%	5.6%
South Africa	1.6%	2.4%	3.1%	3.5%
Tanzania	7.0%	7.8%	7.6%	7.4%
Uganda	4.3%	5.6%	6.3%	6.8%
Africa average	**4.6%**	**5.1%**	**5.2%**	**5.3%**

EXHIBIT 2.7 (*Continued*)

percentage of the population is currently in retirement and what percentage will move into retirement by 2050. This simple statistic is not only a critical component for measuring the impending and growing pension obligation (when combined with retirement period, a presumed discount rate, and per capita income levels), but it also opens the door for understanding the extent of the pension burden. If one retiree is "carried" by 10 workers, that is a far different situation vis-à-vis retirement funding

EXHIBIT 2.8   Country Old Age Dependency Ratios

Country	Old Age Dependency Ratio 2010	Old Age Dependency Ratio 2050	Delta	Average
France	26	45	19	35.5
Germany	31	58	27	44.5
Ireland	17	40	23	28.5
Switzerland	25	51	26	38
Netherlands	23	47	24	35
Brazil	10	34	24	22
China	11	41	30	26
Chile	13	37	24	25
South Africa	7	13	6	10
Japan	35	75	40	55
Canada	20	44	24	32
Australia	20	50	30	35
United Kingdom	25	39	14	32
United States	20	35	15	27.5
Average	**20.8**	**44.0**	**23.2**	**32.4**

Source: From UN published data.

sufficiency than if one worker is carrying three retirees. Let's see how it all stacks up in Exhibit 2.8.

Once again, we see that France, Germany, and Japan are at the top of this list, only this time in reverse order. Japan, which tried so very hard to be conservative in providing for its future pension needs, finds itself in the unenviable position of facing an aging population where one worker is available to support three retirees. The future German worker supports more than one entire retiree and the French worker is almost as burdened. Meanwhile, the United States, China, and Brazil are much better off with three workers for each retiree. This age dependency issue can help us translate the likely ability of these nations to be able to support their pension needs.

The next step in this analysis is to translate all of this data into a meaningful prognosticating tool. The elements are shown in Exhibit 2.9.

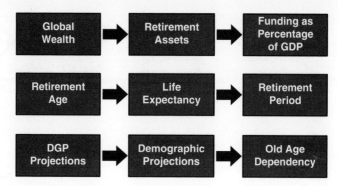

EXHIBIT 2.9   Pension Sufficiency Analytic Flow

The elements are then combined over the projection period of 40 years to produce a retirement need, a funding burden, and a funding gap, which allow us to see the real impact of this analysis on national economic outlook per Exhibit 2.10.

This can all be translated mathematically into a simple equation that is illustrated in Exhibit 2.11 for the global retirement situation and can be used to similarly calculate each country's funding burden status.

Let's walk through the equation in Exhibit 2.11 to clarify. The global average old age dependency ratio is 20 percent, which means that 20 percent of the world is currently in retirement. If we assume an average generation is about 25 years, this does not seem too bad since there are fewer people in retirement than a 30 percent generational split would imply by virtue of a longevity level of 78 years. Thus, we can assume that 20 percent of GDP is represented by this old age dependency ratio. We know that global retirement income expectations run fairly consistently at 60 percent of income, so it is more accurate to multiply that by 60 percent, producing a need of 12 percent

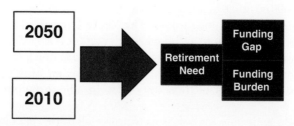

EXHIBIT 2.10   Pension Funding Gap Flow

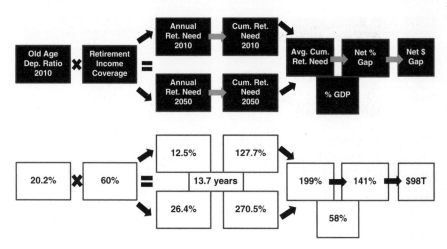

EXHIBIT 2.11 Pension Funding Gap Equation

of GDP. However, if we use the 2050 projected old age dependency ratio of 44 percent (much less positive than the current 20 percent, but predictable by virtue of the heavy Baby Boom generation and the generally aging population), then that need rises to 26 percent after adjusting for the 60 percent.

The next step is to extend that need level out for the indicated retirement period and discount it back using a 5 percent rate. I have done this using both the 2010 and the 2050 old age dependency levels and averaged them to produce an average cumulative funding need expressed as a percentage of GDP. Against this need, I have deducted the current level of funded assets (again expressed as a percentage of GDP) to come to a net funding burden. To generate the funding gap, I have merely multiplied the percentage by current GDP.

What we see is that the world as a whole has a funding need of 199 percent of GDP, partially offset by the 58 percent of funded assets and leaving a net burden of 141 percent of GDP or $98 trillion. Let that number sink in for a few moments while we review how much worse this calculus becomes for many of the developed countries as shown in Exhibit 2.12.

Think about the numbers shown in Exhibit 2.12. They are quite shocking put onto the shoulders of individual countries. Just think about how big we in the United States consider a burden of $7.5 trillion in unfunded pension obligations. When one reads about the public pension market and hears numbers like $4.5 trillion in funding gap, we find that horribly high. Add $3 trillion to that for private gaps and miscellaneous Federal gaps and $7.5 trillion seems massive. And yet, except for an

EXHIBIT 2.12   Country Net Pension Funding Gap

Country	Cum. Retirement Need 2010	Cum. Retirement Need 2050	Avg. Cum. Retirement Need	Net % Gap	Net $ B Gap
France	211%	365%	288%	281%	$ 7,811
Germany	232%	433%	332%	317%	$11,452
Ireland	119%	281%	200%	145%	$ 320
Switzerland	175%	357%	266%	148%	$ 978
Netherlands	172%	351%	262%	106%	$ 884
Brazil	58%	199%	128%	114%	$ 2,854
China	64%	239%	152%	134%	$ 9,781
Chile	76%	216%	146%	85%	$ 230
South Africa	41%	76%	58%	−6%	$ (23)
Japan	226%	484%	355%	293%	$17,169
Canada	149%	329%	239%	155%	$ 2,697
Australia	149%	374%	262%	161%	$ 2,387
United Kingdom	175%	272%	224%	112%	$ 2,713
United States	117%	196%	157%	49%	$ 7,342
14 Countries					$66,595
World	128%	271%	199%	141%	$98,626

aberrant South Africa, the United States has the smallest net gap as a percentage of GDP at a mere 50 percent. Imagine if you were told you only had to save a half-year's salary more to have a fully funded and comfortable retirement.

Now consider where this analysis leaves France, Germany, and Japan. All three have funding gaps that are larger in absolute terms than the United States . . . even though all three combined have a mere 80 percent of the United States level of GDP. These net gaps of 300 percent of GDP or more are enormous by any standard. At least China, with a net gap of 151 percent of GDP produces a funding gap of over $11 trillion, but at least has a GDP, which should grow by 6.9x to be larger than the U.S. GDP by 2050. Japan, with $17.6 trillion has a modestly growing (1.6x) GDP with which to cover this burden.

As if this news was not bad enough, now we need to go one final step and examine how the old age dependency and average income per

EXHIBIT 2.13   Country per Capita Pension Funding Burden

Country	Net % Gap	Adjusted % Gap	10-Year %GDP Burden	20-Year %GDP Burden	20-Year %GDP Burden in $'s p.a. p.p.
France	281%	380%	38%	19%	$4,527
Germany	317%	460%	46%	23%	$5,771
Ireland	145%	175%	17%	9%	$2,442
Switzerland	148%	197%	20%	10%	$3,820
Netherlands	106%	137%	14%	7%	$1,807
Brazil	114%	127%	13%	6%	$ 300
China	134%	151%	15%	8%	$ 194
Chile	85%	97%	10%	5%	$ 296
South Africa	–6%	-6%	-1%	-0%	($ 11)
Japan	293%	450%	45%	23%	$8,877
Canada	155%	194%	19%	10%	$2,553
Australia	161%	201%	20%	10%	$2,631
United Kingdom	112%	149%	15%	7%	$2,057
United States	49%	61%	6%	3%	$1,106
14 Countries	141%	198%	20%	10%	

capita really define the burdens citizens of these countries have to look forward to. Exhibit 2.13 combines these factors for each country in our universe.

What Exhibit 2.13 shows is that after we adjust the gap for the worker/retiree ratio, we can see the actual burden, which is inflated globally by 20 percent, but can get as high as 35 percent in countries like Japan . . . and this is using today's dependency ratios. We know that if we used the projected 2050 dependency ratios, that would go up to 45 and 75 percent, respectively. I did not add that extra layer of pessimism to the analysis for fear of scaring the pants off us all. It is harsh enough to see these burdens ranging from a scant additional "tax" on U.S. citizens of 3 percent per annum for the next 20 years, all the way up to 23 percent of incremental taxation for each worker in Japan for the next two decades. These burden levels are clearly intolerable and do not allow life as we know it to continue on. Therefore, we will need to postulate some other ideas for shouldering this burden.

■ ■ ■

It is quite clear that globally we have ignored the impending retirement crisis brought on by our Baby Boom generation for much too long. Some countries like the Netherlands, Australia, Chile, and Norway have seen the beast coming and made big changes to intercept the future. Unfortunately, most of the rest of the world has not done so and it has left us all in a bit of a pickle. As I explain in the next chapter, solving the problem in the confines of your national boundaries is a good, but not sufficient if the world around you is collapsing under the weight of these obligations. We all recognize that we are an interconnected world, and there simply is no way for any of us to build our walls high enough to ignore this global problem.

Some regions are facing dramatic changes to their circumstances that are coming from a concurrent and compounding impact of slowing growth and pension underfunding. Some are flailing and still pretending they can tinker their way out of the problem or perhaps find some secret growth formula to make this all go away. But, unfortunately, you can't run away from demographics, and demographics are perhaps the biggest part of the problem, as I have tried to show.

The European Union and Japan clearly have the biggest immediate and primary problem. China, with the backfiring of its incredibly impactful one-child policy (perhaps the most effective and far-reaching single public policy ever instituted in the history of mankind) is not far behind is seeing its growth engine screech to a halt from its administered demographic shift. The Anglo countries see fine, and the emerging markets as a class are poised to have yet another feather in their economic cap to thrust them into the center stage, whether they are ready for the responsibility or not. But the most important thing I cannot get out of my mind, as I watch the gyrations of the Greek crisis and the beginnings of a "Grexit" unfold and lead to highly correlated gyrations in other world markets, is that none of us will be able to build our walls high enough, and the global pension crisis will be a primary, secondary, and at least tertiary challenge for us all.

Unlike past economic crises where some group abrogates and another (generally wealthy investor group) takes the pain and moves on, or when national policies are forced to inflate away the problems at the expense of bondholders, this problem is pervasive and runs directly in the face of Maslow's hierarchy of needs. This is about food and shelter. This is about saving our elderly. This is about everyone's right to a healthy life within the best scientific means available. And, mostly, this is about the economic order we leave not for our grandchildren, but our very children.

CHAPTER 3

You Can't Build Your Walls High Enough

The next 40 years of economic life will be dominated by one underlying theme: dealing with the retirement income security of a growing, aging, and longer-living global population. This is a "can't run, can't hide" problem that will affect the lives of almost every human being on the planet. This is what I mean by this chapter's title of "you can't build your walls enough." Whether you are light in your pension account, whether you have more money than Croesus, whether you live in the well-funded Netherlands, or whether you are a put-upon unambitious young male in Japan who sees no future for himself, you cannot escape this problem.

THE PROBLEM OF RETIREMENT INCOME SECURITY

You can segment the world into richer and poorer with regard to funded pension assets, but that does not tell the whole tale. As we have shown, you need to look at the demographics to see how the age dependency impacts the demand for pension funding and the gap that is created. And then you have to look at the amount of burden that creates on the working population. Once you have done that, you need to do some degree of projecting of future GDP growth and population growth in order to determine the degree of problem facing a given country or region. But remember, even Switzerland and The Netherlands are surrounded by countries that have massive and looming pension issues. Indeed, The Netherlands is in the European Union and uses the Euro, where Switzerland is not and does not. But can they still avoid the surrounding problem? Unlike Switzerland's perseverance during World War II, this "war" goes on for decades and has everything to do with Maslow's hierarchy of fundamental human needs. It is hard to imagine that even the relatively insulated and well-prepared countries of the world will not be impacted by a global pension crisis. Think of Switzerland surrounded by Italy, Germany, and France . . . one with a bigger problem than the next with faltering economic growth, aging populations, and massive deficits made monumental by unfunded pension obligations.

Strangely enough, as I started to show in the last chapter, the impact will be far greater on what we now call the developed countries. The emerging markets will be less impacted directly and the more the emerging countries grow, the more the problem will fade away for them and perhaps, eventually, the whole world. Their growth is already strong, and those where population growth is still strong will find themselves growing out of the problem and, of course, learning from the mistakes of the developed countries. Wait, can that be right? Not only is it right, this may be the first time in history where the growth of countries with higher population growth rates and younger populations will create a more stable economic environment rather than a bigger drain on productivity.

We are particularly well-poised for this unique phenomenon because technology transfer and open mass communications via the Internet will allow these countries to leap over the knowledge barriers that have previously impeded growth. This is a particularly poignant issue for those countries like China and many Islamic countries that consciously try to shield their populations from the outside and particularly the Western world by blocking full access to the Internet. This has to be one of the most misguided and shortsighted policies in current vogue. I am reminded of my youth when the Soviet Bloc thought they could prevent the people of Eastern Europe from finding out about the advancing prosperity of the Western Capitalist countries by blocking radio and television signals. Radio Free Europe seems like a funny concept now that Glasnost led to the Wall coming down (you see, you really can't build your walls high enough to keep out reality) and Eastern Europe and Russia are in the midst of their own uber-capitalistic mode. The best thing that can happen to emerging economies is to embrace mass media and use it to connect to the West in as many ways as possible. This might start with outsourcing and using global telecommunications to spur the building of an outsourcing service economy, but that quickly leads to broader technology transfer and entrepreneurship that gives countries the broadest standing they can hope for and enables a true leapfrogging over old infrastructure-burdened "overdeveloped" economies.

In a recent *New York Times Magazine* article on the challenges of income inequality versus growth, technology is said to be possibly to blame for a great deal of this inequality (along with government policies) in what they call S.B.T.C. (skill-biased technical change). And of course, there seems to be broad agreement that "rampant inequality can undermine democracy and economic growth by fostering despair among workers and corruption among the wealthy."[1] The debate goes on to suggest that countries like Finland that have had high tax rates (generally associated with attempts to induce more income equality) have successfully created a high-income technological economy. Meanwhile, southern European countries like Greece, Spain, and Portugal have gone the opposite route and left them and their countrymen in seriously noncompetitive territory. It is fascinating to see that, according to the OECD, "the fastest-growing industrialized economies have remarkably low inequality . . . [where] low-growth countries have high inequality."[2] As it turns out, building your wall higher has the added effect of hitting you in the back of the head via lower growth.

In 1987 as a young executive at Bankers Trust Company in New York (at the time the seventh-largest bank in the United States), I was asked to convert a very successful asset enhancement strategy focused on Latin American sovereign debt into global effort gathering up all the LDC (less developed country) debt from the developing regions of the world and using it to form the basis of a merchant banking business in these predominantly Southern Hemisphere areas known to most at the time as the backwater of the world. While my colleagues busied themselves between the trading hubs of New York, London, Frankfurt, Tokyo, Hong Kong, and Singapore, I was asked to take all the rest (for the most part deep in nonperforming sovereign and often private debt) and try to both reclaim value and build a merchant banking business from the ashes.

If I had been asked to categorize these regions, I would have said that we were 10 years from seeing Latin America come into its own, 20 years for the non-tiger nations of Southeast Asia, 30 years for Eastern Europe (a generational cleansing being needed to remove the negativism of Communism), and 50-plus years needed for Africa to find its way out of the jungle of underdevelopment. My order was more or less correct, but it's fair to say that progress has generally come more quickly across the board than I had anticipated. When asked to name my new kingdom, I stumbled upon a small fund at the IFC (part of the World Bank) that was called the Emerging Markets Fund. This struck me as a particularly upbeat moniker so I took it and called our business the Emerging Markets Department. It was a name that has since spawned dozens of similar banking departments and, indeed, an entire genre of investment vehicles and hedge funds focused on what is now one of the most interesting and productive investment arenas.

---

[1] Adam Davidson, "The Great Divergence," *New York Times Magazine*, January 20, 2013.
[2] Ibid.

In Chapter 10, The Poverty of Nations, I will delve into the global economic landscape more, but for now suffice it to say that for me the transformation of the emerging markets started 25 years ago and will likely peak in about another 25 to 40 years . . . making my original timeframe prediction not so far off the mark.

The biggest driver of this reversal of fortunes will be demographics. That is, a combination of population growth, immigration, the aging of the population at various rates around the world, and the resulting ratio of workers to retirees. This population driver, in combination with the large percentage of various countries' citizenry that will be in retirement and the relatively skewed ratios of retirees to workers, is positioning us sociologically such that we will be less confronted by class or national conflict and perhaps more confronted by generational conflict. This becomes a major theme in the next few years and is beginning to find its way into the popular press.

While we all care to some degree about geopolitical economics, it is clear that when it comes to retirement, our main focus is on ourselves. This is why I began this book with a nightmarish scenario reflecting where you could find yourself in 40 years. But the truth is that for individuals, the retirement calculus is fundamentally the same and the process of projection is very similar. Start by figuring out how much you have set aside for retirement or have accumulated wealth more generically. You then need to project future wealth accumulation through earnings and reinvestment and calculate the decumulation process (how you spend down your savings) over the projected number of years you and your dependents are expected to live. Now you know that you have protected you and your loved ones from the ravages of the unproductive years in the future . . . maybe. You have built your walls around your family. You may well build your walls high enough to seemingly protect yourself from the problem, but have you really insulated yourself altogether?

If national policy demands that the pension-funding gap gets filled from somewhere, isn't it likely that you will get taxed in some manner to fill this gap? Some would say that we are going through the early stages of that process right now in the United States. And if you need a very real example from the front pages, look no further than the Euro crisis. Your first reaction may be that the problems in Greece, Spain, Portugal, and Italy have more to do with overspending and profligate Southern European ways and less about pensions. But this is simply not so. I contend that if you plumb the depths of Angela Merkel's consciousness, you will find an acute awareness that the problem Germany faces with regard to its own looming pension crisis . . . and their severely underfunded status and aging population make Merkel very unwilling to tackle the problems of Southern Europe . . . who ALSO have their own pension crises looming behind the current overborrowing crisis. And the other pillar of the

European Union, France, is, as I showed in Chapter 2, in even worse shape than Germany and entirely unable to shoulder this burden. In fact, given the depth of their problems it might be fairer to remind ourselves that France is perhaps also a part of Southern Europe despite its supposed "pillar of the European Union" status.

Well, if you don't live in Europe and you have built your personal walls really high through prudent saving, you are pretty insulated, right? But how insulated can you be when your state services are being provided by policemen and firefighters who can no longer rely on pensions sponsored by bankrupt state and municipal governments. At the very least, you had better position yourself in a state that has some funding and some answers about how it plans to solve these problems. And can you really escape a growing national, nay, global problem behind high walls?

GENERATIONAL WARFARE OVER THE "PRIVILEGE GAP"

We are living in what *Esquire* magazine recently called The Worst Generation: "The Baby Boomers are the most self-centered, self-seeking, self-interested, self-absorbed, self-indulgent, self-aggrandizing generation in American history."[3] This is the preamble to a very scathing explanation about why generational warfare is both in full swing, but also very global. I believe it tends to overstate the current tension, but may well do a very accurate job of describing what we have to look forward to in the near future.

This is what I have called "The Privilege Gap" because it goes to the heart of perception by the beleaguered younger generations that the Baby Boomers have squandered the Earth's and their nation's resources and taken this sense of entitlement to the extreme of leaving nothing for the younger generations to live on and build on:

> *Since the beginning of the Industrial Revolution, human potential has been consistently growing, generating greater material wealth, more education, wider opportunities — a vast and glorious liberation of human potential. In all that time, everyone, even followers of the most corrupt or most evil of ideologies, believed they were working for a better tomorrow. Not now. The angel of progress has suddenly vanished from the scene.*[4]

In Chapter 2, we spoke of the dramatic impact of 22 percent youth unemployment in France, but what of the United Kingdom at 21.8 percent

---

[3] Stephen Marche, "The War Against Youth," *Esquire*, March 26, 2012.
[4] Ibid.

youth unemployment, Hungary at 26.1 percent, Italy at 28.2 percent, or, hold on to your hat, Spain at 47.8 percent? This "Boomerang Generation," as it is being coined, is increasingly living at home and forced into under-employment situations (if they are lucky) and stalled in creating their own independent lifestyle. This is both ironic and potentially devastating to the developed nations who face the compounding problems of an aging popula-tion and naturally slowing growth:

> At the exact moment when the United States and all other Western countries are trying to deal with aging populations, they are failing to capture the energy and potential of the people who will have to work to support those aging populations.[5]

And one of the more compounding aspects of the generational differ-ence is that while Baby Boomers enjoyed the wealth-creating power of ever appreciating assets—mostly in real estate, but also in equities—that trend had come to an abrupt end. Most of us are acutely aware of the bursting of the housing bubble and the revised sense that "safe as houses" is an expres-sion of a bygone era. We are very rapidly moving from an economy predi-cated on home ownership to a "rentership society" driven by a combination of reduced personal capital and creditworthiness combined with a reduced desire to be homeowners.

I spent much of 2011 and 2012 working hard with the Federal Housing Administration (FHA), a part of the branch of the government called HUD (Housing and Urban Development). "HUD's mission is to create strong, sus-tainable, inclusive communities and quality affordable homes for all."[6] As for FHA, it is HUD's vehicle for providing mortgage insurance on homes so that a broader cross-section of Americans can afford to buy homes. Unfortunately, with the collapse in housing prices and the general unem-ployment problems that have plagued the U.S. economy for the past five years, the default rate on home mortgages has created a huge backlog of pending foreclosures (well beyond the almost 10 million foreclosures we have already suffered in this cycle). The truth is that as the other major housing guarantors (Fannie Mae and Freddie Mac) have become wards of the state and generally closed for new business, as is also the case with many of the various private mortgage insurers, so the FHA has been forced to write the vast majority of mortgage insurance policies and especially so on lower- and middle-income homes.

---

[5] Ibid.
[6] U.S. Department of Housing and Urban Development Mission Statement 2012.

What is the result? Simply stated, FHA, which bears the full faith and credit of the United States on its MMI insurance fund (the only insurance fund of the U.S. government, I might add), is creating a self-perpetuating problem where the less prosperous communities are incurring a disproportionately greater default and foreclosure rate and suffering far greater loss in value. This is a perverse outcome for a policy striving to create greater economic equality. And the point for all of you hiding behind your walls is that the more they do this and the less the economy pulls out of its nosedive, the greater the tab that FHA will be forced to present to the U.S. Treasury and the U.S. taxpayer. The housing crisis that you have successfully avoided by living in a good neighborhood and paying off your mortgage will not leave you unscathed. You can't build your walls high enough.

The younger generations are wise to be careful about home ownership in this environment. We used to ride inflation to boost housing values and minimize mortgage burden, but that simply doesn't happen in a deflationary world. There goes what has been a good family wealth accumulator. What is less obvious than the housing crisis, but equally harmful to the younger generations, is the effect all of this has had on the equity markets. I am not talking about a cyclical dip, but rather a secular compression. As *The Economist* recently noted, "Zheng Liu and Mark Spiegel, economists at the Federal Reserve Bank of San Francisco, found in 2011 that movements in the price-earnings ratio of equities closely track changes in the ratio of middle-aged to old workers, meaning that the p/e ratio is likely to fall."[7]

So there you have it; the ever famous "multiple bump" available in the public equity market is being impacted by the Old Age Dependency ratio. This effectively means that for the next 40 years or so the younger generations may not have the magic IPO markets and will almost certainly not have the advantage of ever rising asset prices (the ubiquitous "carry trade") on which to leverage great wealth accumulation. In fact, it is possible that the leverage that has been our financially tax-advantaged friend for so long may now turn into our enemy, not just on occasion, but perhaps as a matter of course.

The basic arguments against the Baby Boomers in this generational conflict are that they had one of the best economic scenarios in which to prosper and proceeded to squander it and burden the next generations unduly in the process as well. The arguments for the environment focus on the notion that the post-WWII world was rife with opportunity. Education was plentiful and relatively cheap and very financeable. Housing and oil, while shocked in the early 1970s were pretty attractively priced during the generation's accumulation stage. Hell, we were doing so well that we drove the budget to surplus and rewarded ourselves with a tax cut or two. Jobs were abundant and employers were still offering

---

[7] "The Next Crisis: Sponging Boomers," *The Economist,* September 20, 2012.

attractive defined benefit pension plans and, at the very least, attractive defined contribution pension plans with generous employer matching provisions. The Federal Debt level in the United States was at 38 percent of GDP, so while we all worried about Social Security, it was paying for the Greatest Generation before us so at least they were not a real burden on Baby Boomers as they began their accumulating lifestyles and wealth-gathering ways. When you add to that the 12-fold increase in the stock market valuation during the Boomer working life and the huge bond market gains from when rates spiked in the late 1970s, it adds up to a pretty decent setup for a prosperous generation.

I remember in 1982 when my first son was born. I had just leveraged up into my second home at age 26 and had just had a child. My thoughts logically went to the need to start funding his college education. I had several gifts from his grandparents that totaled a whopping $1,500. Being the financially savvy guy that I was, I went shopping for a zero coupon bond targeted for his college years. I called my old business school buddy, nicknamed Gross Bob (we will defer from further explanation, but you can imagine the origin of the name), who was a broker at Kidder Peabody at the time. He put me onto a series of zero coupon bonds issued by the Alaska Housing Finance Authority. They not only were yielding 11 percent, but a municipal issuer, they were also tax exempt. That meant that these bonds would be worth 10x ($15,000) when my son started college. What a deal.

About a month later, I got a letter from Kidder Peabody saying that I owed them margin on my purchase of $150,000 worth of bonds. Despite my wife's concerns (she never did trust Gross Bob), I was very confident that Kidder Peabody had made a simple error. In fact, what I discovered was that Gross Bob had put the principal amount of the bonds into the box where the discounted amount was supposed to go and had, indeed, bought me $150,000 worth of these bonds. But then it dawned on me . . . we had just had a massive bond market rally in the fall of 1982. I called a friend at Salomon Brothers (the issuer of the Alaska Housing Finance Authority bonds) and asked for a price on the $150,000 worth of bonds. The price was up almost 20-fold from where I had bought them. The bonds at discount were now worth almost $30,000. So I gathered up all my resources and begged or borrowed the $28,500 to buy in the position and simultaneously sell them. I made about $28,000 in profit on this riskless trade . . . all in my infant son's tax ID number. That little mistake by Gross Bob and Kidder Peabody pretty much funded my son's college education. That is a lot less likely to happen for the younger generation.

The "Privilege Gap" may be far greater today than we are aware. According to the *New York Times*, the gap is at an unprecedented width:

The wealth gap between households headed by someone over 65 and those headed by someone under 35 is wider than at any point

*since the Federal Reserve Board began keeping consistent data in
1989. The gap in homeownership is the largest since Census Bureau
data began in 1982. The income gap is also at a recorded high;
median inflation-adjusted income for households headed by people
between 25 and 34 has dropped 11 percent in the last decade while
remaining essentially unchanged for the 55-to-64 age group.*[8]

This is the setup for the anti-Boomer arguments, which are well argued
by Jim Tankersley in his piece "Generational Warfare: The Case Against
Parasitic Baby Boomers" appearing in the *National Journal*. In that
Tankersley says:

*Brigham Young University economists Richard Evans and Kerk
Phillips and Boston University economist Laurence Kotlikoff published a paper in January that projected a 1-in-3 chance that the U.S.
economy will reach 'game over' within 30 years. In their definition,
'game over' means that the government's obligations to seniors (thanks
again, boomers) will exceed 100 percent of everyone else's earnings. In
other words, all the young workers in America together won't earn
enough to pay down the government's obligations to their parents.*[9]

This is very consistent with the numbers we have dimensioned in Chapter 2
and, interestingly, would argue that this outcome is a combined product
of the United States debt burden of 74 percent of GDP added to my calculus of
a 50 percent of GDP pension funding gap for a total burden of 124 percent of
GDP set onto the backs of about 65 percent of the U.S. population.

If this is a "game over" position, what does that imply for the rest of
the developed world, where we have shown that the numbers are far more
severe in aggregate on a much smaller portion of their respective populations? I think what it clearly says is that our collective problem will come
upon us much sooner than 40 years.

FEEDING THE WORLD

We used to worry about population growth and feeding the world. When
I was in college in the early 1970s, the focus was on two fundamental
issues: world population growth and how we were going to produce

---

[8] David Leonhardt, "Old v. Young," *New York Times,* June 22, 2012.
[9] Jim Tankersley, "Generational Warfare: The Case Against Parasitic Baby Boomers,"
National Journal, October 20, 2012.

enough food to feed the world (we soon refocused on the shortage of oil as only an oil embargo can galvanize the mind). I had the advantage of attending Cornell University. That, in turn, had many advantages, but perhaps the most relevant for the moment was the large land grant College of Agriculture that dominated the eastern end of the campus. I had traipsed around the world behind my mother for 18 years, following without option in her international development career. This culminated in her being a director of the Food and Agriculture Organization of the United Nations. Where else could I better see the solutions to the very problems FAO was facing, being tested in the labs and fields . . . high-yielding rice and non-lodging high-yield wheat to literally feed the world? FAO has led this charge for 60 years now and the effects have been startlingly good. Improvement in food production, particularly in developing or emerging nations, was robust and began to outpace demand caused by population growth.

I think it was understandable that we worried about whether the earth could feed itself. We were growing our global population exponentially and there were very real barriers to food production. Who knew that both the science AND the sociology would prove to be so malleable and that we would creatively address those issues in far less than a generation? The combination of advances in food science and agriculture at places like Cornell combined with the advances in applied technology in every area from manufacturing to telecommunications. This meshed nicely with the cultural trend away from rural life and toward urbanization. Fewer farmers made for more scale and efficiency, and urban centers made for relatively easy distribution systems. Many argue that food production in the next 50 years will begin to pale by comparison to projected population growth, but I contend that such concerns must logically drop into secondary status in the face of the looming global pension crisis, where population plays such an important role in fueling the growth needed to support the aged population and still providing a platform for further economic growth to support quality of life on an ongoing basis. Exhibit 3.1 shows how the U.N. Food and Agriculture Organization (FAO) sees this issue.

In the past, there was one surefire way to alter the population trend of the nation or world, and that was to go to war. Now we recognize how quickly population growth can be arrested with policy rather than war . . . China has made that clear. It may be obvious or melodramatic to say, but no single policy in the history of mankind has done more to alter the course of history than the one-child policy of China. In one generation, with the help of advances in communications (first broadcast and now Internet), the largest and fastest growing population on Earth has not only been halted, it has actually been permanently altered such that the prevailing cultural belief in China is that the only path to prosperity for both generations lies in a one-child household. This behemoth peaks and starts its downward move in the next 10 to 15 years, as shown in Exhibit 3.2.

EXHIBIT 3.1 Per Capita Food Consumption
FAO calculations based on data from IMF and World Bank.

China

	2010
Total population (thousands)	1,341,335
Population density (persons per square km)	140
Percentage of population under age 15	19.5
Percentage of population age 15-24	16.8
Percentage of population age 15-64	72.4
Percentage of population aged 65+	8.2

	2005–2010
Annual rate of population change (percentage)	0.5
Total fertility (children per woman)	1.64
Under-five mortality (5q0) per 1,000 live births	26
Life expectancy at birth (years)	72.7

Note: data presented for the projection period 2010-2100 refer to the medium fertility variant.

The designations employed and the presentation of material on this map do not imply the expression of any opinion whatsoever on the part of the Secretariat of the United Nations concerning the legal status of any country, territory, city, or area or of its authorities or concerning the delimitation of its frontiers or boundaries.

Population by age groups and sex (absolute numbers)

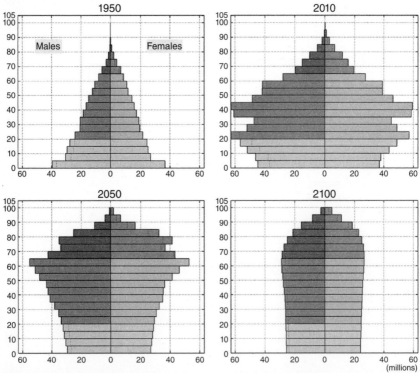

The dotted line indicates the excess male or female population in certain age groups. The data are in thousands or millions.

EXHIBIT 3.2   China Population Trend
Source: United Nations, Department of Economic and Social Affairs, *Population Division (2011): World Population Prospects: The 2010 Revision.*

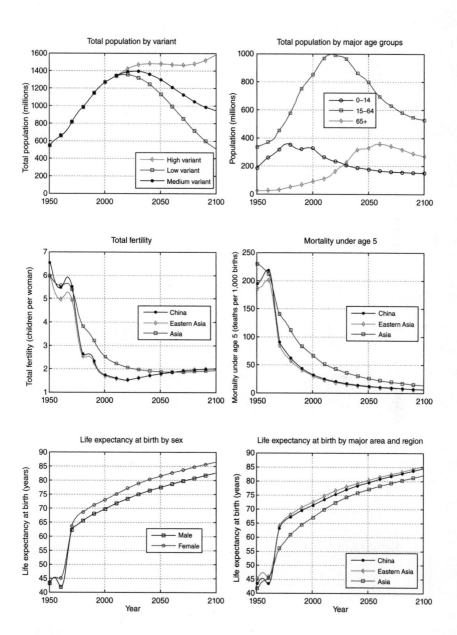

EXHIBIT 3.2 *(Continued)*

EXHIBIT 3.2 (Continued)

China

	1950	1960	1980	2000	2005	2010	2015	2020	2040	2060	2080	2100
Total Population												
Total population (thousands)	550,771	658,270	983,171	1,269,117	1,307,593	1341335	1,369,743	1,387,792	1,360,907	1,211,538	1,048,132	941,042
Population density (persons per square km)	57	69	102	132	136	140	143	145	142	126	109	98
Median age (years)	23.8	21.3	22.4	29.7	32.2	34.5	36.2	38.1	46.4	49.4	48.4	46.2
Dependency rates (percentage)												
Child dependency ratio (a)	84.3	99.6	92.9	56.5	50.7	42.3	37.6	34.9	31.8	35.2	39.4	42.1
Old-age dependency ratio (b)	8.7	8.3	10.5	11.8	12.4	12.7	14.4	18.4	40.1	56.5	60.0	55.9
Total dependency ratio (c)	93.1	107.9	103.4	68.3	63.1	55.0	52.1	53.3	71.9	91.8	99.3	98.0

Rates of population change	1950–1955	1960–1965	1980–1985	2000–2005	2005–2010	2010–2015	2015–2020	2020–2025	2040–2045	2060–2065	2080–2085	2095–2100
Annual rate of population change (percentage)	2.0	1.5	1.4	0.6	0.5	0.4	0.3	0.1	-0.4	-0.7	-0.7	-0.4
Rate of natural increase (per 1,000 population)	19.9	15.5	14.5	6.3	5.4	4.5	2.9	1.3	-4.1	-7.1	-6.5	-4.0
Population doubling time (years) (d)	35	46	48	116	136	–	–	–	–	–	–	–

	1950	1960	1980	2000	2005	2010	2015	2020	2040	2060	2080	2100
Mortality												
Crude death rate per 1,000 population	22.2	21.0	7.0	7.1	7.2	7.5	7.9	8.5	12.9	16.1	16.4	14.6
Infant mortality rate ($1q0$) per 1,000 live births	122	121	38	25	22	20	18	16	11	8	6	5
Under–five mortality ($5q0$) per 1,000 live births	200	208	57	29	26	24	21	19	14	10	7	6
Adult mortality ($45q15$) per 1,000 (e)	467	469	166	131	120	110	101	94	71	55	43	36
Life expectancy at birth (years)	44.6	44.0	67.7	71.6	72.7	73.8	74.7	75.6	78.5	80.8	82.8	84.2
Male life expectancy at birth (years)	44.6	42.0	66.2	70.0	71.1	72.1	73.0	73.8	76.6	78.9	81.0	82.4
Female life expectancy at birth (years)	44.6	46.4	69.2	73.4	74.5	75.6	76.7	77.6	80.6	82.9	85.0	86.3
Life expectancy at age 15 (years)	43.2	43.2	57.4	59.1	59.9	60.8	61.6	62.3	64.8	66.8	68.5	69.8
Life expectancy at age 65 (years)	8.7	8.8	13.9	14.5	15.0	15.5	16.0	16.5	18.1	19.5	20.8	21.8
Fertility												
Crude birth rate per 1,000 population	42.1	36.5	21.5	13.5	12.6	11.9	10.8	9.9	8.8	9.0	9.9	10.5
Total fertility (children per woman)	6.11	5.61	2.61	1.70	1.64	1.56	1.51	1.53	1.73	1.88	1.97	2.01
Sex ratio at birth (males per 100 females)	107	107	107	121	120	118	116	115	111	107	107	107
Net reproduction rate (f)	1.99	1.86	1.16	0.73	0.71	0.69	0.68	0.69	0.80	0.89	0.94	0.96
Mean age childbearing (years)	29.7	29.8	26.4	26.2	26.2	26.7	27.1	27.5	28.6	29.4	29.9	30.2
Births and deaths												
Number of births (thousands)	122,067	124,802	109,459	86,801	83,570	80,852	74,359	68,724	59,096	53,408	50,969	50,043
Number of deaths (thousands)	64,363	71,723	35,792	46,026	47,944	50,692	54,412	59,419	86,475	95,680	84,483	69,163
Births minus deaths (thousands)	57,704	53,079	73,667	40,775	35,626	30,160	19,948	9,306	-27,378	-42,272	-33,514	-19,120
International migration												
Net number of migrants (thousands)	-116	-1,059	-258	-2,298	-1,884	-1,752	-1,899	-1,841	-1,760	-1,379	-854	-417
Net migration rate (per 1,000)	0.0	-0.3	-0.1	-0.4	-0.3	-0.3	-0.3	-0.3	-0.3	-0.2	-0.2	-0.1

a   The child dependency ratio is the ratio of the population aged 0–19 to the population aged 20–64. They are presented as number of dependents per 100 persons of working age (20–64).
b   The old-age dependency ratio is the ratio of the population aged 65 years or over to the population aged 20–64. They are presented as number of dependents per 100 persons of working age (20–64).
c   The total dependency ratio is the ratio of the population aged 0–19 and that aged 65+ to the population aged 20–64. They are presented as number of dependents per 100 persons of working age (20–64).
d   The population doubling time corresponds to the number of years required for the total population to double in size if the annual rate of population change would remain constant. Doubling time is computed only for fast-growing populations with growth rates exceeding 0.5 percent.
e   Adult mortality is expressed as deaths under age 60 per 1,000 alive at age 15 and represents the probability of dying between age 15 and age 60 ($45q15$).
f   The net reproduction rate is expressed as number of daughters per woman and represents the average number of daughters a hypothetical cohort of women would have at the end of their reproductive period if they were subject during their whole lives to the fertility rates and the mortality rates of a given period.

China

Total population (2009): Estimated to be consistent with all the censuses up to 2000, the 2005 sample census, the official population estimates for 2008, and with estimates of the subsequent trends in fertility, mortality, and international migration.

Total fertility: Based on official estimates of total fertility through 1990, and on adjusted official estimates of total fertility for 1991 to 2008. Researches using education, immunization, or policy information are taken as reference. Studies using additional assumptions are also considered.

Infant and child mortality: Based on official estimates of infant and child mortality through 2000. The demographic impact of AIDS has been factored into the mortality estimates.

Life expectancy at birth: Based on official estimates of life tables through 2000. The demographic impact of AIDS has been factored into the mortality estimates.

International migration: Based on estimates of net international migration derived as the difference between overall population growth and natural increase through 2005, and on the numbers of international migration admitted by the main receiving countries.

EXHIBIT 3.2 (*Continued*)

As for food, the pace of food production growth has been outpacing population growth for more than 20 years (Exhibit 3.3). The result has been a steady drop in what FAO calls the "food-insecure population," and this would be nonexistent altogether were it not for economic distribution barriers. It turns out that these problems were surmountable, and all the while the inexorable demographic monster of an aging population with less money to support retirement income and fewer young citizens to provide a reliable public safety net were creeping up on us while we were worrying about population and food supply.

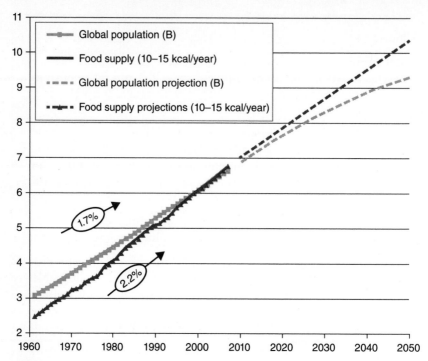

EXHIBIT 3.3 Global Population and Food Supply, 1961 to 2051
Source: Data from UN sources. FAO statistics database: http://faostat.fao.org/
site/609/DesktopDefault.aspx?PageID=609#ancor and population database: http://
esa.un.org/unpd/wpp/index.htm.

POST-CRISIS POLICY ADJUSTMENTS

It is unfortunate that it takes an economic "heart attack" to cause policy
adjustments that improve the situation, but that seems to be the way the
world works. The Great Depression is thought to have brought about Social
Security, but it really has its roots in the English Poor Laws enacted in
mother England in 1601 and brought over on the Mayflower in 1620 as
part of the Puritan Ethic and Anglo history of caring for the poor, aged,
and indigent. This fervent sense of self-determination and independence that
came with the Puritan Ethics made this the exception in social policy, not
the norm. In the mid-nineteenth century after the Civil War (yet again a
major public policy driven by a social "heart attack"), the first American
pensions were established specifically for war veterans. When the Great

Depression brought hardship to the masses and turned need into the norm, this provided the breeding ground for both a host of state pension systems and then the Social Security Act in 1935. See Exhibit 3.4 for a visual of what the first Social Security card looked like.

And America was not the first place to create a social insurance scheme. By the time 1935 rolled around, there were 30 other countries (mostly in Europe) that had similar schemes. The original was, ironically enough, in Germany in 1889 and prompted by Otto von Bismarck.

The rise in private pensions in the United States, while somewhat predating World War II, really took place because of World War II. During the war years, there were limits placed on wage increases and this led to companies using non-wage benefits like pension benefits to induce workers to stay in place. Remember, this was an era of labor shortage and employers were competing for top talent with whatever worked. At the same time, the one-two punch of a Great Depression followed very closely by a Great War made for peace-seeking workers who wanted little more than to work for a fair wage and retire at a comfortable age in peace and tranquility. I believe that it was this extreme quest for retirement income security that gave rise to the severe overextension of the defined benefit pension scheme to the point of creating high worker expectations and eventually debilitating burdens on slowly aging corporations.

EXHIBIT 3.4   Social Security Card
Source: http://reavel.files.wordpress.com/2008/08/social_security_card2.gif.

We are simply much better at salving current wounds than we are at thinking through the full ramifications of our policy choices. From the hardships of the Great Depression and World War II, we have positioned ourselves, and the children of these eras (a.k.a. The Baby Boom Generation), to expect retirement income security at high levels provided by the mother corporation or mother nation. For a few decades, we wallowed in self-pity and perhaps self-indulgence until someone started doing some pension math and figured out that this might all end badly if we did not make a midcourse correction.

It's not as though we were totally oblivious to all these demographic trends, social phenomena, and the pension math. As the Big Kahuna in responsible governance, the United States set up the Employee Retirement Income Security Act (ERISA legislation) in 1973. But the discipline of long-term retirement saving is a very difficult and unnatural act, even for frugal people. For Baby Boomers and nascent Emerging Market populations, it is more than unnatural, it is downright unlikely. As a member of the Baby Boomer generation (I fall smack in the middle of the bulge), I can say with great personal conviction that we are far too gratification-focused for our own good. We are only now waking up to the realities that our overextended lifestyles, financial miscalculations, and "live-in-the-moment" ways are now due and payable.

The Employee Retirement Income Security Act of 1974 (ERISA) is a statute that establishes minimum standards for private sector pension plans. It was created to protect employee benefit plan participants and their beneficiaries through codes of action for fiduciaries and by requiring the full disclosure of financial details of the plans by employers, as well as providing income tax rules on transactions linked to employee benefits. It is enforced by the Department of Labor and the Department of the Treasury.

ERISA can be traced to President Kennedy's Committee on Corporate Pension Plans established in 1961. It was the failure of Studebaker in 1963, which was unable to provide its employees with their promised pension benefits that spurred legislation to address the funding and disclosure shortcomings. It was eventually NBC's 1970 television special called *Pensions: The Broken Promise* that garnered the public support for reform pensions and to enact ERISA in 1974.

How ironic that what looked "broken" in 1970 was a damn sight better than the situation we face today, despite the existence of ERISA and all the national legislations and regulations around the world that modeled themselves after granddaddy ERISA.

THE DEMOGRAPHIC MONSTER STALKING US

As it turns out, you can outrun a food shortage problem (thank you, FAO) and even a population growth problem (bravo, China), but who can outrun the demographic monster created by an aging work force, slowing population growth, slowing economic growth, and profligate spending that ignores retirement savings in favor of pretending that a pay-as-you-go approach will suffice? It turns out that very few can. We talk in Chapter 10 about how Chile has largely done so. But alas, I will repeat my Cassandra-like warning that no one can build their walls high enough to escape this problem. The world likes to think that it solved its problems after World War II and that peace and prosperity (ignoring several regional conflicts along the way) have made for a harmonious world for generations to come.

Unfortunately, while we were all hiding under our desks worrying about nuclear winter, we should have been doing some math and figuring out that the post-World War II Baby Boom that was a direct result of our belief that "all is well with the world" has had two debilitating effects:

1. We created a demographic bulge that in and of itself creates a financial burden when combined with accelerating longevity trends.
2. We created a generation that was driven by instant gratification and entitlement that was prepared to borrow from the future to finance its lifestyle today, thereby creating the very dangerous "privilege gap" that will set generation against generation as we all seek to enjoy the lifestyle we all thought we were due.

CHAPTER 4

Money Matters

ERISA not only set out stringent protective rules for establishing and administering and controlling pensions, but it actually "created" the modern money management industry governed by the principles of what is called Modern Portfolio Theory such that pension savings might have a chance of keeping pace with the visible growing need. I would like to take a moment to review what we in "the biz" call MPT.

ENTER MODERN PORTFOLIO THEORY

If you need to understand why this is important, just consider the equation 15/35/50 where for every $15 you put into retirement savings (presumably over a 40 year retirement lifecycle), you should accumulate $35 in compounding before retirement and an added $50 postretirement, assuming you drawdown at 60 percent of your preretirement income. This is actually quite logical if you stop to consider the compounding math and the timeframes involved in retirement cycles. And the funny point is that this assumes an investment return of only 5 percent, and if we raised that to 10 percent, almost 99 percent of the value comes from compound return earnings. The point is simply that how your money is invested is far more important than the amount you save (actually somewhere between 6 and 100 times more important). And, in addition, it only gets more important in the later periods once the retirement pool is accumulated. Thus, pensions must rely heavily on their investment schemes to succeed in providing retirement income security.

By the same token, bad investment results can be devastatingly impactful on retirement income security, so it is fair to say that any investment scheme deployed, since we all know that there is no reward without risk, must focus heavily on risk management in how it is deployed. If there is one concept we all learn in business school, it is that perhaps the only "free lunch" in finance is diversification. This means that diversification is critically important in reducing risk while allowing the optimization of return . . . both vital concepts in pension fund management. Let me point out that these concepts are equally important to any investment scheme, not just pension fund management, but what differentiates pension fund management is the long-term nature of the retirement cycle and thus the impact (as shown in the prior paragraph) that the investment return has on the amount of money available to satisfy retirement income security.

So let's discuss what Modern Portfolio Theory means. To do this requires a quick trip down economic memory lane. Nobel laureate Harry Markowitz started it all with the notion that optimized returns for given risk levels could be best obtained through mathematically chosen diversified portfolios of assets. His Efficient Frontier model was the basis of much of what we were all taught in the 70s. Assume a normal distribution of returns for different asset classes. Find the correlation among those assets. Assume rationality and efficient markets. Then select the optimal portfolio and off you go. Good enough for a Nobel Prize, but unfortunately not good enough for the reality of the markets over time (more on that later).

We then had John Maynard Keynes, the classical macroeconomist who weighed in with the beginnings of behavioral finance and the importance of holding cash in a portfolio. He said the three reasons for holding cash were:

1. The Transaction Motive—we need it for everyday living.
2. The Precautionary Motive—keep it safe.
3. The Speculative Motive—it earns a steady return, which, during some cycles is a good return unto itself . . . and, of course, you keep some dry powder to jump on opportunities when they arise.

This seems obvious to us, but it started the thinking about behavioral elements in portfolio management and led to much more financial theory.

James Tobin, another Nobel laureate, followed up on this Keynesian work on cash versus risk assets and came up with the theory of separation, which basically states that one can find the proper mix of multiple asset classes by using the NPV (net present value) of the assets and then overlay cash (as a risk-free asset) to come up with the optimal portfolio.

This work led to Bill Sharpe (yet again, another Nobel laureate) and the creation of the capital asset pricing model (CAPM) that dominated business school education in the 1970s. He refined the concept of systematic versus non-systematic risk and forged the foundation of what we now call the separation of alpha and beta. Systematic risk is undiversifiable risk, which is most often called market risk (but generally thought of as specific market or market sector risk). You can neutralize this risk, but if you want to be in that market or asset class that is the risk you live with as the economy fluctuates. Nonsystematic risk is idiosyncratic risk or, more simply, the risk of a specific security within an asset class. It is a risk that is chosen by the investor and thus relates mostly to his or her specific point of view on that security and its likely absolute and relative value.

THE SEARCH FOR ALPHA

While there is much more economic theory we could go over, you now know enough of the history of economic or portfolio thought to understand that portfolio theory wants to segregate beta or market risk from alpha or selection risk. Alpha is actually somewhat more complex than that and demands a bit more explanation because it is like the Holy Grail of portfolio theory. Everybody wants alpha. Everybody wants to outperform the market. Mimicking the market is relatively easy and mundane. Indexing, while not quite as easy as you might think (consider the challenges of rebalancing your portfolio as the "random walk" of returns causes a daily fluctuation in the tracking of a static index composition), is generally considered a fairly straightforward investment proposition. No one feels special doing it and no one gets paid a lot of money for doing it . . . or at least shouldn't.

Alpha is actually the risk-adjusted measure of excess return. That relates to beta in that it implies the value of the selection of a specific security versus the market return. That is what we define as excess return. Naturally, since no return is generally had without risk, the issue of interest is the amount of excess return only after you have adjusted for the added risk you are taking. If the investing world was truly "perfect" (as in the perfect market hypothesis), there would be no alpha because the amount of excess return available from any security would be offset by the risk being taken to achieve it. But because the investing world is, indeed, not perfect in reality, there are opportunities to garner true alpha or true excess return without a concomitant increase in risk.

Alpha is generated if investment returns exceed a benchmark or index if the risk taken is similar to that benchmark or index. Alpha can also be generated if investment returns are equivalent to a benchmark or index if *less* risk is taken than the benchmark or index.

So now that you know how we define alpha, where exactly does it come from? The easiest answer to that question is that it comes from the esoteric concept of manager skill, which, while very true, is too simplistic and opaque to give you a reasonable sense of where and how the secret sauce of alpha comes from. Since I have the nerve to teach a graduate level course at Cornell University's Johnson Graduate School of Management titled "The Search for Alpha," I figured I had better come up with a better answer than that as to the source of alpha.

Let's start with yet another quick trip down memory lane to understand the history or evolution of alpha, at least in the context of pension fund management (phew, that means we do not need to go back to the Phoenicians, but can start about 50 years ago). To begin with I will note that if man has been worried about saving for the future for his 10,000 years on this earth, all the accumulated portfolio management wisdom does not equal the depth of thought or focus on this issue of portfolio management that we have had in these past 50 years. In the pre-ERISA years (yes, in this business, the birth of ERISA is somewhat likened to the coming of Christ), pension management was a sort of Stone Age affair that was dominated by what was called balanced fund management. It was mostly done by banks and insurance companies for pension funds and it consisted of roughly allocating a wad of the portfolio like 60 percent to equities and putting the other 40 percent into bonds and cash. That seemed pretty balanced in its day and, given the relatively new and limited supply of publicly traded equities, the emphasis was on investing in the "nifty fifty" stocks so as to keep the portfolio "blue chip" or high quality. Now, in fairness, the pace of change was quite a bit different in that day, so perhaps this approach was as good as it got for that moment in history.

With the advent of ERISA, it became clear that portfolio management needed to be more diligent in its selection criteria and management process. What also became inherently clear was that relative performance was perhaps as or more important than absolute performance. This all spawned the concepts of benchmarks and style boxes. A benchmark is exactly what it sounds like, something by which the overlords of pensions could determine whether this particular pension fund was being managed well in terms of how the market was performing . . . that is, relative performance. A style box is a logical outcome of the proliferation of equities and eventually other instruments in the market from which managers could select. Equities were taking on new characteristics at this time and one could segment them into styles such as growth orientation versus value orientation or on the basis of the size of the companies from small capitalizations to large capitalizations. While there are many ways to create style boxes, perhaps the most ubiquitous for equities was the one shown in Exhibit 4.1.

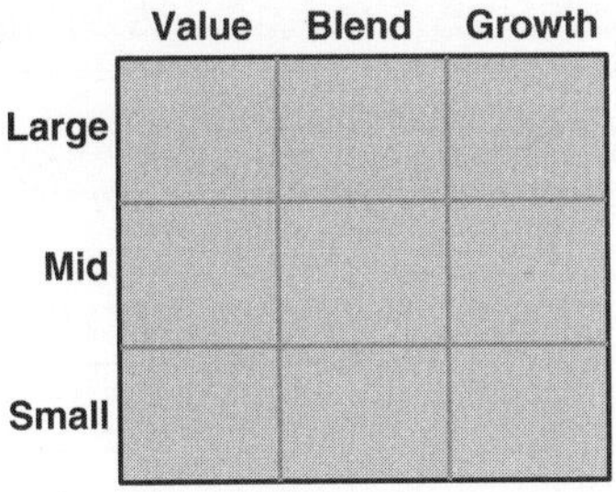

EXHIBIT 4.1   Style Boxes

What this style box does is simply segment managers into nine boxes based on these two self-explanatory dimensions of the capitalization size of the entity for which a security or portfolio was being considered (mostly objective) and the investment style (value or growth) that entity represented (somewhat subjective). It suggests that managers had to define their investment orientation so as to explain to pension funds how they were seeking alpha and from which arena of securities they were choosing. It highlighted the beginning of a distinct trend toward specialization in money management. It was, of course, just the beginning of what would grow to be an even far more specialized array of money managers. Exhibit 4.2 shows examples of expanded style boxes for equities and bonds.

THE AGE OF DERIVATIVES

Searching for alpha using benchmarks and style boxes during the 1960s and 1970s resulted in an increased sophistication and segmentation of money managers. Then in the early 1980s, a new phenomenon entered the scene to great impact: the derivative instrument market was created. Now *derivatives* has always been a scary sounding word to people outside the trading markets. You can tell that something is being derived from something else, but few words could do a better job of evoking a mad scientist at work with dangerous chemicals than *derivatives*. The concept bears an anecdote or two to help explain from whence these strange new instruments came.

The year was 1983 and, as a young creative banker at Bankers Trust, I was thrust into a role to come up with new products for the largest of our multinational clients (those would be large corporations whose operations spanned the globe and required financing in a multitude of currencies and locales). By far the biggest problem being faced by these corporations was interest rate risk. Just as a reminder, it was in late 1979 that the world

Expanded Stock Mutual Fund Style Box

Style	Market Capitalization				Location
	Large	Mid	Small	Micro	
Aggressive					Domestic
					International
					Emerging Markets
Growth					Domestic
					International
					Emerging Markets
Blend					Domestic
					International
					Emerging Markets
Value					Domestic
					International
					Emerging Markets

Expanded Bond Mutual Fund Style Box

Debtor >	United States														
	Corporate			Treasury			Federal Agency			National Municipal			State-Specific Municipal		
Duration >	Sh	In	Lg	Sh	In	Lg	Sh	In	Lg	Sh	In	Lg	Sh	In	Lg
Very High															
High				░	░	░									
Medium				░	░	░									
Low				░	░	░									
Very Low				░	░	░									

^Quality

░░░ = Not an option. All U.S. Treasury securities are considered to be very high quality .

Debtor >	International					
	Developed Markets			Emerging Markets		
Duration >	Sh	In	Lg	Sh	In	Lg
Very High						
High						
Medium						
Low						
Very Low						

^Quality

Duration = Short, Intermediate, or Long
(Duration is the proper measure of interest rate sensitivity)

EXHIBIT 4.2 Extended Style Boxes
Source: www.investing-in-mutual-funds.com/bullettour22.html.

of finance changed dramatically. That is when Paul Volcker, the newly appointed Chairman of the Federal Reserve launched his attack on inflation by announcing his monetary policy changes that sent interest rates skyrocketing. Interest rates became extremely volatile and, as corporations struggled to cope, they desperately needed some way to hedge their interest rate costs . . . a major cost of doing business in a modern economy.

In response, the futures markets in Chicago launched contracts on interest rates to give market participants a vehicle to go long or short interest rates (and currencies . . . which had been on the exchanges since the death of Bretton Woods' fixed exchange rates unleashed their volatility inducements). Now the history of futures contracts shows us that most contracts get launched just when they are most needed and when volatility creates a brisk amount of market movement to allow traders to have a wild and potentially profitable ride. Grains were the first commodity traded on the futures markets (hence their origin in Chicago at the center of the farming belt) and that occurred directly following the Civil War. Meats began actively trading after World War I, and then metals began trading after World War II, interest rates after 1979, and oil actively after the first Gulf War. Do you see the pattern? Market trauma is followed by the introduction of futures contracts to give market participants a means to hedge their exposures.

So in 1983 Bankers Trust assigned me the task of forming what was called an FCM (Futures Commission Merchant), which we called (not so creatively) BT Futures. We set up on all the major futures exchanges including the Chicago Board of Trade, Chicago Mercantile Exchange, COMEX (New York), LIFFE (London), and SIMEX (Singapore). I went out and had the pleasure of getting pit certified in Chicago and then hired up teams of traders to man our desks on those exchanges so that Bankers Trust could have eyes and ears on the markets in a direct manner and have full execution capability. I will return to this notion when we discuss the concept of arbitrage, but let it be noted that not everyone who traded in the cash markets was quite so aggressive as to position themselves directly in the new futures contract markets, but we determined that these instruments were simply too similar to cash instruments and too useful in their ability to facilitate shorting the market to *not* be directly involved in a big way.

The idea of BT Futures was to transact the bank's own trading needs on the exchanges and to provide those multinational corporation clients a mechanism to be able to hedge their interest rate risks. Transacting for the bank was pretty routine in that it was not so strategic as really pure but efficient execution. For corporate clients, it was another matter altogether. We needed to construct hedging procedures such that a company could identify its interest rate risk, construct a hedging strategy, identify the best instruments to buy or sell, execute, monitor, and track the results of the hedges.

If that sounds like a lot of work to you, it was, and it also sounded like a lot of work to the clients. Some engaged and their Treasury Departments got very into the process of hedging (not surprisingly, these were companies that regularly hedged other commodity exposures in the course of their normal operations), but most claimed not to have the personnel to do such a new activity and wanted us to do it for them. This was problematic.

When faced with a new problem (in this case, an extreme need and a desire for us to "do it for them"), one innovates. In this case, innovation struck me on the fourth hole at Westchester Country Club one fine Saturday morning. I was playing golf with a pal who was the head of the Swap Department at Salomon Brothers (in those days, swaps were agency deals arranged between counterparties without Salomon acting as principal in the trade, but rather as a pure intermediary). He brought along another friend from Salomon, who ran the futures business, so that he and I could get to know one another. Since Salomon Brothers was at the top of the investment banking food chain in those days, the talk went to how burdensome it was for both of the two bankers to have to fly around the world behind John Gutfreund, the managing partner, to explain swaps and futures. They had just come back from Kuala Lumpur and were talking of their trips next week to Ulan Bator (seriously). I made the simple observation that they should do a deal where only one went on each trip and spoke about both product areas, it being obvious to me that the two topics were extremely similar and related. They both laughed and told me to tee off because neither of them understood the others' arena and that idea would never work.

This revelation hit me like a ton of bricks. How could it be that a swaps guy didn't see the similarity that futures contracts held and how could a futures guy not recognize that a swap was just a contractual form of a futures contract? Well, it seemed they didn't, Wall Street specialization being what it was. I can remember rushing my way through the round of golf to go home and model a swap using futures contracts on my computer. I quickly realized that shorting the contracts in successive and what we called "stacked" array and pricing that against the swap prices available did not lead to an attractive construct. This puzzled me. How could the market be that perfect when the biggest player was clearly not familiar with the similarities in these instruments? Had I just been jerked around by my pal at Salomon Brothers? And then the penny dropped. I recalculated the construct by going long the contract (something that no banks were generally doing since they went long in the cash markets and used the futures markets to go short) and "stacking" them out three years to replicate a three-year swap. There was an arbitrage of 70 basis points (0.7 percent), which in the traded debt markets was considered massive.

The next day I constructed a $10 million swap and called our Capital Markets area (they did the swap intermediation at Bankers Trust) to offer them the price. After making sure I was not crazy, they immediately accepted the offer and agreed to the deal. Now, understand, I had been trying to find interest rate risk hedging products for corporations and here I had conjured up a product that did the exact opposite. This was an investment swap for someone who wanted to take on more interest rate risk at a given price. As it turned out, the Capital Markets Group had quite a number of investment clients that wanted and needed such contracts just like I had clients that wanted and needed the short side of this contract. So the next thing I knew, I was being paid a visit by the two heads of the Capital Markets Group, who only rarely ventured onto the trading floor. They had a simple request. Could I do a $100 million swap at the same level I had just done? Judging by the ease with which I had been able to buy the last contracts, I felt confident that I could do that, but feigned a bit of concern so as to improve the price a snick. We agreed and off I went and bought over 2,000 contracts on the exchange.

That day I had lunch with my boss, the head of Liability Management at the bank, and I proudly told him what I had done. He almost choked on his sushi. He screamed at me, "You just used up the entire futures contract allocation of the whole bank!" After administering the Heimlich maneuver on him, I explained that since the firm's limits were net limits and I had gone long the contract, I had done the exact opposite and had *doubled* the firm's futures contract capability. This did not calm him as I had expected. Such was the uniqueness of the concept of going long a futures contract in that day. We rushed back to the trading floor and only after gathering a dozen trading professionals and risk management people did things calm down, and everyone became modestly satisfied that I had not given away the bank.

Now, many times people say that such-and-such was a defining moment when the spark of life began. In this case, I think that is a fair characterization since it was shortly after this trade that the Trading Department and the Capital Markets Group formed a joint venture to do more of these structured swaps and that JV became known as the Derivatives Department of Bankers Trust. And for any and all who know the marketplace, Bankers Trust is the granddaddy of derivatives shops, from whence most professionals in the market came. So there you have it, the birth of derivatives, spawned on the fourth hole at Westchester Country Club.

Along the way in this little anecdote, you should have also noticed the smooth transition from interest rate hedging as a practice for corporate borrowers to interest derivative contract usage by investment clients. Yes, derivatives were and are very useful tools for both borrowers and investors. Why? Because, at their core, derivatives are instruments that parse risk.

What does that mean? It means that you can break apart otherwise composite instruments or securities and separate them into their component risk forms and allow investors to pick and choose which risks they want to take and hold and which risks they would rather avoid. This is a very powerful concept and quite central to the evolution of alpha since risk separation lies at the heart of optimal portfolio construction.

THE BIRTH OF HEDGE FUNDS

The timing of this development of derivatives was perfect because it directly preceded the Roaring 90s when the bull market made everybody oblivious to risk because, quite frankly, everything seemed to be going up and up. It's wonderful when trees can grow to the sky. Derivatives were occasionally used to parse and minimize risk, but they quickly evolved into instruments with tremendous imbedded leverage to allow investors to double and triple dip on risk to their appetite's content. The refinement of futures markets and forward contracts as well as more sophisticated derivatives allowed the work of Fisher Black and Myron Scholes, who pioneered the famous Black-Scholes model of option valuation to flourish and make derivatives a vastly greater spectrum of symmetrical and asymmetrical risk tools. What this fundamentally meant is that in the Roaring 90s, the markets became quite adept and tuned to the use of sophisticated products that involved significant amounts of structuring and any number of derivative instruments. Everyone was happy, and none more than the technology markets, which were booming both in terms of innovation and in terms of the quantum leap of the Internet and all the possibilities that such a development portended. That and a roaring market that could find excuses and means to structure around any concerns created the tech bubble with which we are all familiar.

When the NASDAQ died in March 2000, it ushered in a new era in investment. It turned out that trees did *not* grow to the sky, and as the markets collapsed in what seemed like a massive cyclical adjustment, the really sophisticated investors that had learned their lessons well about risk parsing had formed these vehicles called hedge funds and they, unlike the markets in general, were weathering the storm quite nicely, and in some cases prospering in this period of high volatility. This caught the attention of many investors including pension fund managers, who watched their brethren in the endowment and foundation (E&F) markets (most notably David Swenson at Yale University) reap the rewards of being invested with managers who knew how to take full advantage of both turbulent markets and hedge against a negative beta risk that was correcting itself *in extremis*. This may have been the first real lesson in seeing real alpha in action that many institutional investors had. While traditional equity managers proved yet again that they were heavily beta-driven and subject to the whims of the market, hedge fund managers were producing good returns in down markets and showing that market-neutral did not mean "no return" and that alpha was something very achievable.

Allow me to digress on hedge fund history for a moment. Some will say that hedge funds are as old as the Phoenicians, but the term itself was coined in 1949 by Alfred Winslow Jones who started the first modern hedge fund. Pretty interesting that just as World War II "created" the modern pension fund, it also "created" the modern hedge fund. Jones believed in unconstrained investing so he basically opened a boutique that invested primarily in equity long/short trades, trying to take advantage of both directions in market movements and the ability to pick winners and losers to his advantage. He would make leveraged long trades using margin and sell short using the cash from the margin to finance the borrowing of the stocks he was shorting. We will learn a lot more about the intricacies of this form of trading in Chapter 7 when we discuss shorting, but, for now, just realize that A.W. Jones was doing this when others were not and when more sophisticated instruments like derivatives were not available. This is like showing great respect for the man who chiseled his way into the first rock wheel.

Many people would be surprised to learn that Warren Buffett also launched a hedge fund in 1956. Everyone thinks of Buffett as a value-oriented long-term investor, but they fail to realize that he needed to accumulate capital to be able to take such a posture. And that he did via a hedge fund and eventually by taking smart but very large bets in the catastrophic risk market through Berkshire Hathaway. By the time most Americans became aware of the legend that is Warren Buffett, he had already made his big nut and was able to invest in the manner we have all come to admire. But he has never stopped judiciously underwriting catastrophic risk and his primary disciple in this arena, Ajit Jain, is one of the people rumored to be a Buffett successor. I guess once a risk junkie, always a risk junkie.

With Harry Markowitz coming on the scene in 1964 with MPT and eventually George Soros hitting the long currency ball in 1992, hedge funds had gradually filtered into the investing consciousness of mostly high net worth individuals and the E&F crowd at places like Yale and Harvard.

ALPHA/BETA SEPARATION

While hedge funds were blasting away at alpha creation, the real thrust of alpha/beta separation vis-à-vis pension funds was in the area of index fund management. More and more pension fund managers became devotees of the Efficient Market Theory, which says that you basically can't beat the market. The corollary to this is that, if you can't beat the market and most of your traditional equity managers have very high beta components and, indeed, in aggregate do not usually beat the market, then why pay higher fees to perform at or below the market when you can pay much less to the new breed of passive managers who manage index funds in bulk for very little in fees? The logic was compelling and more and more pension funds moved large blocks of assets to passive managers for fees that fell and fell as the scale play of indexation forced fierce competition among three of these managers (State Street Bank, Barclays Global Investors, and Bankers Trust).

It was Jack Welch of GE who said he wants to be number one or two in whatever market he competes in. You can add my name to that roster as well as I can honestly say that playing the passive management game from the number three spot was absolutely no fun. I can remember one particular mandate competition for a $1 billion pool of money to manage in an S&P 500 Index replication strategy. We finally won the bid for zero basis points in fees. That's right: zero basis points. How does that work? You give away the management for the ability to lend the securities and keep the lending income. Again, we will explain this more in Chapter 7, but suffice it to say, these are slim margins for managing money.

Meanwhile, the pension funds are loving this new beta play. They wanted to stay in equities in large part at that time because they were allowed by current accounting convention to not have to mark the portfolio to market. They were relatively immune to volatility swings and, as long-term investors, they had plenty of recent vintage research to show that equity had superior long-term performance to bonds or cash, so long as you didn't mind the volatility (also hang onto that thought when we discuss liability-driven investing and the changes in accounting that have eventually unhinged this thinking).

It is somewhat ironic that pension funds now live in the schizophrenia of seeking beta and seeking alpha separately. It happens to be very logical and efficient when you understand the market pricing and dynamics, but it still sounds funny to say that they want both—from different vendors.

It is even funnier if you realize how many hedge funds, especially quantitatively driven hedge funds, came into being. Remember how I mentioned that indexing is not as simple as the pricing and the name implies? Well, it is actually quite quantitative to structure and run a passive or index fund. To optimize you must actually replicate the index without buying into each and every stock. This requires significant statistical work that needs constant updating. And, indeed, the way in which passive managers are generally evaluated is to look at their "tracking error" or the amount they are off the index over time. It does not take quantitative managers long to realize that there are aspects to indexing that are illogical and that "give away" return for the sake of minimizing tracking error. When a quant manager sees this, he is inclined to suggest to the client to allow for some "tilting" of the fund to take advantage of the low-hanging fruit at the risk of seeing the tracking error rise (presumably in a positive direction). In fact, many quant hedge fund strategies were born on the passive management desks. It is no wonder that Barclays Global (both a huge passive manager and exchange-traded fund sponsor [another form of index product]) is also one of the bigger hedge fund platforms in the market.

The result of all this alpha/beta separation has been a squeeze on traditional equity money managers. Between cheap beta on the one side and expensive, turbo-charged, performance fee–driven hedge funds seeking alpha on the other, the traditional manager has been left with very little space on which to stand. You can see this squeeze in the reduced allocations to traditional equity managers by pension funds.

THE ORIGINS OF ALPHA

Anything that is so sought after as alpha must have several defining characteristics. To begin with, let's discuss where it comes from. We know it is manager skill, but there must be more to it than that. For alpha to exist, there must be mispricings or anomalies to exploit, inefficiencies or arbitrages to be exact. The secret to hedge funds being able to avail themselves of these anomalies lies in the highly constrained nature of most institutional investing. That same ERISA that protects pension funds from bad things happening to them also serves to dramatically constrain them. Hedge funds do not, for the most part, live in these constraints. Indeed, hedge fund investing is generally known as unconstrained investing. There are fewer risk controls, no restrictions on using derivatives and other sophisticated structures, no foreign content or the use of foreign exchange contracts, generally no limits on leverage except what is stated in their own prospectuses, no limitation on shorting or the borrowing and lending of securities to accommodate that activity, and historically much less regulatory constraint. We delve more into seeking alpha in Chapter 6, when we discuss pension fund use of alternative investments in greater depth.

STATIC VERSUS DYNAMIC ASSETS AND LIABILITIES

Let's take you through a few basic quantitative concepts that you'll need to understand as to how the wealth in the world can be leveraged to help remedy the pension crisis.

From a pension perspective, we are going to treat every country, state, and municipality as if it were a company. Just for fun, let's also pretend this is an Accounting 101 course. The holy grail of the first day of every beginning accounting class is "A – L = SE," showing that Assets (what one has), minus Liabilities (what one owes), equals Stockholder's equity (what one is worth). For the most part, think of pension planning as a company perpetually targeting zero stockholders' equity (or slightly negative). At first this seems strange, but it makes sense considering that each pension is an arm of a company/state and so on, whose sole purpose is to provide pension income/benefits for retirees. Think about it— if assets are significantly higher than liabilities, thereby boosting stockholders' equity, those assets would be better used elsewhere in the firm. Conversely, if you owe significantly more to pensioners than you have assets on hand to pay out, it's unlikely pensioners will be receiving their monthly checks.

Now let's consider the more common way pension assets and liabilities are referred to: funded status. Pension assets divided by pension liabilities = funded status. Typically, entities target 80 to 100 percent funded status. In other words, they target having 80 to 100 percent of the assets on hand to meet their projected pension liabilities. Please note that the operative word in that sentence is *projected*—which brings us to the final point in this introduction to pension accounting. Similar to the stock versus flow concept in business, accounting, and economics, pension assets and liabilities can be both static and dynamic.

At a given point in time, one can observe a static value of assets specifically set aside for pension liabilities—that is a monetary value at an exact point in time. However, it is important to notice that fund performance is both absolute and relative. The return from period to period is absolute, but it is relative to both the size of the pension liability and to the return the fund expected.

Example 1: Time Value of Money with Static Liabilities

Think of this in terms of betting on ponies at the races. Let's say I, for instance, borrow $1 million to bet. I expect that I'll be able to win over the course of the year enough to give myself a 10 percent return. Steve (an unsavory lender) is going to charge me 8 percent to borrow that $1 million for a year, so if I meet my expectations, I'll end up with $100,000 – $80,000 = $20,000 profit. Likewise, if I had made only 6 percent, I would have lost $60,000 – $80,000 = ($20,000). In this case, the liability was static. I knew I had to pay the lender $1 million in one year, plus a fixed interest rate.

Example 2: Time Value of Money and Expected Return

Now let's make this a bit more complicated. Instead of one lump sum of $1 million, Steve agrees to give me 3.5 percent of his yearly salary every year until he retires for me to go bet at the race track. He makes $120,000 (for simplicity purposes we'll keep that constant) and he's 25 years old. He hopes to retire at 67—leaving 42 years for me to make/lose money on his investment and for him to accumulate principal yearly payments of $4,200. In this case, I predict that my expected annual winnings will be 7.5 percent of the accumulated principal and return. If I hit my expected return of 7.5 percent exactly in each of the 42 years, the lender will receive $1,111,733 to retire with when he is 67—which is a 6.3x return. Sounds great, right? Now, consider if I'd only made 5.5 percent per year—after 42 years, I'd hand over $647,222 instead, a 3.67x return. The point is that asset values will realistically fluctuate with return. However, this example didn't establish a specific liability amount. Rather, it was as if Steve had invested in a security and annually enhanced his stake. (Note: for simplicity, this example excludes several costs, including transaction costs and what I charge him to gamble/manage his money.)

Example 3: Matching Assets with Dynamic Liabilities

Now let's really kick it into high gear so you can get a sense of how complex pensions really are. Suppose Steve from the previous example is now under my employ. He makes $120,000, and each year I contribute the equivalent of 3.5 percent of his salary, or $4,200, and put it into a pool of assets I use to gamble with at the track. This may seem ridiculous to you, but it's easier than trying to teach bond, equity, and option math.

Anyway, I promise that when he retires at 67, I'll give him 70 percent of his final salary until he passes away. This is more complex than the prior two examples, because the liability is dynamic. What does that mean? Well, it's 70 percent × ($120,000) = $84,000—so I need to put away enough to pay him $84,000. But I don't know how long it will be that I will have to provide this income for Steve. He is a relatively healthy guy and, statistically, I think he should probably live till he's 83. Instead of giving him a lump sum as in the previous examples, I need to figure out how much I need to put into his account each year, given an expected return, an expected duration (how long will Steve live?), and a discount rate to account for risk.

Expected return moves inversely with the liability. For instance, if I drop the expected return on his pool from 7.0 to 6.5 percent—I predict I will be making fewer winnings on his pool of assets, so the liability to meet his account increases. More simply, I can't depend on winning 7.0 percent anymore, so in order to make sure I'll have enough to pay him in retirement,

I need to add to his account. We also need to consider the discount rate. Without getting too far into the weeds, pension liabilities need to be discounted by some rate, which accounts for taking on investment risk and indicates whether risk is likely to change as the duration of the liabilities increase. This is particularly important when you are analyzing liabilities that extend 25 to 50 years into the future. Historically, pensions have used a risk-free rate (rates of return on U.S. treasuries), expected rates of return on assets, and the return of high-grade corporate bonds to discount pension liabilities. Coming back to our example, I need to constantly assess what the liability of Steve's retirement account will be. We saw the significant difference in example two between a 5.5 and a 7.5 percent return. As expected return fell, my liability increased. It's the tricky part of accrual accounting, where no cash actually changes hands.

The final example brought to light some of the key elements that make pension planning so difficult. And if you need one takeaway, let it be that pension liabilities are dynamic. As you add more plan participants, liabilities become even more dynamic. If I were to add 100 employees, I would need to estimate how long each will live and when they will begin receiving payments. I'd need to estimate how each one's compensation will increase/decrease (the $120,000 constant salary was a significant oversimplification). Then, I'd need to estimate my returns and the rate I'll use to discount the projected future returns. Longevity, duration, investment returns, discount rates, and capital markets all influence the estimation of what the current liability is and how much I should add each year to meet that liability.

And, of course, when it rains it pours, and many of these variables attack pensions' funding status all at once. Consider the current environment in 2012. Equity, fixed income, and alternatives, on aggregate, are producing lackluster return. And, even the big hitters like CalPERS, the California Public Employees' Retirement Systems, have cut target expected rates of return from 7.75 to 7.50 percent (on June 30, 2012). To rub salt on an open wound, short-term constant maturity treasury rates are hovering around zero, with one-month securities yielding 0.09 percent and the 30-year yielding a mere 2.84 percent. Expected returns are falling, so the liability increases, and assets will not grow as quickly. Treasury rates are near zero and have fallen significantly in the past seven years, so the liabilities increase.

SUMMING UP

So let's think about what we have learned in this chapter. Fundamentally, when it comes to pensions, money matters . . . a lot. The manner in which it is managed in portfolio, the manner in which risk is mitigated, and even the fees that are paid to manage money matter (they can add up to a substantial amount of "haircut" to the returns your retirement pool can garner). Understanding some of the new-fangled tools that are being used like derivatives and hedge funds is getting more and more essential to understanding the chances of meeting the pension obligations, which are mounting each and every day for us all. And finally, getting some basic understanding of the arcane manner in which pension liabilities and assets are juxtaposed, so as to better understand the degree of difficulty that pension managers have in navigating these complex waters, is quite valuable. We are not trying to turn anyone into an investment guru or an actuary, but rather to give you a few tools to enable you to grasp the magnitude of the problem and start to assess the means available to solve the problem.

CHAPTER 5

Reinventing Retirement

The world of retirement is generally broken into two distinct categories; defined benefit plans and defined contribution plans. There are other forms coming into the picture called hybrid plans, which are clearly a blend of these two building block styles. Before you can really understand the state of the pension universe you really do need to understand the distinction between these two types of plans and the problems and pros and cons that each enjoy.

DEFINED BENEFIT PLANS

A defined benefit plan promises the participant a specific monetary benefit at retirement and may state this as an exact amount or a portion of the final or average final salary earned. Monthly benefits are sometimes calculated via a formula that incorporates a participant's years of service in addition to absolute or average salary level. Participants are not required to make investment decisions and these are generally made by a professional pension management team whether the fund is a private or public fund. Those teams may or may not manage some or all of the money themselves or tender it out to outside managers. A defined benefit plan is sometimes referred to as a fully funded pension plan, which is clearly a gross misnomer if applied generically since full funding would obviate the need for this very book and this is decidedly *not* the case in many, many plans.

The advantages of defined benefit plans are primarily that they provide participants with (as their name implies) a defined array of benefits at retirement rather than a monetary sum that may or may not satisfy the benefit needs of the participant. These defined benefits include guaranteed retirement income security for the life of the participant and often the life of the participant's spouse. There are often cost of living adjustments and sometimes post-retirement medical coverage (less and less the case). These plans give participants the feeling that they bear no investment risk. But recent notable failures and the impending crisis that may face the Pension Benefit Guaranty Corporation (the ultimate guarantor of pension plans in the United States, which we discuss further in Chapter 9) makes this heretofore assumption somewhat suspect. What is clear is that defined benefit plans offer participants professional management of their funds. Perhaps most important, defined benefit plans are very "paternalistic" and are not dependent on the participant's ability to save or budget their retirement resources. They cradle participants in a cocoon of comfort by providing them with benefits rather than money. This is the ultimate Maslowian vehicle because it addresses the exact hierarchy of fundamental needs for retirees.

The disadvantages of defined benefit plans begin with the fact that they are extremely difficult for participants to understand, either in their working years or in their post-retirement years. This is probably fine if all is well and the participant remains in the bosom of the plan sponsor for many years and through retirement. However, these plans are not terribly beneficial to employees who leave before retirement. This is so both because the actuarial basis favors those who stay until the bitter end (remember, these were generally designed as employment retention tools) and because they are not portable and therefore not in keeping with modern employment trends, which tend toward far greater mobility and self-determination.

There are also tremendous disadvantages to the sponsors of a defined benefit plans. This is clearly the most notable aspect of these plans since the aging of the workforce and the sponsors themselves have created tremendous burdens and dislocations to companies and public sponsors to the point of many financial analysts viewing pensions as the tail that is starting to wag the dog. The cumulative nature of defined pension plans combined with increased longevity has created long-tail risks for sponsors and often deadly financial burdens. This is a classic case of an exacerbation of generational conflict in that a growing number of companies and public sponsors find themselves torn by the dilemma of paying older retirees or continuing to be able to afford to pay younger, in-force employees and provide them even modest versions of the very pensions whose obligations are dragging down these sponsors.

DEFINED CONTRIBUTION PLANS

A defined contribution plan provides an individual, self-directed retirement account for each participant. There are no specified benefits per se, but the amount of retirement funding available to the participant is based on the amount the participant and perhaps the employer (assuming the employer is matching contributions) contributed into the plan and the reinvestment value of those amounts. Thus, the amount of retirement income security is directly impacted by the individual participant's savings pattern, the generosity of the employer, and, perhaps most importantly, the investment program put in place and maintained by the participant him- or herself. This pool is subject to the whims of market gains and loses. There are no promises of any set monthly payments at retirement. The most common examples of defined contribution plans include 401(k) plans (for private corporate sponsors), 403(b) plans (for educational institutions), and 457 plans (for the growing number of state and municipal sponsors that are resorting to this mechanism). There are also a growing number of other plans, such as employee stock ownership plans and profit sharing plans, which bear many similarities to these traditional forms of defined contribution plans.

The advantages of defined contribution plans are most often stated as their being an attractive tax-deferred retirement savings medium where participants have a significant say in how much they choose to save (most often funded through easy payroll deductions), how their money is invested and at retirement are given access to lump sum distributions that are furthermore eligible for special 10-year averaging for tax purposes. Compared to defined benefit plans, these plans are generally much more easily understood by participants and, since they are valued daily most often, they are tracked quite closely by most participants.

Employers like defined contribution plans because they are, by definition, well defined in terms of any obligations that the employer has to its employees and it leaves virtually all decisions about how much to save and how to invest it up to the participants themselves and pretty much leaves the employer out of it. Many employers also used defined contribution plans to allow employees to invest in the company stock (sometimes the plans were slanted unreasonably to encourage this), but the Enron and WorldCom debacles have caused these practices to be significantly curtailed.

The disadvantages of defined contribution plans include that they are less than effective vehicles for building a sufficient retirement fund for those who enter the process late in life or simply fail to sufficiently save. There is very little policing of this in the United States, though other countries such as the Netherlands and Chile have enacted more stringent rules for both employee and employer contributions. In all cases, though, participants bear their own investment risk and since we have already shown that anywhere from 85 to 99 percent of the funds available for retirement come from the returns garnered through the pre- and postretirement investment process, this is a great deal of risk to place on unsophisticated investors. As I show in Chapter 9, some studies show that individuals habitually underperform professional money managers by as much as 10 percent, and the most "gentle" surveys show that there is at least a 2 percent disadvantage to individuals investing on their own. I am not inclined to again show you how much that means over a retirement lifecycle so suffice it to say that it may well make all the difference in the degree of sufficiency of the retirement pools.

WHO'S THE CLIENT AFTER ALL?

In 1992 I was asked to take charge of Bankers Trust's full complement of pension and employee benefit activities. We called it The Retirement Services Group and we were the third largest trust bank at the time and handled the custody, master trust, and securities lending for a vast array of the pensions in the United States and abroad. In addition, we had been one of the first and now were the biggest provider of defined contribution pension management services, which we called the Participant Services Group. We handled all the large 401(k) plans and had recently taken on the 1 million–participant General Motors account.

To understand how this "instivdual" market works, you need to realize that while we are serving the needs of the participants, it is the sponsoring institution that hires us and directs us as to how the services will be provided per the ERISA requirements. That means we serve all 1 million GM participants (active and retired), but our master is the GM Treasury Department.

This service was working on a monthly, quarterly, or semi-annual reporting cycle depending on the desires of the sponsor. We batch-processed the accounts for valuation on those cycles, most often quarterly. When we discussed providing valuations more often we were regularly told by the sponsors that this was unwarranted and actually bad for participants because it promoted churning in their investment selections and was simply too distracting to employees and generally unproductive (you will recall that churning tends to hurt most individual performance based on bad market timing). This was fine since most of the accounts were in what are called commingled accounts, which simply means that we offered style "buckets" within which participants could choose to invest part of their money. This was the cheapest way to scale the costs of money management and the Treasury Departments were being prudent stewards for their participants.

One of the new mavericks in the defined contribution field was this little mutual fund company called Fidelity (which was not really so little, even then). Fidelity saw the processing or recordkeeping of defined contribution plans as a very messy systems-intensive process that was better left to experienced banks like Bankers Trust. What they wanted was the lucrative money management business for flows into their mutual funds, which could replace the commingled "buckets" currently in use. They were gaining traction with sponsors since more and more individuals were familiar with Fidelity and other branded mutual fund products. But sponsors insisted that the recordkeeping be bundled with the money management. So Fidelity came to Bankers Trust and asked that we form a JV with them where we provide all the recordkeeping and they do all the money management. Besides the obvious exclusivity concerns this presented, we were also less than happy to cede the money management business, which we too saw as very lucrative. We had our eye on the mutual fund business as well. So we turned Fidelity down, figuring that would slow them down, so confident were we that recordkeeping was a challenge few would be able to undertake successfully.

But Fidelity forged ahead and built a recordkeeping system and they did it the same way one would expect that a mutual fund company might. They were already required to give clients daily valuations, so they built their system to provide daily valuations to plan participants. We knew that would not make plan sponsors happy. But we were wrong. Plan sponsors were increasingly bowing to the pressure from their participants for access to name brand fund product and daily valuation. Suddenly, the sponsor community reversed field and demanded daily valuation and we were sitting there with huge and expensive legacy batch systems that were simply not designed for that sort of activity. It cost hundreds of millions of dollars and several years to revamp and by then, Fidelity had become king of the defined contribution recordkeeping hill and the other fund managers were not far behind. We were sitting by the side of the road wondering how our buggy whip had become obsolete when we had done exactly what our clients had asked us to do.

THE CHANGING LANDSCAPE

With a few exceptions, there is a clear trend of plan sponsors moving away from the defined benefit plans of old toward more portable and flexible defined contribution plans that will dominate the retirement landscape of tomorrow. The beneficiaries of defined benefit plans typically secure a large portion of their pension benefits in the later stages of their careers, and thus, only true firm "lifers" are able to reap the full benefits defined benefit plans offer. As lifetime positions at a single firm are increasingly rare, defined contribution plans that allow employees to take their accumulated benefits with them from firm to firm are more pragmatic. The investment risk is transferred to the plan beneficiary, but the accounts are transferable from firm to firm.

From the employer perspective, traditionally defined benefit plans are simply becoming too cumbersome to maintain. Firms need to estimate how much employees will make at the peak of their careers and how long they will live. They need to determine expected portfolio return, and the magnitude of annual employer pension contributions. Rates are near zero and the lackluster equity returns are too often accompanied by excess volatility. Just like bond prices, pension liabilities move inversely with rates.

To make things worse, FASB ASC 715 requires that pension funded status be reported on consolidated balance sheets (as an asset or a liability)[1] and FAS 158b may eventually require that investment losses from pension investment flow through to the income statement and statement of cash flows.[2] Firms expend significant capital to remain up-to-date on the rapidly changing accounting and regulatory environment.

The concern is the following: so many companies have pension obligations that dwarf their market capitalizations. For instance, before the GM/Prudential pension buyout (a transaction we will analyze in Chapter 9), GM had global pension liabilities of approximately $134.7 billion ($25.4 billion of which was unfunded) compared to a market capitalization of just $30.7 billion.[3] That sounds like a pension company that happens to make cars, rather than a car company offering retirement benefits. This is the tail wagging the dog and highlights another source of pension risk, and why so many plan sponsors are searching for ways to de-risk their respective portfolios. Addressing pension obligations detracts from companies' focus on their core businesses.

Another gift for defined benefit plans sponsors came in the recently passed "Moving Ahead for Progress in the 21st Century Act," otherwise known as Map-21. This bipartisan bill signed into law by President Obama July 6, 2012 increased the premiums that the Pension Benefit Guarantee Corporation (PBGC) charges for single and multi-employer plans.[4] Single employer premiums jumped 20 percent from $35 to $42 per person in 2012, and will increase another 17 percent in 2013. Similarly, multi-employer premiums will jump over 22 percent from $9 to $11 in 2013. Variable premiums charged on underfunded pensions will increase as well—yet another incremental cost defined benefit plans will need to incur.

---

[1] www.deloitte.com/assets/Dcom-UnitedStates/Local%20Assets/Documents/AERS/us_assur_Financial_Reporting_Alert_09-5.pdf.

[2] www.fasb.org/summary/stsum158.shtml.

[3] www.pionline.com/article/20120822/REG/120819895.

[4] www.dot.gov/map21.

THE PERFECT STORM

It is said that defined benefit plans are like the fishing boat from Gloucester that has traveled too far beyond the Grand Banks and has encountered the Perfect Storm. In the case of pension funds, the Perfect Storm in the United States has come in the form of four forces that have come in sufficient force as to be deadly in and of themselves, but in combination are truly lethal to defined benefit plans.

The first deadly force has come in the form of the accounting changes described in the earlier part of this chapter. Between FASB ASC 715 and FASB 158, the accountants have ganged up on private pension plans at a moment in their lifecycle where these "old dog" company sponsors have found that the weight of their tails is simply too heavy for the dog to maneuver. Now the accounting is forcing the dog to be defined each and every quarter by his big old tail such that every blip in the market value of the pension plan is swamping the accounting of the underlying business. This causes private pension fund managers to think very carefully about their portfolios, not so much in terms of optimizing returns, but perhaps in ways to minimize volatility. This is particularly perverse for pension funds since they have this wonderful advantage over many other investors in that the retirement cycle enables them to think very long term and garner what the financial world calls the illiquidity premium (except if you can't afford to think long term anymore because the ups and down of the market cause you agita every quarter).

The second deadly force has come from our friends at the Department of Labor and Congress in the form of The Pension Protection Act of 2006. Regulation in the pension arena has many good things about it and the intentions are usually always good, but the unintended consequences can be very harsh. In this case, the PPA imposes a number of requirements on pension plans in recognition of the underfunding problem (and probably due in part to the concern that the PBGC ultimately ends up owning all these problems when underfunded pension plans drag their sponsor companies underwater for the last time). This mostly has to do with the amount of time that grossly underfunded plans have to refill their coffers to rise above the dangerous underfunding threshold. If the accounting rule changes make for accounting angst every reporting period, the PPA requirements smack sponsor companies directly in the face by severely increasing their cash contribution requirements just at a moment in their lives when they can least afford it. This would be the equivalent of imposing a heavy tax burden on a dying man specifically because his impending death worries you that he will leave obligations that cannot otherwise be met. It might be fair to say that this sort of taxation might very well create a self-fulfilling prophecy in that it might indeed hasten death rather than protect anyone.

The third force of nature acting on pension funds is perhaps cyclical if you believe that we are in a cyclical market correction rather than a secular or very long decline in equity markets. Naturally, right after enactment of the PPA in 2006 we entered into yet another steep financial crisis that has knocked the stuffing out of pension plan portfolios and significantly reduced funding levels. As we see in the case of both the accounting and now the contribution requirements of the PPA, such an adjustment creates a worrisome force on pension plan managers like never before. Even if the corrections are cyclical and funding levels come back into line, the memories of these swings are so fresh as to induce managers to think seriously about how they can avoid these pressures the next time a correction throws them into that hot seat. This sort of learned response might be great when training Pavlov's dog, but it is not at all clear that it helps pension fund managers grow their plan assets in an optimal manner. When managers are forced to play defense and not offense against the constant grinding of the market and the pension liability dragon that stalks them, they are not necessarily doing what's right for their participants.

This brings us to the fourth force of nature, the actions of others in similar predicaments in different parts of the world. Remember that the pension crisis is a global problem and like planning any strategy it is important to keep an eye on the "competition." Pension plans do not technically compete against one another; at least not head-to-head in the way that companies compete. We have discussed the importance of relative performance, so it is clear that the world does benchmark pension plans against one another, but additionally, since pensions are governed by different laws and accounting standards in different countries while literally trying to solve the same financial equation using assets and considering liabilities (admittedly for slightly different populations), they do watch one another. In many cases, the United States is often the leader, but in the past few years it is fair to say that other countries have shown some interesting leadership moves.

This is most notable in the case of the United Kingdom. They enacted similar legislation to the PPA and the international accounting standards that are used by U.K. pension plans had recently implemented similar provision to FASB 158. All of this happened about two years before the U.S. market changes so U.K. pension plans became a bellwether and U.S. managers watched as the United Kingdom had a significant increase in plan freezes and then went straight on to plan terminations and full risk transfers using a defeasance structure called a plan buyout. None of this went unnoticed by U.S. pension managers.

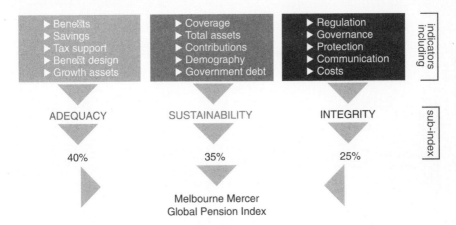

EXHIBIT 5.1   Calculating the Melbourne Mercer Global Pension Index
Source: Australian Center for Financial Studies and Mercer, October, 2011.

Additionally, there are now organizations like Towers Watson and Mercer that spend time benchmarking global pension schemes. Towers Watson has tended to focus on sufficiency versus GDP where Mercer has taken a much more extensive look through their Melbourne Mercer Global Pension Index at the adequacy, sustainability, and integrity of the various national pension schemes and rated each one as shown in Exhibit 5.1. This rating occurs without a "curve" and grades countries on an absolute scale in terms of how likely they are to meet the needs of their participants. Again, all of these indicators are not missed on pension fund managers and they all add to the angst to act to adjust their plans to reflect the present and coming dangers.

Exhibit 5.2 is from McKinsey and shows how all these forces come together into the Perfect Pension Storm and have the impact that volatility management and risk management come to the fore. This might be a good thing for plans that are at or near full funding, but this can equally be a bad thing for plans that are significantly underfunded and far from their goals. The important thing for us to consider is how these forces of nature are causing managers to alter their pension and portfolio management to address the concerns and what impact this has on the adequacy, sustainability, and integrity of those plans.

Increasing volatility flows through to company financials, rates are low and liabilities are increasing, yields of investment strategies are insufficient to bridge the gap between dwindling assets and ballooning liabilities, accounting and regulatory costs are overbearing, and catering to defined benefit plans is detracting from the core businesses these pensions were

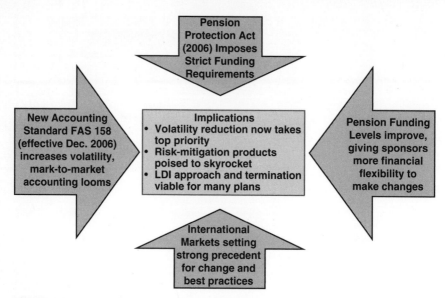

EXHIBIT 5.2   The Pension Perfect Volatility Storm
McKinsey & Co.- The Coming Shakeout in the Defined Benefit Market –2007

created to support. We explain some of these forces more in Chapter 8, but the point to make here is that defined benefit plans are under extreme pressure from a perfect storm of forces. Is it any wonder that fewer and fewer sponsors are offering DB Plans and those that already have them are quickly moving to freeze their plans in one form or another to cauterize their exposure.

With reversion taxes taking all the upside of overfunding out of the equation and the Pension Protection Act of 2006 increasing the cost of underfunding makeups, defined benefit plan sponsors have been turning to a process called freezing their defined benefit plans. There are various types of plan freezes that they can put in place; closed freezes, soft freezes, and hard freezes. This smorgasbord of icy choices is all about determining who sponsors want to exclude from future accrual of benefits. Maybe they just want to close the plan to new employees. Perhaps they want to stop accrual for out-of-service ex-employees and retirees. Or maybe they want to stop all accruals altogether (this represents 85 percent of the freezes being enacted). Freezing a plan is the first step toward full termination, but ERISA has very strict rules for how plans must be terminated (we will discuss that in Chapters 8 and 10).

You can see from the following Towers Watson 10-year trend shown as Exhibit 5.3, the world is moving away from defined benefit to defined contribution plans—whether retirees like it or not.

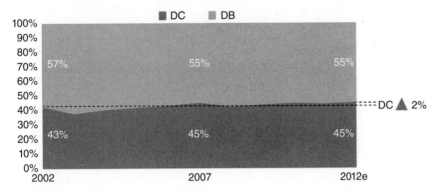

EXHIBIT 5.3   Global DB/DC Asset Split
Source: Towers Watson Global Pension Asset Survey 2012.

What is most interesting about the timing of this trend is that it comes just at the point where the first Baby Boomers are reaching retirement age and are starting to grapple with the sufficiency of their defined contribution lump sums. This is not an altogether obvious picture to a recent retiree. There are many calculators available to give estimates, but also many assumptions that must be made as to longevity and various needs including and perhaps most notably medical care.

It would not be surprising to see the start of a retiree backlash against defined contribution plans in this environment. What seemed like a nice thing in youth, self-determination and independence has a way of becoming very scary in older age. The truth is that most people are not driven to wealth for wealth's sake, but rather to buy a certain lifestyle. In retirement, that lifestyle is mostly a function of the benefits we receive from reputable and reliable providers. The high-flying 401(k) investors of yesteryear may quickly reverse field and wish that they had state or corporate pension plans to lean on.

CHAPTER 6

Alternatives Are Not Only for the Rich and Famous

Half of the pension equation is about assets, so this would be an unfulfilling treatise on the pension crisis without some degree of focus on the fundamental trends underway in the asset management industry. A review of pension assets must start with a broad overview of the investment management industry, but must then move quickly toward a review of the more recent growth in alternative investments and especially hedge funds. (I will reference other alternative assets like private equity, venture capital, real estate, and so on, but the real trend to watch now is hedge funds.)

PENSION ASSETS AND THE MOVE TOWARD ALTERNATIVE ASSETS

Given the attention that the investment management industry (not to mention the world at large) has put on hedge funds and the relatively unregulated and secretive nature of the breed, this chapter seeks to answer the question of what exactly is going on in the industry and where it is going. The intention is to give readers an overview of the hedge fund space from the perspective of what comprises it, who the participants are (managers, investors, support areas, and intermediaries), how hedge funds are assessed and measured both individually and in portfolio, how investors access hedge funds, and what major issues face the industry. This is increasingly becoming an institutional market and, as such, very much about pension funds.

I want to cover the investment landscape and how those trends, such as the enactment of ERISA and the evolution of mutual funds, developed the framework for defined benefit pension management, defined contribution pension management, high-net-worth investing, and retail investing. The chapter spends time explaining and dimensioning these various arenas in order to set the stage for the evolution from balanced fund investing to relative return/style box approaches to modern portfolio theory investing and now to alpha/beta separation asset allocation.

In order to have a complete contextual understanding of the hedge fund universe, it needs to be explained and dimensioned with a brief history of major events in its development. Our focus is on giving readers a sense of who the players are in the market and what investment styles have come and gone and exist today. We include a review of how the investor base in hedge funds has and is shifting and what implications that has for the market.

We need to spend some time discussing the structural side of hedge funds so that everyone understands the legal constructs used that permit hedge funds to carry on business as relatively unregulated entities and how this is quickly changing in ways that directly affect the pension industry. There are a bevy of "post-crisis" regulatory changes that affect the hedge fund industry that are quite striking in how they impact the original unconstrained nature of the hedge fund beast. There are onshore and offshore structures that need to be understood in at least a simple manner. The primary service providers including prime brokers, administrators, and other providers must also be reviewed because, as we will see, they can be an unexpectedly perverse source of risk if not properly understood.

The challenges for investors in assessing hedge funds need to be a major topic for this book. Bernie Madoff and the various feeder funds, which blindly put investor money into a severely undiligenced fund situation, pretty much brought to a halt the "easy" approach of relying on a fund of funds manager to make all these decisions for a pension fund manager. While funds of funds are still used by some and some inertial investment remains in that space, the new-age pension manager wants and needs to understand both systematic and nonsystematic risks on his or her own. We must therefore cover the challenges of due diligence, the attempts to rate hedge funds, and the all-important risk assessment approaches available to investors. Investors need to be able to assess, select, and compose portfolios; blend hedge funds into traditional portfolios; understand the risk dynamics of individual and portfolios of hedge funds; and then monitor, rebalance, and report on performance. This is both about understanding where their risks lie and where their return expectations should be, as well as whether they are getting the alpha for which they are paying.

This chapter also explores the way in which hedge funds are offered to the investing public. This includes pricing issues as well as structural and marketing approaches and trends. We cover single strategy funds, funds of hedge funds, hedge fund platforms, and newer efforts to wrap hedge funds into private equity vehicle offerings (seeding programs). We also discuss the new 130/30 strategies and what they mean to hedge funds and investors.

This chapter then ends with a review of trends and opinions from various thought leaders about where the industry is headed.

THE GREAT HEDGE FUND DEBATE

The history of hedge funds, which we briefly reviewed in Chapter 4, tells us that, while unconstrained investing and absolute return investing have been around for thousands of years, the precise form of hedge funds began in the mid-twentieth century. It began to get broad notice in the Roaring 90s when investor names like Soros, Robertson, and Steinhardt began making piles of money with their hedge funds.

But it was not until the bursting of the Internet bubble and the general market crash in 2000 that institutional investors (beyond the brave souls in the endowment world like David Swensen at Yale) began to take serious notice as the lack of hedging in their long-only investing left them with big market losses and nowhere to turn for uncorrelated returns and true diversification. In the early part of the new millennium, institutional investors started piling into hedge funds, first through something called a fund of funds and gradually into direct fund investments. It was at this moment that the array of hedge funds began to proliferate for a variety of reasons, leaving investors with truly too many funds to choose from as the list began to approach 9,000 funds.

Then, when the markets came crashing down with the financial crisis in the fall of 2008 (a topic we discuss later in this and the next chapter) and many hedge funds failed to provide the diversified returns they had promised because they were far too beta-centric and correlations in general collapsed, people decried the end of the hedge fund era despite the exceptional performance of managers like John Paulson (with his famous bear bet on U.S. residential housing). Hedge funds did see a mild retrenchment, but not long after the collapse they were back on the rebuilding path with institutional participation even stronger yet, for many reasons we will discuss.

Take a look at the Hedge Fund Research (HFR) asset charts in Exhibits 6.1 and 6.2 for the hedge fund industry showing the growth to $2.1 trillion in assets, and look at the charts showing the number of managers: with over 7,600 direct hedge fund managers and another 2,600 fund of funds managers.

It is instructive also to look at the growth of hedge funds as a function of funds liquidated and launched as in Exhibit 6.3.

It is the nature of the industry to be entrepreneurial and for most fund managers to stay in business for an average term of about seven years. Most managers either run out their arbitrage or their motivation by then.

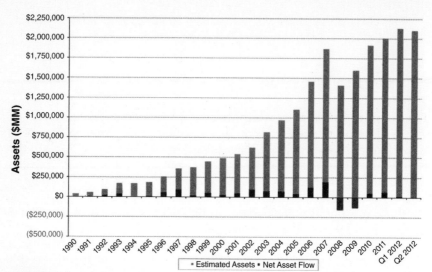

EXHIBIT 6.1   Hedge Fund Growth in AUM
Source: HFR Global Hedge Fund Industry Report—Second Quarter 2012.

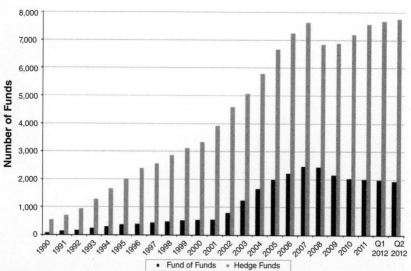

EXHIBIT 6.2   Hedge Fund Growth in Number of Funds
Source: HFR Global Hedge Fund Industry Report—Second Quarter 2012.

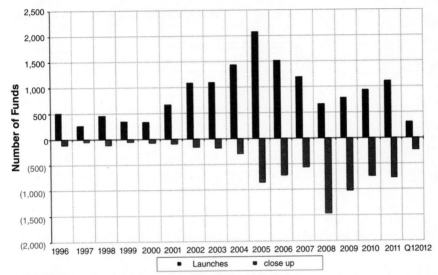

EXHIBIT 6.3 Hedge Funds Launched and Liquidated
Source: HFR Global Hedge Fund Industry Report—Second Quarter 2012.

They either flame out or get so wealthy as to no longer care to endure the rigors of fiduciary duties. Very few managers have found a successful path to monetize their platform beyond their personal and direct involvement (the exceptions being Fortress and Och Ziff, neither of which have performed particularly well post-offering). This fact is quite relevant in comparative performance analysis of the sector by naturally eliminating failed managers. This phenomenon is called the "survivorship bias."

What Exhibit 6.3 shows is that the new launch and failure rate have both risen of late, with far more liquidation growth than launch growth. Such is the postfinancial crises state of affairs in the industry.

So why do hedge funds exist at all? There are several key theories and, not to get too classical, but I call the first of them the Darwinian and Newtonian theories:

- Darwinian reasoning is fundamentally about survival of the fittest, and clearly the best of breed in investing wants to do what hedge funds allow them to do: be unconstrained, make lots of money for their acumen, and be allowed to manage their own money at the same time (eating their own cooking). They revel in the thought that they win and win big if they are good and, if not, they (or, more likely, the other guy) move on.
- The Newtonian thought is one of the parsing of risk that we discussed in Chapter 4 when we spoke of derivatives. Various people have spoken

of "particle finance" as the business of being able to dissect financial risk to its primary colors and load up on cheaply priced assets and sell expensively priced assets. The way one determines value or "cheapness" is a function of risk/reward. There is nothing better than derivatives to do this with securities, and hedge funds are as or more adept at using derivatives than anyone. Remember, constrained investors like mutual funds generally cannot use derivatives in many forms.

To get more basic about the rationale for hedge funds, the proof has also been in the pudding. Certainly from 1988 through 1998, it is hard to say that hedge funds did not do better than long-only investors. There was a moment at the end of the Roaring 90s when the market raced ahead before it came crashing back to earth in 2000, but all the Darwinian and Newtonian theories would not make up for inferior performance, so it is safe to say that hedge funds exist because they outperform other forms of investing on a rather decided and regular basis (we will discuss some recent theories espoused by Simon Lack a bit later that attempt to counter this fact).

And then there is the issue of absolute returns or asymmetrical risk. What does that mean? It means that everyone wants all the upside volatility the market has to offer and none of the downside volatility. There have been many studies done about human behavior in investing and it is absolutely fair to say that individuals have risk preferences that clearly state that they will give up some bit of upside if they can protect the downside. If this sounds like a feeding ground for options technology, you are absolutely correct. Indeed, options are the ultimate asymmetrical instrument and, in general, derivatives market participants are the most adept at options technology. This has made hedge fund managers the best able to deliver asymmetrical risk configurations labeled as absolute return strategies. The ultimate version of this comes in what is called a market neutral strategy, where the manager delivers pure alpha or outperformance to investors without any of the market risk—a nice trick if you can do it—consistently.

Now individual investors care less about correlations than institutional investors do, but with the push into hedge funds by institutional money it is fair to say that hedge funds also exist because they are far better at delivering uncorrelated risk than long-only managers are. This would be completely true if they all eschewed beta in favor of alpha, but they do not. The shakeout in terms of non-correlated risk came in 2008 when correlations collapsed. As Warren Buffett is fond of saying, "Only when the tide goes out do you discover who's been swimming naked." Nonetheless, hedge funds are generally better at delivering uncorrelated risk, so that stands as a valid *raison d'état*.

And let us not forget the last and most compelling, if somewhat raw, reason why hedge funds exist: greed. Gordon Gekko said it clearly in the movie *Wall Street*, "Greed is good." In this case, it is greed on all sides. This is the best form in which good managers can get paid for their skill . . . and they get paid *very* well for it. But also, money chases the best returns and that is what investors do. You can easily call this a subset of Darwinian thinking, but I like letting greed stand on its own.

So let's now look at performance in Exhibit 6.4.

First, let's look at five-year performance by hedge fund type as defined by HFR. Note that the last two return profiles are for the Barclay's Aggregate Bond Index and the S&P 500 Index. Now, look at Exhibit 6.5, which shows an even longer period with cumulative returns, using the HRFI Fund Weighted Composite Index, which is the closest proxy for the entire hedge fund universe.

It does not take a statistical genius to see that a cumulative graph may tend to visually distort the most recent performance reality. To see beyond that, let's look at the most recent 12-month performance in Exhibit 6.6.

What the data in Exhibit 6.6 show is that it's been a rough year, actually a rough two years, for hedge funds with only one category (relative value—asset backed) showing better returns than either the bond or stock index.

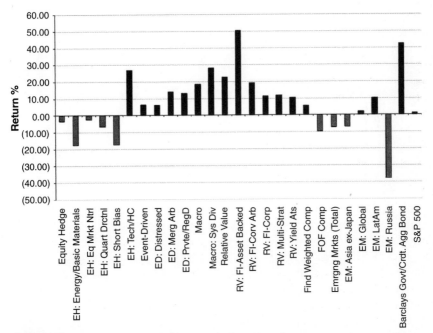

EXHIBIT 6.4 Cumulative Long-Term Hedge Fund Performance
Source: HFR Global Hedge Fund Industry Report—Second Quarter 2012.

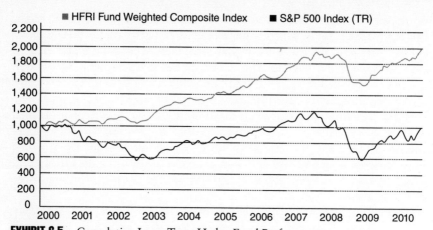

EXHIBIT 6.5   Cumulative Long-Term Hedge Fund Performance
Source: HFR Global Hedge Fund Industry Report—Second Quarter 2012 and Standard & Poor's

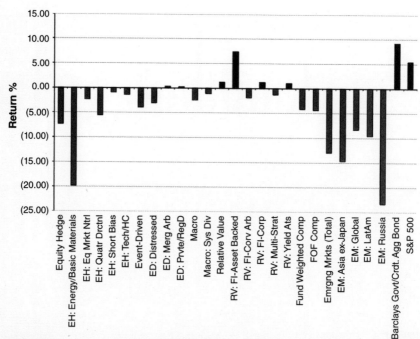

EXHIBIT 6.6   One-Year Hedge Fund Performance (2011)
Source: HFR Global Hedge Fund Industry Report—Second Quarter 2012.

That comes at a moment when Simon Lack, an ex-banker with J.P. Morgan, chose to write his exposé on the industry called *The Hedge Fund Mirage*, published in 2012 by John Wiley & Sons (also the publisher of this book). In that book, he made a number of contentions about hedge funds that basically suggest that the performance has been far worse than investors understand. The bottom line, according to Lack, is that between 1998 and 2010, 98 percent of all earnings from hedge funds went to the managers or the aggregators (fund of funds managers) leaving a mere 2 percent for the investor, whose capital is at work and at risk. This is shown in the following Exhibit 6.7.

Everybody's Fees

Year	Average HF AUM* (BNs)	Real Investor Profits (BNs)	Estimated HF Fees (BNs)**	Estimated FOF Fees (BNs)	Total Fees	Net Real Investor Profits (BNs)	Industry Share of Total Profits
1998	$ 131	$ 10	$ 7	$ 1	$ 7	$ 10	44%
1999	$ 166	$ 36	$ 14	$ 1	$ 15	$ 35	30%
2000	$ 213	$ 17	$ 12	$ 1	$ 13	$ 16	44%
2001	$ 279	$ 13	$ 12	$ 1	$ 13	$ 12	52%
2002	$ 414	$ 12	$ 13	$ 2	$ 15	$ 11	58%
2003	$ 666	$ 82	$ 36	$ 3	$ 38	$ 79	33%
2004	$1,027	$ 14	$ 27	$ 5	$ 32	$ 9	78%
2005	$1,295	–$ 6	$ 35	$ 7	$ 42	–$ 13	143%
2006	$1,537	$ 67	$ 66	$ 9	$ 75	$ 58	56%
2007	$1,925	–$ 11	$ 59	$11	$ 70	–$ 21	144%
2008	$1,797	–$448	$ 36	$10	$ 46	–$458	NM
2009	$1,506	$200	$ 30	$ 7	$ 37	$193	16%
2010	$1,624	$ 83	$ 32	$ 6	$ 38	$ 77	33%
Total		$ 70	$379	$61	$440	$ 9	98%

*Source: BarclayHedge
**Assumes no incentive fees, as many funds were still below their high-water marks following 2008.

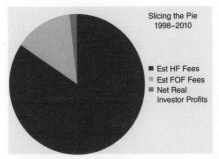

EXHIBIT 6.7 Simon Lack's Hedge Fund Miracle
Source: HFR Global Hedge Fund Industry Report, Second Quarter 2012, from *The Hedge Fund Mirage* by Simon Lack (Hoboken, NJ: John Wiley & Sons, 2012).

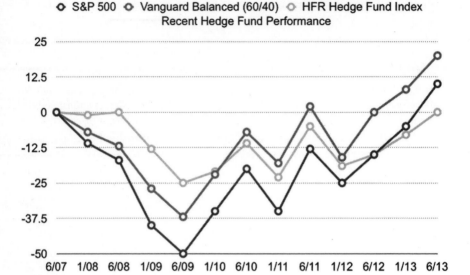

EXHIBIT 6.8   Hedge Fund Reversal of Fortune

The reaction to the book by the industry and specifically by the Alternative Investment Management Association (AIMA) was summarized in a research paper called "Methodological, Mathematical and Factual Errors in *The Hedge Fund Mirage*."

The matter of greatest interest is not whether Lack or AIMA is correct, but that hedge fund returns have marginalized (secularly or cyclically) to the point where there is a legitimate debate. Even Bloomberg points this out, as shown in Exhibit 6.8.

When the issue boils down to whether one should use dollar-weighted returns (Lack) versus time-weighted returns (AIMA), meaning those who looked at this for individual investors (who chose when to enter or exit the fund) rather than the fund, it's clear that returns for the whole category are recently not what anyone hoped. What I believe everyone, especially Lack, would agree with is that there is a greater need than ever to differentiate between managers delivering true alpha and those collecting high fees and underperforming.

THE INSTITUTIONALIZATION OF HEDGE FUNDS

All of these recent performance issues notwithstanding, institutional investors have hedge funds in their sights and are not swayed to reconsider based on this. There is one perspective that the "perfect storm" we described with underfunding and increased impact of volatility has driven pension funds to play "catch-up" by reaching for yield if they are already way behind and a liability-driven approach is not possible (more on that in Chapter 8). Exhibit 6.9 shows the institutional flows pouring into hedge funds, while Exhibit 6.10 shows where they are generally coming from.

This might be exacerbated at some pension funds by the move to passive management and the generally dampened market outlook of late (notwithstanding the 2013 rally we are experiencing as I write this . . .). We can see in the following Exhibit 6.11 the steady growth in passive and ETF (mostly passive) instruments. The overlay of alpha from hedge funds is a topic coming up regularly in pension trustee boardrooms.

The growth of hedge fund allocations is not limited to pension funds, but is also seen in the endowment and foundation area (where, as we have previously said, the activity is quite longstanding) as well as the sovereign wealth funds. (See Exhibit 6.12.)

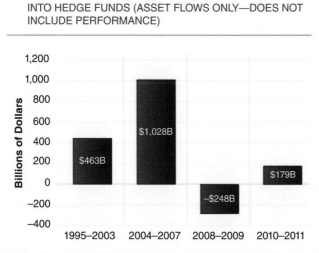

EXHIBIT 6.9   Institutional Hedge Fund Flows
Source: "Institutional Investment in Hedge Funds: Evolving Investor Portfolio Construction Drives Product Convergence," Citi Prime Finance, June 2012.

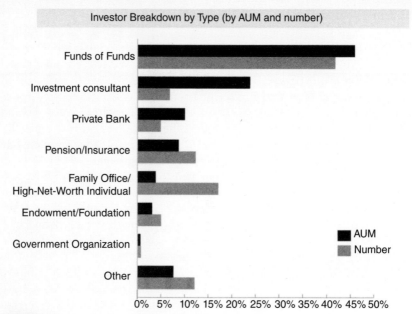

Investor Breakdown by Type (by AUM and number)

EXHIBIT 6.10 Institutional Hedge Fund Segmentation
Source: Deutsche Bank—2012 Alternative Investment Survey.

The fact that hedge fund allocations are growing is hard to refute and the fact that this is happening during a bad performance cycle for hedge funds, when a major market debate is underway about the value of hedge fund investing, is a testament to several things. First, it speaks to the slow and steady long-term view of the institutional investor market. It also speaks to the long history of success by hedge funds and perhaps the specific outperformance of enough very good hedge funds, even during this period, such that investors believe they can select the next breed of winners.

The real question to ask is how this influx of institutional money is going to alter the hedge fund market itself. The obvious issue is whether the influx will chase returns and alpha out of the system and effectively collapse the arbitrages that they are built upon by sheer dint of the volume of money that seeks to be invested. I would argue that managers self-police this issue pretty well given that their own money is likely to be diluted in its returns in the process and most institutional managers making large allocations watch the market capacity constraints pretty closely.

I think the much bigger impact is on the business model of hedge fund investing itself. This "unconstrained" space has been a bit of a cottage industry with a bare bones approach to the back office and client service

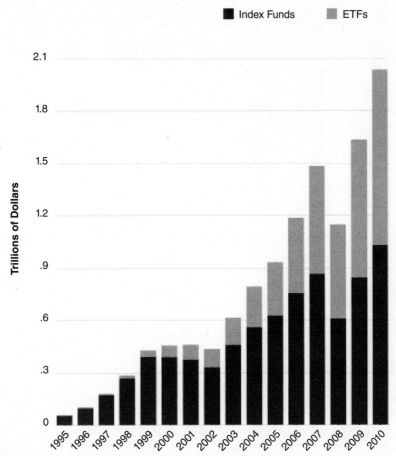

EXHIBIT 6.11   Growth in Passive Index and ETF Funds

Source: "Institutional Investment in Hedge Funds: Evolving Investor Portfolio Construction Drives Product Convergence," Citi Prime Finance, June 2012.

arenas. Some change is clearly mandated by the new, sterner regulatory environment. Since 2008, this has not just come from the U.S. regulatory community, but increasingly from the European and Asian (much less so) markets. Exhibit 6.13 shows the areas of concern.

Let's look at the most recent data on hedge fund allocations in institutional portfolios altogether. Citibank Prime Finance shows the growth in two stages (Exhibits 6.14 and 6.15). Exhibit 6.14 shows 2003 to 2007, where the share goes from 2.4 to 9.2 percent, while passive strategies grow from 7 to 10.1 percent (hence further proving the alpha/beta separation).

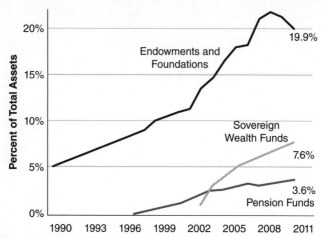

EXHIBIT 6.12   Institutional Hedge Fund Segmentation
Source: "Institutional Investment in Hedge Funds: Evolving Investor Portfolio Construction Drives Product Convergence," Citi Prime Finance, June 2012.

And then from 2007 to 2011 in Exhibit 6.15, we see hedge funds growing from 9.2 up to 10.5 percent, while passive strategies grew from 10.3 to 15 percent. The refinement in Exhibit 6.15 is that there is further breakout of active equities from active fixed income. This allows us to see that *more* than the full amount of allocation shift for the hedge fund and passive increases came from active equity. This should tell us yet again that the volatility impact of the "perfect storm" is, indeed, driving managers to do several things. They are shifting out of higher volatility equities. They are moving from traditional managers and breaking that up into passive managers/high alpha managers (presumably with less volatility by some degree of market neutrality).

One of the interesting suggestions over the past few years has come from McKinsey, the world-class consulting firm. They produced a report called "The Coming Shakeout in the Defined Benefit Market," which discussed the alternatives facing the largely underfunded defined benefit pension plans of the world. Their construct was to do what McKinsey does so well: Put it in a matrix. In this case, it was a matrix showing the financial flexibility of the sponsoring company and the plan status (frozen or unfrozen). The interesting outcome of the matrix was to suggest that the investment allocations of these companies would be driven by their positioning on this matrix. Those that could innovate might look to take advantage of their situation and use their plans to do so. Those without financial flexibility would either wait

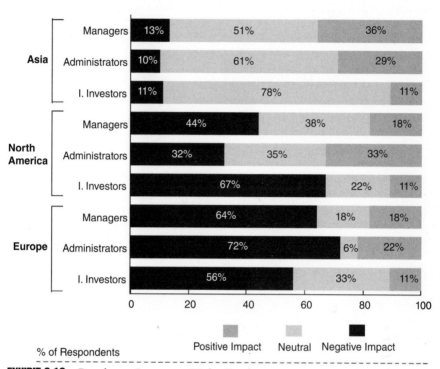

What do you think will be the impact of forthcoming regulations in the below regions on worldwide growth of alternative investments?

EXHIBIT 6.13   Regulatory Impact on Hedge Funds
Source: Deutsche Bank—2012 Alternative Investment Survey.

and pray or roll the dice and take on perhaps more alpha risk. Those stuck in the middle would either use solutions like liability-driven investing (LDI, as discussed in Chapter 8) or work toward termination (Chapter 9). The real outcome of this analysis implied that many more pension plans would seek the "hail Mary" play and invest more heavily in hedge funds, which they have effectively done. See Exhibit 6.16.

So with all this new money seeking a bigger return to help fill the under-funding gap, which alternatives areas do you suppose got the lion's share of the allocations? If you guessed hedge funds, you win. Recognizing that this survey by Deutsche Bank (Exhibit 6.17) was done in 2011, it is fair to say that the same answers came back for most of the past five or six years from the pension plan respondents to this institutional investor survey.

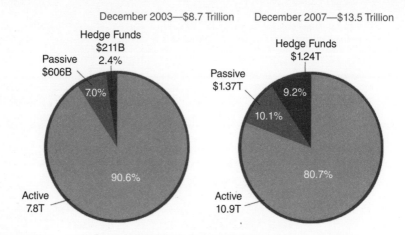

Comparison of Institutional AUM Pools by Investment Type

EXHIBIT 6.14 Hedge Fund Allocations by Institutions (2003 through 2007)
Source: "Institutional Investment in Hedge Funds: Evolving Investor Portfolio Construction Drives Product Convergence," Citi Prime Finance, June 2012.

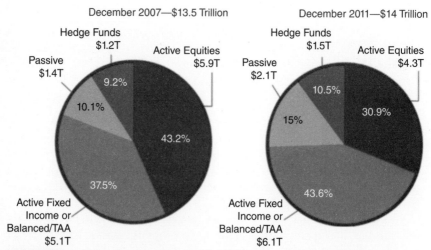

EXHIBIT 6.15 Hedge Fund Allocations by Institutions (2007 through 2011)
Source: "Institutional Investment in Hedge Funds: Evolving Investor Portfolio Construction Drives Product Convergence," Citi Prime Finance, June 2012.

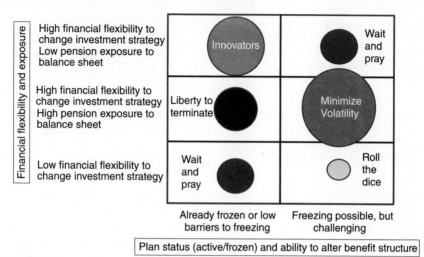

EXHIBIT 6.16 McKinsey Solution Segmentation
Source: "The Coming Shakeout in the Defined Benefit Market," McKinsey & Co., 2007.

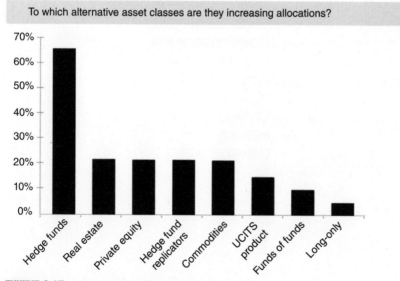

EXHIBIT 6.17 Alternative Allocations
Source: Deutsche Bank—2012 Alternative Investment Survey.

This is actually a good list of other alternative classes. The two obvious ones are real estate and private equity. The rest on this list are really other names for hedge funds. Replicators are effectively hedge funds, and commodities are usually packaged as CTA hedge funds. UCITS products are just packaged hedge funds used under EU regulations. And of course, fund of funds are just bundled hedge funds.

Now let's look at the impact all this money flowing into hedge funds has had on the hedge fund market. Generally, one would think this is only good, but keep in mind that compared to high net-worth individuals and family offices—and perhaps even endowments and foundations—pension funds swing a *much* bigger stick with investment managers since they allocate larger blocks of money and they have much more rigorous standards of diligence and tracking. Pension funds are the big dogs of the neighborhood, and if you want to run with the big dogs, you have to play the game "their way."

"Their way" means a much more controlled, regulated, transparent, and generally buttoned-up approach to what had grown up as a cottage industry. Let's start by looking at what investors think are the biggest issues their managers face now. See Exhibit 6.18.

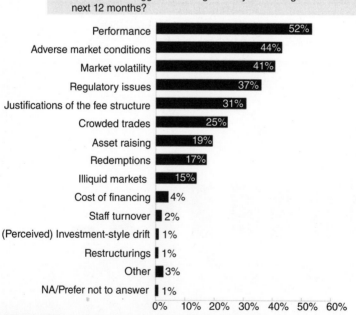

EXHIBIT 6.18 Hedge Fund Manager Challenges
Source: Deutsche Bank—2012 Alternative Investment Survey.

It's funny because to read this list of what factors investors use to assess managers, one would think that it's all about performance and investment style (see Exhibit 6.19).

But when you look more deeply at the rigorous requirements that institutional investors (particularly pension funds) put on their managers, you see that they are asking them to fundamentally change their way of doing business. As you can see in Exhibit 6.20, hedge fund managers like to shift their arbitrage bets and "drift" to opportunities by creating multistrategy funds; hardly the clarity of investment philosophy that ranks #1 on investors' hit parade. Managers prefer to manage risk "dynamically" from the trading desk—not the sort of risk management infrastructure #2 requires. Identifying the source of alpha and providing transparency (#4 and #6) are anathema to managers, who are secrecy hounds. Well, at least both can agree on liquidity terms—oops, more liquidity for investors means less flexibility for managers . . . same for redemptions, fees, and so on. And all these added separations of duties and reporting requirements cost money. And telling a manager how many prime brokers he should use, well, that's downright insulting.

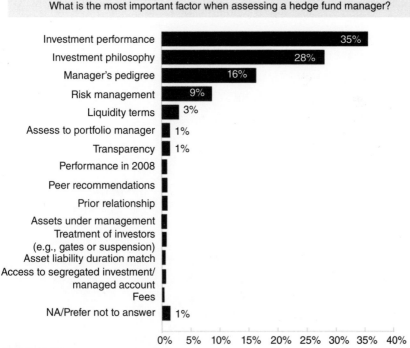

EXHIBIT 6.19 Hedge Fund Selection Criteria
Deutsche Bank—2012 Alternative Investment Survey

Important or very important factors in the selection of hedge fund managers (% of respondents)

EXHIBIT 6.20   Hedge Fund Selection Criteria
Source: Deutsche Bank—2012 Alternative Investment Survey.

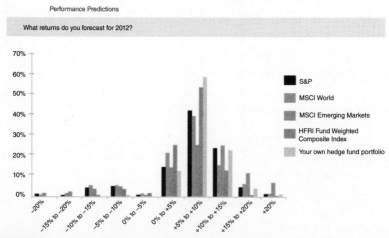

EXHIBIT 6.21   Investor Hedge Fund Performance Predictions
Source: Deutsche Bank—2012 Alternative Investment Survey.

The point made in Exhibits 6.19 and 6.20 is simply that the institution-alization of the investor base is having the effect of institutionalizing the hedge fund business model. That and the increase in regulation is making the business less profitable and, in some instances, less attractive to manag-ers. Not to worry, there is still plenty of juice to interest most managers, but it is certainly fair to say that some of these institutional elements are cramping managers' style and cutting in on returns for both managers and investors.

Nonetheless, hope springs eternal and if we look at the projected re-turns found in the Deutsche Bank survey in Exhibit 6.21 we see that the market is still expecting a lot from hedge funds—but is it enough to fill the underfunded pension bucket?

Next up, we discuss alpha operations, operational risk, securities lend-ing, and ratio lending, among other things to put a fine point on the hedge fund discussion.

CHAPTER 7

The Long and the Short of It . . . Trust Me

O ne of the most interesting, profitable, and yet pernicious aspects of the securities markets and money management revolves around shorting and the borrowing of securities to perform this function. As pension funds ease into the deep end of the asset management pool, they begin to encounter these issues and the rewards and risks are enormous, as I try to explain in this chapter.

This chapter focuses on the elements of the asset management industry that most critically add to success, but that are outside the traditional realm of investment strategy. It is generally understood today that risk is comprised of many elements and includes a significant component of operational risk. In the same way, return is often described as being comprised of systemic and specific elements or beta and alpha. Much confusion exists around the delineation of alpha and beta, and alpha is sometimes thought to be better characterized as exotic beta or beta is characterized as synthetic alpha. There are, however, operational elements of the investment process that clearly add or detract significant value from returns just like operational risk can add to or detract from overall risk.

These operational elements that add to returns are called many things, but the one thing you need to be very careful *not* to call them is "operational alpha." When I started teaching my course about how alpha can come from how a manager operates the back office, I logically called my course "NBA 5470: Operational Alpha" as part of my Alpha Series ("The Search for Alpha," "Operational Alpha," and "Liability-Driven Alpha"). Several months later, I was contacted by the Cornell University Legal Department, who had been contacted by KCG IP Holdings LLC with a threatening letter demanding that I cease and desist using what they claim is a copyrighted name, "Operational Alpha," which is owned by KCG IP Holdings LLC. KCG is the intellectual property holding company of Ken Griffin of Citadel, one of the most successful hedge fund groups. Griffin is one of the foremost hedge fund managers in the world. In fact, it is fair to say that Ken Griffin is in the pantheon of hedge fund managers along with George Soros, Julian Robertson, James Simons, Steven Cohen, Ray Dalio, and John Paulson.

Now, after getting over my amazement that the term was copyrighted and that Ken Griffin would bother to chase an academic violator, I decided that I could use this tidbit to my academic advantage. I now call NBA 5470 "The Short Side of Alpha*" with the * being that KCG IP Holdings LLC and Ken Griffin thought the concept of "Operational Alpha" was so important that he wants sole use of the term . . . something that should be a meaningful indicator to students that there is something here they should learn about.

(A side note about the significance in course titles is that my third course was originally called "Defined Benefit Pension Plans in Transition." That title netted me seven students. With the change of title to "Liability-Driven Alpha [third in the Alpha Series]," I now average 50 to 60 students. Marketing is all around us.)

ALPHA FROM OPERATIONS

The more mature a market or investment strategy becomes, or the more difficult the return environment, the more important generating alpha from operations becomes. This element of investment performance is generally overlooked and misunderstood. It is often the case that hedge funds and investment managers in general relegate it to back-office processing clerks or simply leave it in the hands of prime brokers, when it should be attended to with far greater care. At pension funds, this function has often been left in the hands of custodians and/or master trustees—equally a mistake, as we next show.

Asset management (most notably the hedge fund industry, but also the new arenas of 130/30 investing) that is unconstrained in terms of being able to use shorting, leverage, and derivatives as a significant part of investment strategy has a significantly greater operational burden than do long-only managers. These activities depend very heavily on securities financing to accommodate their strategies. The arcane and opaque world of securities finance, and specifically securities lending, has been a primary driver of broker/dealer profitability over the past 15 years. It has also supported the securities processing businesses of major banks for over 40 years. During the current financial crisis, no activity has come under more scrutiny and become more widely debated (not to mention being more widely misunderstood) than stock shorting activity. In fact, there has even been a new moniker created for this arcane species called Shadow Banking. This $3+ trillion arena is a key element in a successful investment strategy for both managers and, indeed, for large institutional investors, and everyone from the SEC to the European Union to securities litigators are trying hard to shine a light into the corners of this shadowy world.

Securities lending drives prime brokerage and therefore drives Wall Street profitability. Securities lending is necessary to shorting, which is one of the handful of major alpha generators for hedge fund managers. Securities lending drives custodial revenues and therefore drives the bulk of securities processing. Securities lending drives the profitability of passive or index strategy management and therefore drives the profitability of large traditional managers and many mutual fund and ETF managers (a large topic unto itself these days). That means it's an important profit center for instruments critical to retail and "instividual" markets that are central to defined contribution markets and retirement savings generally. And securities lending has become a significant driver of pension fund returns and as such is a driver of the next demographic stage of the world economy.

Understanding how shorting, securities finance, and rehypothecation and securities lending take place and how the business is conducted are critical skills for anyone in the asset management business and the pension management business. It is not widely discussed or widely taught in business schools because it is only understood by a very few professionals, and yet it is increasingly essential to a broad array of professionals in and students heading toward capital markets, sales and trading, and even general finance careers.

This chapter explains the history, practices, risks, rewards, participants, and controversies of this relatively obscure but vitally important financial function.

OPERATIONAL RISK

Before we go into securities lending, let's review the importance of operational risk in investment management (and especially hedge fund management). As explained in the last chapter, institutional investors are demanding more evidence of controlled operational risk, so this is important stuff to managers and investors alike. Most of the great hedge fund failures have had significant elements of operational risk. Operational breakdowns such as illiquidity, misreporting, and excessive leverage or prime broker counterparty risk concentration are at the center of most of these failures including Granite, LTCM, Beacon Hill, Bayou, Marin Capital (no relation),

Ameranth, Bear Stearns High Grade Funds (unfortunately, too much relation), Madoff, and even MF Global.

Hedge fund collapses often begin when an unusual market event causes
the portfolio to quickly fall in value. When leverage is involved, as margin
calls and investor redemptions increase, the hedge fund is forced to either
liquidate the portfolio or be acquired by another firm. The cycle is almost
self-fulfilling. It is so common because the sources of alpha involve the very
elements that are problematic in adverse circumstances: shorting, hedging,
rehypothecating, leverage, prime broker risk, gating, suspended redemptions, lock-ups, exit fees, and, ultimately, manager skill or the lack thereof.
The process looks like Exhibit 7.1, with the dotted line signifying the demar-
cation between survival and inevitable demise.

Holly Miller, one of the foremost experts on hedge fund operational risk
has put together her list of the top 10 operational risks (the list follows). I
have then added examples to her list that makes it come to life from specific
experiences.

1. **Complacency:** Trivializing and disregarding risks—LTCM and many
   more.
2. **Blind leading the blind:** Overextended and underqualified managers—
   many emerging markets managers on platforms with limited EM experience.
3. **Novices, apprentices, and soloists:** Inadequate training and cross-
   training—many platforms allow managers to work remotely, in solo.
4. **Dropped batons:** Hand-offs—in many funds I have seen, operational
   and compliance procedures often fall by the wayside over time and with
   personnel turnover.

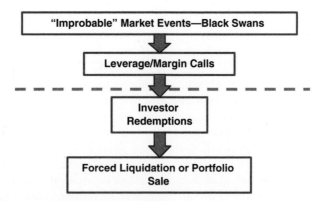

EXHIBIT 7.1   The Hedge Fund Death Spiral

5. **Naïve reliance on technology:** The downside of automation—we owned Measurisk, a hedge fund VaR risk platform that simply couldn't do its job with certain funds where sufficient modeling did not exist.
6. **Playbooks:** Workflow documentation—it *rarely* exists sufficiently.
7. **Amalgamated assignments:** Segregation of duties—the now-infamous NewCastle Funds at Bear were rife with conflicted arrangements, blurring the segregation of trading and operational areas. We corrected this, but the tendencies were indicators of attitudinal flaws.
8. **Reconciliation gaps:** A false sense of security—when running the 401(k) business, it was clear that unreconciled errors were common bases for larger failures.
9. **Poor planning and response times:** Changes in the firm, the marketplace, and the regulatory environment—this is most evident in the multiple failures in the mortgage-backed securities markets.
10. **Reading the fine print:** Know thy legal entities—there are many examples, but the most famous is the Plus Funds case, where director liability indemnity overlap breached the segregation of the separate account structure.[1]

Generally what are needed are processes and controls particularly in the all-important accurate pricing and valuation realm. It goes beyond processing to timely reporting, transparency, and risk management. They want all those things from the last chapter that institutional investors demand so that they can feel comfortable with thorough diligence of the funds or funds of funds. The Madoff cascading risk scenario where no real operational due diligence was conducted on Madoff for decades simply cannot happen anymore.

When we look at what characterizes hedge funds today, we see newly developed derivative instruments giving managers more opportunity for arbitrage and leverage. We see increased investment in illiquid securities and more and more information arbitrage (with concomitant indictments for insider trading). We see evolving investment strategies leading to trade crowding (especially in quantitative strategies), dilution of relative value arbitrages, and hedge funds that are looking more like broker-dealers as they activate trading in securities finance and securities. This all translates into one thing: more operational risk.

SECURITIES LENDING HISTORY

In fact, when you stop to consider almost all of the sources of alpha, what you find is a preponderance of one common element. That element involves

[1] Holly Miller, Stone House Consulting, LLC.

securities finance and securities lending. And where there is collateralized financing involving securities, counterparty risk is right behind. This has particularly become a major concern to regulators after the failure of Lehman; the near failures of Bear, Merrill, and AIG; and then the abject failure four years later to plug the holes as evidenced in the events of MF Global's collapse. It is the world of securities finance that operates in the most opaque nether regions of Wall Street that has given rise to the term *shadow banking* and the resultant regulatory maelstrom around this arcane arena. It is not unusual that many complex financial products or transactions are not well understood by the politicians and lawmakers . . . and sometimes even the regulators.

But what distinguishes securities finance is that it is so misunderstood by Wall Street professionals and management and really only known well to the actual practitioners in the equity derivatives and prime brokerage areas. I am even surprised how little is taught about securities lending in business schools. When my students contact me after graduation, they often say that the small amount of securities lending education I give them has given them a differential advantage in the market. This is all pretty amazing, and I attribute it largely to the huge profitability of the practice and Wall Street's preference that it all stays in the shadows.

Now securities lending is not a new practice. When I joined Bankers Trust in 1976, my first assignment was in an area called Eastern Financial. We handled all the banks and insurance companies in the Northeast, and I was assigned to the New England team. What I was out selling was one thing predominantly, bringing the trust and portfolio assets of these banks and insurers into the new paperless world of "dematerialization" of securities, which were now being handled through depositaries like DTC and the Fed Book Entry system. This was as opposed to holding physical securities in their vaults where they were difficult to transact. These banks and insurers now needed to use a custodian to handle their securities, even though the custodians themselves didn't often handle the physical securities either, but did all the things needed to control the transactions and give the bank or insurer the comfort that a trustee or fiduciary was watching their assets for them.

One particular small savings bank that I convinced to use Bankers Trust as custodian actually sent their 70-year-old securities clerk named Mildred to New York with two separate locked suitcases. One had the security certificates and the other had the signed powers documents needed to make the securities negotiable. I had to take Mildred's picture outside our 16 Wall Street office with both suitcases. She then insisted on taking the cases into the vault, a place I had not seen since my week of vault duty, when all new officers had to take a one-week shift of being there each night for the physical locking of the vault. I tried to explain that we had secure rail cars to carry securities into the vault, but she insisted on seeing it herself. There she carefully unloaded both cases, and she and I had to sign each security. Imagine her shock when she learned that the next day we would send the vast majority of the securities (all except the odd municipal or restricted shares) to DTC, and we would never see them again except on portfolio lists.

What I have not yet explained is that we really didn't have good cost accounting systems that could tell us if we made or lost money on the custody service. It was all so new and complex that this was not as surprising as it sounds. We priced the service on the basis of the competition's pricing (and they were likely doing the same). There were really only four or five players that were in the game (BT, Chase, State Street, Northern, and Mellon, with BONY a small also-ran). I doubt anyone was priced to make money because we were all in a disruptive (by virtue of DTC) land grab. And, oh yeah, there was securities lending.

Securities lending was why we were in the game, even then. Since there were no hedge funds or equity derivatives to speak of then, the demand or securities lending was purely operational. Other brokers needed to borrow securities to cover failed deliveries (a declining problem with DTC) and the relatively small amount of shorting going on—if any regulators were even watching that in those days. Poor old Mildred was never even told that we planned to lend her beloved securities. Her boss, a retired farmer who was now the chairman of this little country bank, heard only one thing: that allowing us to lend his securities would save him enough on custody charges that he would be able to tell his board that the whole transition saved them money, including the cost of Mildred's train ride to the big city.

THE SECURITIES LENDING MARKET

This is a really big globalizing market. There are about $50 trillion in equities in the world with about $16 trillion of that considered "lendable." Of that there has often been a utilization level of 20 percent, meaning that it is not unusual for there to be over $3 trillion in securities out on loan at any time. And of course, this is just equities, and bonds, which are perhaps lent even more than equities (though generally with lower fees), more than double those numbers. This qualifies this as a very big market by any standards. As to their global nature, it is true that over 60 percent of the equity securities loaned are U.S. equities, but European and Asian securities are coming on strong, and every day another emerging market crosses over the hurdle of fearing the impact of short-selling and approves securities lending, albeit with great trepidation. The market is highly intermediated and very, very opaque.

It is interesting that in an era when regulators have spent great energy insuring best execution tracking for cash market activities, there is no such tracking of securities lending transactions. Basically, the intermediaries can charge or extract whatever the market will bear. In addition, with no good price discovery capability (these are all private trades that do not get "printed" on an exchange and thereby shared with all market participants), market participants simply have no way of determining if they have been fairly treated by their intermediary. Surprisingly, this opacity goes for the sophisticated hedge funds on one side of the trade and the sleepy pension funds on the other side. We go into this much more deeply later in the chapter.

The numerical example I like to use to get the attention of my students involves just how important securities lending is to Wall Street. Let's start by realizing that a large Wall Street broker/dealer interfaces mostly with the securities finance market through its prime brokerage business. Prime brokerage is not fundamentally different from regular brokerage, but it is a 15-year-old or so business that focuses heavily on hedge funds. This is because hedge funds have higher trading volumes and certainly borrow more securities than any other market sector. The prime brokerage areas of large broker/dealers were making $11 to 12 billion per year in revenues (I haven't seen updated numbers on this, but it's still in this order of magnitude). For many big banks like Goldman Sachs, Morgan Stanley, or Bear Stearns, the prime brokerage business represented 20 to 25 percent of the profits of the bank.

Within the prime brokerage areas, it is common knowledge that the securities finance activities represent over 100 percent of the profitability of the area. That means many of the other activities other than securities finance are loss leaders to make sure the prime gets the lion's share of the securities lending activity. (Sounds a bit like the old custody stories from 1976, doesn't it?) So it is fair to say that securities lending represented 20 to 25 percent of the broker/dealers' profits.

In valuing banks, analysts differentiate annuity businesses (those that are there cranking out profits year after year) from transactional businesses (trading or investment banking for instance). As a rough rule of thumb, annuity income is worth a multiple of transactional income for the logical reason that it can be counted on in ways that trading profits and investment banking fees cannot be. This leads me to suggest that more than half of the value of big Wall Street banks comes directly from securities lending. Think about the emergency sale of Bear Stearns to JPMorgan Chase in 2008. The only things that were valued were the large prime brokerage business and the building. Wow, no wonder they want to keep this all a deep, dark secret.

Now go back to those big processing banks like State Street, BONY Mellon (now merged), and Northern Trust. Have you been noticing all the litigation aimed at them in the past few years? It has been focused on two ancillary activities to the custody product suite. One that got lots of profile (because it's pretty easy to understand) was that they were using off-market FX rates in the international securities transactions for pension clients. FX was a massively important profit center or the custody business of these processing banks. And the other was the litigation against the custodians over securities-lining activities that ended up costing pension clients lots and lots of money. The custodians all pretty much salved over those wounds with major cash settlements of hundreds of millions of dollars into their STIFs (short-term investment funds), and even that did not stop the flurry of litigation which is ongoing. This received less general public attention because while the numbers were large, the underlying issues are very complex.

And last, but not least, look at major investment managers, particularly those like BlackRock (the largest money manager in the world) and again State Street, who are both big passive managers and managers of the relatively new vehicles called exchange-traded funds (ETFs). Both activities rely heavily on securities lending revenues and those activities (which too often do not accrue to the asset owners, but rather to the managers) are coming under attack by regulators and in the press. In fact, BlackRock is also now the target of big litigation by pension funds over its securities lending splits on its ETF products[2] . . . and it's just the beginning, I suspect. Again, when I ran the asset management business of Bankers Trust, we were, as I mentioned, the third largest passive manager. I recall bidding on an S&P 500 index mandate and pricing it at zero. That is no misprint— we offered to manage a $1 billion index mandate for a big Canadian pension fund for nothing, other than the right to lend the portfolio and keep those fees.

Pause for a moment and ask yourself who might be very, very dependent on securities lending. Well, before 2008 the three worlds of prime finance, money management, and global custody were more split than combined. Now, of course, that is no longer so. With JPMorgan Chase's purchase of Bear Stearns, JPM has now positioned itself as a major prime broker, a major money manager, and one of the four major custodian banks. That pretty much puts JPM on all sides of this trade as an intermediary serving hedge funds, pension funds, running hedge funds, and doing almost everything in between. That's a pretty unique and interesting situation. As an analyst, I would say that's a great advantage to JPM given the current profitability of the securities finance business. As a more broadly thinking person, however, one might worry that if the regulators and the market participants decide it's

[2] Steve Johnson and David Ricketts, "U.S. Pension Funds Sue BlackRock," *Financial Times,* February 4, 2013.

time for more transparency in this arcane area (yes, some of that is already underway), then that profitability might evaporate. What is it that Buffett likes to say about low tide and bathing suits? The question is, how will these business models fare when transparency takes the tide out?

So with big broker dealers, big custodians, and big money managers all relying so heavily on securities lending as a primary revenue source, and keeping things very hush-hush, there must be something going on here at the expense of someone. Well, guess who's at the top of that someone's list? Correct, pension funds. It's time for us to delve further.

SECURITIES LENDING FLOW, PROCESS, AND MECHANICS

Exhibit 7.2 contains a basic primer on securities lending flows.

At the left, you start with the owners of large pools of securities, the so-called beneficial owners, which are often, but not always, pension funds or mutual funds. They have securities that are sitting idly by and are available to be lent. It's funny that I would say that these assets are idle, because in theory the funds are invested in these securities and they are doing exactly what they are supposed to in representing the claims on those interests and accruing dividends, interest, and/or changing value as the marketplace dictates. But in another sense, they are idle because they could be used in the securities lending market to help others facilitate transactions without changing the nature of the economic interest they primarily serve to represent (the exception being perhaps the loss of voting rights).

On the right of Exhibit 7.2, you have hedge funds as the primary borrower of securities, primarily for purposes of shorting, the rules around which have tightened of late and require those who short to locate the security they want to short at the same time that they are executing the trade.

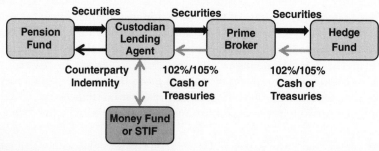

EXHIBIT 7.2   Securities Lending Flows

The reason for this is fairly obvious; regulators and market participants do not want people to speculatively short securities and create undue negative volatility and disrupt securities markets. It is like fire insurance. You wouldn't want just anyone to write an insurance policy against your property because it might create a perverse incentive to see it burned down. Just as insurance companies require evidence of an insurable interest, securities markets require the party shorting a stock to be able to prove that he can borrow the stock and keep it on hold to fill the short if need be. In this way, there cannot be shorting that exceeds the available supply of securities; and more specifically, keeps the available supply on hand and accessible for borrowing.

So hedge funds are looking to borrow securities and pension funds, and mutual funds have securities available to be borrowed. Now enter the intermediaries. This market is highly intermediated, which is to say the intermediaries very tightly control the flows, the mechanics, and the data, not to mention the price discovery process. The intermediaries that act on behalf of the borrowers or hedge funds are the prime brokers. When a hedge fund wants to borrow XYZ security, it tells its prime, who immediately tells the hedge fund whether they can locate XYZ, and then, and only then, will transact to allow the hedge fund to book the short. The prime will then communicate with the custodian community (presuming they do not already have XYZ in their own positions) looking for the security. This is actually a very high-tech and automated process for many securities, but is handled more "hands on" for hard-to-locate securities with the primes really earning their keep with their hedge fund clients by always knowing where to find hard-to-source securities.

The custodians are the intermediary that interfaces with the beneficial owners. This process happens in a much longer-term process with pension funds and mutual funds by the custodians getting securities lending agency agreements for their existing custodian clients. Under those arrangements, there is generally a revenue split agreed (usually 15 to 20 percent of the revenue going to the agent bank). In addition, since the norm in the U.S. securities lending market is that cash collateral is provided in an amount of 102 percent of the market value of the lent securities (marked-to-market daily), there is also a need to agree on the manner in which that cash collateral is invested. Much of the revenues from lending come from the reinvestment of this cash collateral, though some revenue also may come from what are called rebates of fees from the borrower. So it is critically important to understand that the intermediation on the beneficial owner side is for both placement of securities loans, but ALSO the management of the cash collateral. Most agent banks will argue that the two functions are inextricably linked, but they are indeed two separate functions. One other function of

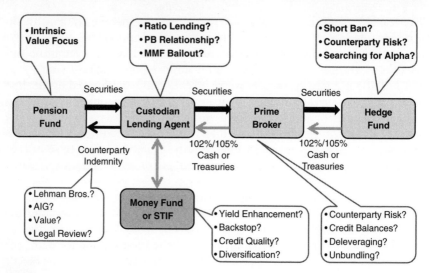

EXHIBIT 7.3   Disruptions in the Securities Lending Market

the agent bank intermediary is that it provides the beneficial owner a full counterparty indemnification. This is functionally important to get pension funds and mutual funds over the hurdle of who is being lent their securities (the cash collateral notwithstanding), and it allows the smooth operation of this operationally intensive function since the intraday processing demands to place securities, retract securities (say, if the fund has sold a position or wants to vote a position), and invest collateral funds is quite extensive.

Exhibit 7.3 really highlights all the disruption we have seen in the securities lending markets in the past five years and gives us a roadmap for some important issues for pension funds.

Hedge Funds

The market gyrations here and around the world in 2008 caused a regulatory overreaction such that shorting was banned to prevent panic selling or perhaps predatory shorting. This ban was focused on mostly financial institutions since shorting might impact leveraged institutions more, given the immediate stricture in the availability of credit at that moment. It was almost immediately lifted in the United States because we were fortunate to have a Treasury Secretary who (regardless of whether you are a fan or not of Hank Paulson or the Bush Administration) understood the capital markets very well. The United Kingdom was not so fortunate and suffered a much longer ban on shorting, and there was even talk of a permanent ban, an action which would have effectively killed London as a financial center.

There were even private company overreactions, which are quite notable. As Morgan Stanley's John Mack (no neophyte to capital markets) was getting hammered by the shorting community and the credit default swap rates on Morgan Stanley were going through the roof and signaling imminent collapse (which was the chicken and which was the egg we will never know), Mack lashed out against "predatory" hedge funds that were shorting his stock. This had an immediate and somewhat impactful effect on Morgan Stanley's rather large prime brokerage business because it smacked of nonsupport for what some would say were Morgan Stanley's most important clients.

Hedge funds were also worried about their counterparty risk exposure in addition to sourcing enough borrowing power from their prime brokers to support their trading needs. Heavy concentrations in exposure to one or two primes had the potentially negative effect of both putting the cash balances of the hedge funds at risk (a very real event for those who had suffered through or just witnessed the Bear Stearns and then Lehman Brothers collapses). In addition, the tightness of credit was causing primes to lend only to their most valuable hedge fund clients.

Prime Brokers

As for the primes, they had their own maelstrom with which to deal. They too had massive amounts of counterparty risk within the broker/dealer community and to their hedge fund clients (everyone was suddenly struggling to survive). They had heretofore had pretty free access to the cash balances of their hedge fund clients to fund their operations (more on rehypothecation later), and now that was drying up as hedge funds started cutting deals with banks to hold their credit balances, banks being viewed as more sound than broker/dealers (better 20 times leverage than 35 times leverage).

In the midst of this, primes themselves were having a harder time sourcing credit as everyone pulled in their credit horns. As we have shown, this was a critically important earning source for broker/dealers and having that activity fall off as banks were inspecting the brokers' P&L with microscopes was clearly not a good thing. Meanwhile, the accelerating push to multiple primes and unbundling (not just cash balances, but other services as well) brought the prime brokerage business under even greater business pressure.

Custodian Banks

The biggest clients of the major custodian banks are not the pension funds, but the prime brokers. When the primes are hurting, the custodians are hurting. But in the meantime, during the financial crisis, the volumes of short sales were down, but the spreads or cost of borrowing were going through the roof, making for good lending revenues overall.

So while the actual lending fee business was healing itself somewhat by virtue of blown out spreads (note the disruption in spreads when the financial crisis hit, as shown in Exhibit 7.4), the much more profitable and important cash reinvestment activity was running into its own buzz saw. You may recall that the money fund business, which is predicated on constant valuations and daily earnings credits, did something that sounded bad; they started to "break the buck," which means their values fell enough to create a valuation problem. Why did the buck break? AAA-rated securities were suddenly thought to be worth less than par and thus not really AAA after all. These structured products were built on *asset-backed securities*, another term for mortgage-backed securities, which, in 2007 to 2008 had gone into freefall with the collapse of housing values. So all that cash collateral that has to be returned to the borrowers when they return the securities is suddenly either devaluing or not liquid at all. Good thing there's that indemnity . . . except that indemnity doesn't cover reinvestment losses.

Securities lending is an activity that adds a small amount of incremental revenue to beneficial owners that lend the securities despite the fact that agency banks and prime brokers make massive profits. They only do it out of the desperate need to enhance investment returns and because it is considered to have minimal risk. But the question that needs to be asked is whether these vaunted custodians were doing their

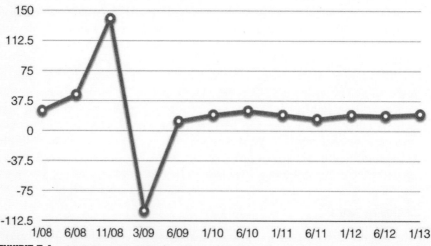

EXHIBIT 7.4   S&P Securities Lending Spread Index

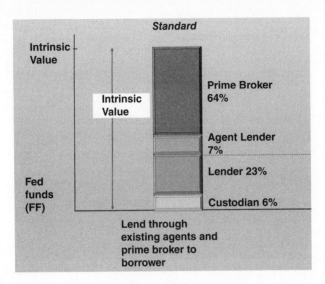

EXHIBIT 7.5   Intrinsic Value Sharing in Securities Lending

fiduciary best in advising and executing trades where they take minimal risk and the pension and mutual fund clients take most of the risk and get far less of the reward than the intermediaries do. Let's see how this pie is really cut up (approximately and based on extensive anecdotal evidence since there is insufficient transparency to determine otherwise) in Exhibit 7.5.

What Exhibit 7.5 shows is that it is estimated that of the intrinsic value in the lending of securities, only 23 percent accrues to the benefit of the beneficial owners, with the intermediaries taking the other 77 percent. This split is hard to empirically prove given the paucity of data made available by the intermediaries, but from privately obtained data, these numbers offer good approximations and are quite logical based on public numbers that are available for aggregate loan volumes, profitability of prime brokerage units, and securities lending profits at major custodian banks. What should these splits look like for the risks being taken by pension and mutual funds? Well, obviously this is a matter of perspective, but in my mind, at the very least, the splits should look like Exhibit 7.6 with the borrower savings either going to the prime broker or perhaps to the hedge fund borrower itself if it choose to disintermediate and participate directly in the market (as some hedge funds are starting to do).

We could double the value to lenders and come much closer to a proper risk/reward ratio for lenders if these splits were adjusted as shown in

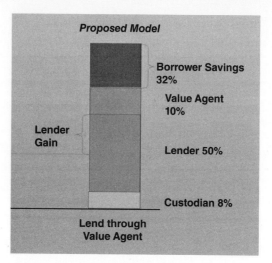

EXHIBIT 7.6   Proposed Intrinsic Value Split

Exhibit 7.6. We leave it open for consideration as to whether the 32 percent shown in dark gray should go to prime brokers or directly to hedge funds. It's hard to imagine feeling sorry for hedge funds, but the more pension funds invest in them, the more I am compelled to hope that hedge funds become more active participants in the securities lending markets like Citadel, Paloma, and several risk arbitrage funds have done. This is a big pot of spread that is captured by intermediaries and maintained through lack of adequate transparency. I am confident that this will gradually change, but Wall Street and custodians (not to mention money managers of ETFs) are clinging to this revenue source in these turbulent times in financial services like a cat on a curtain.

Beneficial Owners

So with all this going on with hedge funds, prime brokers, and custodian banks (all relatively sophisticated users of securities finance), what exactly happens to the hapless pension fund or mutual fund that simply wants to enhance yields a bit at the margin? To say that this deep end of the asset management pool is fraught with danger seems trite. To say that beneficial owners are compelled to go into these deep waters seems strange. But both of these are true. Therefore, I would like to use two examples to explain just how much both of these statements are true: ratio lending and rehypothecation.

RATIO LENDING

First, let's deal with the pernicious side of the equation. Think about a custodian that has a mandate to lend the securities of a long-time custodian client, a nice friendly midwestern pension fund, perhaps one that is underfunded and in need of extra income from wherever it can get it. Last year the client lent out 15 percent of the lendable portfolio and produced, say, $1 million in added revenues, a not-insignificant amount to the pension fund. Since the agent lender gets 20 percent, the custodian earned $250k. But wait, the custodian also invests the cash collateral in its STIF funds for the pension fund as part of the exercise. In a low 2 percent environment, this means that it averaged about $62.5 million in managed cash collateral. Assuming the custodian charged a normal amount of 10 basis points (1/10 of 1 percent) for the management fee, which means it made an extra $62.5k on that for a total of $312.5k. Let's assume that this situation does not offend the pension fund even though the split is really 76/24 and not 80/20 as explicitly agreed.

Now suppose some smart young MBA (say, for instance, one of my more aggressive and less ethical students) goes to work at the custodian in the securities lending area and is mandated to raise the securities lending revenues (remember, the most profitable area in the bank—the one that subsidized the entire custody operation). What he thinks is that he needs to find a way to boost the portion of loaned securities beyond the 15 percent already accomplished. He is skilled in the black arts of securities lending (thanks, Rich) and realizes that while there are many securities in the portfolio that are considered "general collateral" and not in high demand, there are a few gems that are called "hard to borrow" that are worth a lot to prime brokers who want to impress their hedge fund clients in their ability to locate these gems so they can more easily short them (say, like Herbalife shares for Bill Ackman and Pershing Square).

The MBA comes up with a very bright idea: Why not bundle the Herbalife shares with a bunch of the general collateral shares and then get prime brokers to bid that up based on how much of the general collateral they will take in addition to the Herbalife? It won't cost the prime brokers too much in an easy money environment because the fees on general collateral securities are small, and when money is relatively cheap, all the prime broker is doing is borrowing money to lay out as cash collateral and getting most of the earnings credit back in the form of what is called a rebate from the custodian. So say Mr. MBA gets Prime ABC to offer a 10:1 ratio of general collateral to Herbalife. If the pension fund owns $10 million of Herbalife, that means he can lend not only that, but another $100 million in general collateral stock.

On the surface you are going to say that doesn't sound bad for the pension fund since even at lower fees, that added $50 million might net only

1/10 of the earnings value, that will still generate an added $200k to the pot—$160k of which goes to the pension fund and $40k of which goes to the custodian. Not much for Mr. MBA to get a bonus on . . . but wait. We forgot to add the money management fees on the $100 million. That produces another $100k for the custodian. Now the pension fund has earned $1.16 million and the custodian has earned $452.5k, a split of 72/28 with the fund getting the incremental $160k and the custodian getting an incremental $140k. Do this a few times over with all the "hard to borrow" securities and Mr. MBA can rack up some considerable profits and bonuses, and the pension fund client is happy because he's earning more, too. All is well.

But wait a minute, since there is no free lunch in life (that gets taught on day one in business school), where is the risk here? The risk is squarely on the back of the pension fund, which now has $162.5 million in cash collateral investments instead of $62.5 million and all he has to show for it is an added $160k in income. To understand that risk, think of it this way: depending on how much AAA-rated ABS exposure the STIF fund in question had, a mere 16 basis point (again, 16/100 of 1 percent) "breaking" of the buck would eradicate the incremental profit earned by this exposure. And needless to say, the profits of the custodian would have been untouched.

This practice I describe actually has a name, *ratio lending*, and it is perhaps the most severe example of custodian abuse of a beneficial owner client in that it causes bad risk/reward trades (the general collateral trades) to get booked by the custodian on behalf of their fiduciary client and thereby pumps up the volume of cash collateral managed by the custodian. Since the custodian bears the counterparty risk but not the reinvestment risk, this is truly fraudulent activity because it benefits the custodian while hurting the beneficial owner.

If ratio lending is a purposeful case of fraud (perpetrated in this example by my MBA student who understood where the money was being made in securities lending), then my next example is perhaps worse in that it is equally driven by overly aggressive custodian/money manager intermediaries, but is inadvertent and borne of ignorance, but even *more* harmful to our desperate pension fund. It follows the megatrends of investing in that it traces the alpha/beta split, the drift of indexing into quantitative hedge fund management, the perils of prime brokerage and securities lending, and the rehypothecation of securities. If you don't know what that all means, buckle up.

THE REHYPOTHECATION TWO-STEP

Imagine the same midwestern pension fund that is trying through the efforts of its $60k/year manager to do the right thing for the fund. He carefully selects his custodian and fiduciary and he has read all about the perfect market hypothesis and is a believer in passive management, so he has the custodian put his funds in an index fund for low-fee safekeeping that matches the market without trying to outperform. He sleeps well with this approach.

The custodian/money manager (recognize that all major custodians have chosen to be money managers in addition, since it would be foolish to allow trusted client relationships to go underexploited) decides that in addition to the index fund products it offers, it should examine, analyze, and then offer some products that build off these index funds in ways that add marginally more risk and offer outsized reward. In the indexing world, this took the form of "tilting" index funds and eventually offering them in what has become known as 130/30 form. 130/30 (recognizing that the ratio is arbitrary and could just as easily be 120/20 or 140/40) is the idea that you take the indexed portfolio and select some obvious shorts up to 30 percent and cover that directional exposure by leveraging the portfolio and adding another 30 percent to the strongest of your long positions. Hence, you have 130 percent exposure to the long side, counteracted by 30 percent exposure to the short side, with a net resulting more or less "balanced" or market-neutral portfolio that uses manager selection skill to double up on the most obvious strong stocks and short the most obvious weak ones. From a portfolio construction sense, this gets expressed as a modest increase in tracking error to the index, which should add nicely to the positive side, creating a positive alpha component to add to the beta of the index.

This is all sensible portfolio construction mechanics that should work within the bounds suggested and the success of which (measured as positive alpha) is embedded in the selection process and outcome. This is how it gets sold to our midwestern pension fund friend, and it seems to make a reasonable amount of sense. And of course, in order to execute on the short side of this strategy, the custodian, who theoretically could do the locating of stocks needed for shorting himself (the custodian being the guardian of all that beneficial owner stock in the securities lending pools), does not want to upset its largest clients, the prime brokers, by appearing to be in competition with them, so the custodian hires a prime broker to execute on these trades. Maybe they both tell this to the pension fund or maybe they don't, but the pension fund still sleeps well at night because the custodian is his fiduciary and his assets are all ring-fenced in the custody arrangement that governs his relationship.

What is ring-fencing? Well, the reason a pension fund puts its assets in trust with the custodian is so that they will always be segregated and never at risk for any financial failure of the custodian. This is only logical. The pension fund wants to make sure that if the unthinkable happens and the custodian bank goes into bankruptcy, his assets will be ring-fenced and segregated and not subject to creditor claims. It is what trust relationships are all about and is a basic tenet of trust banking.

But a funny thing happened on the way to the market. The custodian inadvertently un-ring-fenced the assets when he gave them to a prime broker. The basis of the prime brokerage agreement (a document that most often was not approved by or even shown to the pension client) calls for the broker to have access to all of the assets of the fund that is being put with the brokerage within the confines of the regulations governing brokers. In the United States, brokers can rehypothecate (a fancy word for lend) the securities to obtain cash, which, in theory, is needed to borrow securities to execute the shorts for the fund. This is effectively the way in which the 130/30 fund generates the leverage to increase its long positions to 130 and put on the 30 of shorts. So, the prime will have to lend out something like 30 percent of the portfolio to get the cash needed to buy 30 percent more longs and borrow the securities needed to sell the 30 percent shorts. The regulations, recognizing the fast-paced nature of this market, the 102 percent cash collateral needs, and the immediacy of the margining calls allows brokers to rehypothecate (lend) 140 percent of the client securities necessary. This translates in this example to 42 percent of the portfolio if fully utilized. (A side note here—which I will come back to later—is that in the United Kingdom the regulations do not limit rehypothecation to 140 percent, but rather allow the broker to rehypothecate 100 percent of the client securities if it so chooses.)

Let's look at Exhibit 7.7 and walk through what is happening.

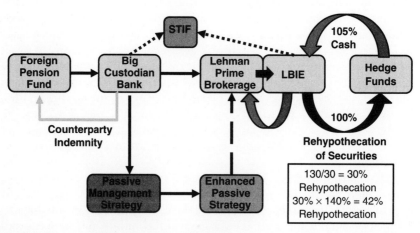

EXHIBIT 7.7   The Rehypothecation Two-Step

What started as a conservative passive strategy got morphed (or sold) into an "enhanced" passive strategy (certainly enhanced for the custodian/ money manager, but not necessarily for the pension fund client). That morph required the use of a prime broker who needs to enter into securities lending trades on behalf of this new enhanced fund. Now at this point, this would be little different from the pension fund deciding to go into securities lending for incremental revenue, except in that program he would get a counterparty indemnity whereas in this situation he is unwittingly entering into a securities lending arrangement without all the normal risk disclosures and decidedly without the benefit of a counterparty indemnity. That is likely something he would never do if he had realized it was happening. Simply telling him that he will be using a prime broker is not full disclosure. And it leaves the client exposed to the credit risk of the prime broker to the tune of 42 percent of the portfolio. Unless that prime broker moves the account to its U.K. affiliate, wherein the entire portfolio is exposed to the broker's creditors.

Stop for a moment and reflect on the events that led up to the distressed sale of Bear Stearns (a large prime broker) and then the failure of Lehman Brothers (also a large prime broker). In both instances, it is now clear that those primes were using client cash (*as they were allowed to*) to lend to themselves for general corporate purposes. Those purposes became rather extreme in the final days, so moving prime accounts to the United Kingdom to allow access to the full amounts of cash was a very tempting tactic. Does this remind you of an even more recent event? MF Global seems to have pursued a similar financing tactic to the tune of $1.6 billion of client funds that got rehypothecated fully from the U.K. affiliate and the funds used to fund the dire corporate needs of a failing broker dealer. It won't take shadow banking investigators too long to realize that the hole in the shadow is largest in the United Kingdom and that the entire shadowy world of securities finance is riddled with holes through which client money flows.

In the case of our midwestern pension fund, the simple and safe passive strategy got put into something with purportedly marginally more risk and absolutely no disclosure that it was being placed outside the fiduciary ring-fence. The adoption of a prime brokerage element and then the shifting of that to a U.K. prime brokerage put the risk levels here into territory completely unfamiliar to the pension fund but in a place where the custodian (a true expert in the arena of securities lending and counterparty risk) should have known and disclosed the risks and, at the very least, offered a counterparty indemnity. It was like insisting that a bungee jumper wear a harness, but when a roller coaster ride incorporated the finishing flourish of a bungee jump, the harness was excluded. Not only did the coaster rider not understand that there was a bungee jump at the end, he never suspected that there would be no harness. Many of these cases are in litigation now and being disposed of wisely by the custodians in favor of the pension clients.

■ ■ ■

What we should take from all of this is simply that when the unfunded liability burden of pension funds logically drives them to take more risk in several forms (hedge fund alpha exposure, securities lending, etc.), it gets more and more complex and sophisticated, and the deep end of the pool is more shark-infested.

CHAPTER 8

Liability-Driven Alpha

Liability-driven investing (LDI) is an approach to pension investing that focuses on calibrating investments to match plan liabilities with plan assets. While this seems to be logical and make sense, it actually runs contrary to much of modern institutional investing wisdom. Perhaps the biggest reason for this is that most pension funds are quite separate in their management of liabilities (the province of the actuaries and pension consultants) and their management of assets (the province of the investment management team and investment consultants). Pension plans certainly have liabilities, and managers certainly invest employer pension contributions to generate enough income to meet those liabilities. However, prior to the last five years, it was quite commonplace to have poor investment results followed directly by investment decisions that further enhanced risk. They followed the classic "Hail Mary" passive approach to investing.

I call this Liability-Driven Alpha, and the name once again comes from the classroom. When I formulated the course, I was motivated by a desire to ensure that more of Johnson's investment management graduates better understood the pension market. My original focus was on the move to terminate defined benefit plans. The course title in early 2008 was "Defined Benefit Pension Plans in Transition." As I mentioned in Chapter 7, that scintillating title drew all of seven students where my "Search for Alpha" course had drawn 50 students. Now it's hard for pension funds to ever stack up on the charts as high as hedge funds, but they didn't need to be that boring, either. So I changed the name of the course to "Liability-Driven Alpha" (not trademarked by anyone, to my knowledge). Ever since, the course has drawn over 50 students with more or less the same theme: again, all by the power of marketing.

Let's assume a plan sponsor falls short of the 7.5 percent "expected return" three years in a row. (As a side note, the majority of pension plans have been using unrealistic return assumptions—but keep this on the backburner for now)—so what does the plan sponsor do? This brings me back to the movie *Swingers*, when Vince Vaughn and John Favreau are sitting at a blackjack table next to an unsavory biker dude, an inebriated chain-smoking young woman, and a geriatric night owl who's Mrs. "*Winner winner chicken dinner.*" Everyone places their bets and John Favreau (Mikey) draws an ace. Vince Vaughn says, "Double-down . . . you always, *always* double down on 11." He hits . . . gets a three, and the dealer gets blackjack.

This is exactly what asset managers have been doing to address pension shortfalls. Risk profiles have increased as pension underfunding has increased, as did allocations to extremely speculative and illiquid securities. Unfortunately, not everyone is a Monday morning hero, and now pension plans are faced with underfunded liabilities, significant volatility, and generally considerably greater illiquidity.

In order to really understand how liability-driven investing (LDI) has become so crucial for pension investing, we need to review a few pieces of landmark legislation. The Pension Protection Act of 2006 (PPA) is often understood as an addendum to ERISA, aiming to further protect plan beneficiaries (based on intent, not effectiveness). The key points include:

- Increasing plan funded status to fully funded (100 percent funded ratio) with any unfunded portion amortized over a seven-year timeframe[1]
- Imposing financial penalties on underfunded pension plans[2]
- Reducing performance smoothing[3]
- Most notably, it determined the specific corporate bond rates to be used in discounting pension liabilities.[4] The bond yields correspond chronologically to three distinct segments of pension plan duration.[5]

The second key piece of oversight is FAS 158, which requires defined benefit plan sponsors to report their funded/unfunded liabilities, health care, and retirement costs on their balance sheets.[6]

---

[1] "CRS Report for Congress," CRS-3,RL33703 www.worldatwork.org/waw/adimLink?id=15322.

[2] Towers Watson, "PPA Establishes New Rules for Multiemployer Plans," *Endangered and Critical Status*, www.watsonwyatt.com/us/pubs/insider/showarticle.asp?ArticleID=16628.

[3] Scott J. Macey, "An Emerging Assessment of The Pension Protection Act (June 2009)," www.aon.com/attachments/pension_protection_act.pdf.

[4] Segments 1, 2, & 3, Corporate Bond Yield Curve: www.gpo.gov/fdsys/pkg/PLAW-109publ280/pdf/PLAW-109publ280.pdf.

[5] Pension Protection Act 2006, 20, www.gpo.gov/fdsys/pkg/PLAW-109publ280/pdf/PLAW-109publ280.pdf.

[6] "Appendix F: pp. 139–141," www.fasb.org/cs/BlobServer?blobkey=id&smp;blobwhere=1175820923452&blobheader=application%2Fpdf&blobcol=urldata&blobtable=MungoBlobs.

PPA and FAS 158 drastically change pension planning, obligation volatility, and pension cost management. These were particularly onerous for firms given the global investment environment. The Pension Protection Act and FAS 158 were both promulgated in 2006, and PPA was implemented in stages through 2011. FAS 158 had even more draconian measures that called for ultimate income statement impact from pension obligations, but that has been postponed (due mostly to the severe recent environment).

PAINTING THE RECENT PENSION LANDSCAPE

In August of 2007, the markets began to collapse and the Fed dropped rates steadily for the next five years—after which they remained hovering around zero indefinitely. As the Federal Funds Rate and the Discount Rate fell, so did the corporate bond rates used to discount pension liabilities. So even though the number of employees hadn't changed, salaries remained stable, and life expectancies were similar, seemingly overnight pension liabilities ballooned. Everyone was afraid of the collapse of the global financial system, and there was a flight to relative security—away from equities. Without high equity exposure, pension funds were forced to reduce their respective target returns. Pension liabilities were high, expected returns to meet those liabilities dropped markedly, and new legislation requiring improved funded status was implemented. Furthermore, companies were otherwise already struggling, and the additional balance sheet volatility (and indirect income statement volatility) became crippling.

So what would you expect pension managers to do? They really needed to address three issues:

1. Reducing financial statement and pension liability volatility
2. Improving funded status
3. Assuring that plan assets are either positioned directly against obligations, or are substantial enough to facilitate pension risk transfer (covered in the next chapter)

These three points focus on growing assets or mitigating the effects of liabilities, and are commonly categorized as "liability hedging" and "return seeking."[7]

---

[7] Matthew Nili, "Capital Efficiency Matters," BlackRock Multi-Asset Client Solutions, https://www2.blackrock.com/webcore/litService/search/getDocument.seam? contentId=1111134370&Source=SEARCH&Venue=PUB_INS.

In order to understand liability-driven investing (LDI), you must first realize that LDI will look and feel different for every single plan. It is much more intricate than simply moving allocations from equities to long duration bonds. So before implementing LDI strategies, each firm needs to analyze its specific fund status to custom tailor an LDI program. Each will need to determine how costly excess volatility flowing through to the income statement and balance sheet really is to regular business. Each will need to analyze the real funded ratio, using more realistic return expectations, government bond segment discount rates, and up-to-date actuarial projections.

Using this analysis, firms can determine the appropriate split of *liability hedging* and *return seeking*. Essentially, how much do they need to buffer the blows of volatility, and how much do they need catch up on the performance side? It is very likely that pension investment consultants and actuaries will play integral roles in this stage and need to be consulted on a much more regular basis. Small moves in interest rates and investment return will necessitate portfolio rebalancing and new risk mitigation. And these changes will need to directly pertain to the specific goals of a given plan. Is the goal 100 percent funded status? Perhaps the plan wants to derisk through a pension buyout but wants to limit financial statement volatility in the short run. These considerations will define the parameters of the LDI program.

At the most basic level, LDI will mark a shift to increased fixed income allocations, matching bond durations with the projected maturities of plan liabilities. This seems like a prudent thing to do, especially the closer a plan is to fully funded status. However, there is always a trade-off. This is particularly so when rates are near zero, as it is difficult to achieve any substantial return on fixed income portfolios. This is not unlike the situation at the moment.

RISKS

Plans must use more sophisticated approaches to account for interest rate risk, bond risk, and equity/return-enhancing risk in a holistic model, incorporating the current status of the plan. The following pages describe these three risks.

Interest Rate Risk

As interest rates move, so do the value of the plan liabilities. LDI implementation should aim to neutralize or minimize the effects of short-term interest rate risk and long-term interest rate uncertainty. Interest rate risk exists on both the asset and the liability side. On the liability side, interest rates affect return, as when interest rates fall (yields), bond prices rise, and typical fixed income strategies suffer. The extent to which this affects a portfolio will, again, be plan specific. There are several ways plans can address this. First, plans can purchase fixed income investments with maturities that align with projected payouts to beneficiaries. Then plans can try to enhance the predictability of likely rates in the future, by purchasing interest rate swaps to hedge against interest rate movement, lock in rates, and project an appropriate discounting yield curve.[8]

Bond Risk

As previously mentioned, the Pension Protection Act of 2006 mandates specific discount rates for three different duration segments of pension liabilities based on corporate bond rates. The rates address maturities of 0 to 5 years, 5 to 15 years, and 15 years+.[9] This risk is twofold. First, a movement to LDI will increase exposure to various maturities of both government-issued and corporate-issued bonds. So, the most obvious risk is that the value of corporate bonds will change with movements in interest rates, affecting the value and volatility of the portfolio. However, the more critical risk/opportunity is the three-segment discounting of pension liabilities. As corporate rates are used to discount pension liabilities, they directly impact the funded status of plans, the return on portfolios more heavily concentrated in fixed income, and the volatility of required pension contributions. Plans can utilize bond swaps and duration matching to address this risk. Plans can also use options to capitalize on inevitable rate increases.

While Ben Bernanke seems to suggest rates will not rise in the near future, eventually, as the U.S. economy strengthens and unemployment falls, interest rates will rise. As Fed rates rise, so will those of corporate bonds, and plans will want to capitalize on this trend. Remember, in the short run it is essential for plans to mitigate volatility and match assets with liabilities, but this is done most often at the cost of reduced return. As corporate bond interest rates rise, so will the rates used to discount pension liabilities. Plans can lock in stability now with duration matching and the use of derivatives, but they can also make money on the interest rate upswing by selling options short. Bond risk most directly affects the *liability hedging* side.

---

[8] Jan Baars, Leah Kelly, Petr Kocourek, and Epco van der Lende, "Liability Driven Investing: Hedging Inflation and Interest Rate Risk," Global Asset Management: Multi-Asset Solutions Research Papers, November 5, 2012, www.cfsgam.com.au/uploadedFiles/CFSGAM/PdfResearch/121116_MAS_Research_Paper_5_Liability_Driven_Investing.pdf.

[9] www.gpo.gov/fdsys/pkg/PLAW-109publ280/pdf/PLAW-109publ280.pdf.

Return-Seeking Risk

While liability-driven investing does typically mark a movement toward fixed income, one should not expect portfolios to convert solely to debt securities. In fact, other asset classes will still be extremely important to the long-term sustainability and/or transferability of plans.[10] But the use of other classes will be driven by similar objectives to those of LDI. Equities, for instance, will still play an integral role in the return-seeking portion of U.S. plans—particularly for severely underfunded plans. The greater the shift toward fixed income, the more likely a plan's required contribution will increase in the short run. If a plan is underfunded and already struggling to reduce the "unfunded liabilities" line-item on the balance sheet, it will need to maintain significant equity exposure, but must do so with an LDI approach. First off, we will see greater investments in diversified equities: U.S. multinationals, emerging markets, global equities, and equity derivatives. While equity returns are not directly correlated to the interest rate environment, rates represent the opportunity cost and/or cost of borrowing for U.S. firms. So exposure to inexpensive global equities and U.S. multinationals will increase. This will necessitate the disaggregation of alpha (to remind you, excess risk adjusted return) from beta (return generated from systematic market risk). Various subsets of global equities can now be purchased inexpensively through market indices. Plans will look to growth areas in search of alpha and get cheap beta exposure through market indices. Managers will also use portable alpha strategies, which take on direct equity risk to enhance return, while simultaneously shorting a market index of industry/subset/market of the long positions. This will create a de facto market neutral position that can simulate certain alternative investment strategies on a cost-effective basis.

BASIC LDI GUIDELINES

Plans will also maintain other asset classes and investment vehicles including hedge funds, private equity, and real estate, but the vetting mechanism to determine if a particular investment is prudent for plan objectives will be guided by LDI. Timelines, expected rates of return, risk analysis, and suitability will all be sensitive to liability maturities and the volatility impact on each chronological segment. Again, LDI will leverage fixed income and bond/asset duration matching, but it will also inform other asset class and vehicle investments.

---

[10]https://institutional.vanguard.com/iam/pdf/Paul_transcript.pdf.

All LDI investing will have to be considered in light of costs and plan goals. To round out this chapter, here are four basic guidelines to keep in mind:

1. **Evaluate:** Despite what you may have read, there is no LDI silver bullet. And all LDI implementation will be different. The first step is to analyze the liabilities of a plan, the assets currently available to meet those liabilities, and the effects of financial statement volatility on the firm.

2. **Determine** the respective needs for liability hedging and return seeking assets. For large plans that are well funded and simply need to reduce volatility, there will be a much greater focus on liability hedging, matching fixed income investments with obligation maturities. For smaller or less well-funded plans, there will be a greater focus on return-seeking assets. These funds will need to custom-tailor investment implementation to cater to the volatility, return, and maturity considerations of an LDI approach. For all classes, focus will turn to servicing plan liabilities and limiting volatility rather than solely focusing on return. High alpha and cheap beta strategies will become more prevalent and investment in alternatives will necessitate greater sensitivity to liquidity and transparency.

3. **Reevaluate, recalibrate, and reanalyze regularly!** Pension assets and liabilities are dynamic. Asset managers, accountants, actuaries, and pension consultants need to constantly monitor return assumptions, duration, hedging positions, and risk.

4. **Account for risk!** Interest rate risk, investment risk, bond risk, equity risk, alternatives risk, and so on. It is both necessary and prudent to do so. Further, carefully analyzed risk can actually be a great source of alpha. One can increase investment return and mitigate risk through well-reasoned risk analysis.

Liability-driven investing is perhaps the best single tool for pension fund management readily available for managers today. Its best feature is that it properly combines the liability need and the asset outcome into one investing strategy. It focuses on limiting volatility, which has become the biggest dragon in the kingdom of the pension manager (thanks to regulators, accountants, and the markets in general). It is a far easier tool to employ for pension funds that are closer to fully funded and much harder for those that are under water. Nevertheless, the lessons it provides are useful to all pension funds and it provides the first step in the inevitable march to freezing pension plan obligation and eventually transferring the risk altogether. Anything that moves plans in that direction is generally good for participants since it improves the assurance of retirement income security.

CHAPTER 9

Power Tools for Pensions

We have now spent a fair bit of time outlining the problems that create the global pension crisis. It should be vividly clear that they are real, they are pressing, and they will not go away by themselves or with simple policy tweaks. We have focused on explaining the importance of investment techniques in attacking this problem. In fact, in the simplistic assets and liabilities sense, how you organize your assets is virtually all you can do to address the immediate problem. Naturally, that assumes that you are not inclined to be revisionist when it comes to liability obligations. I was recently asked about corruption and fraud in pension fund liabilities and it is clear that, in particular, public funds suffer from this to some degree in the manner in which long-standing employees are allowed to manipulate the system in their final years of employment to take advantage and maximize their retirement payout. This can be egregious in the form of fake jobs and receiving multiple pensions and it can be more subtle in padding the last few years of compensation (either with raises or, more often, overtime) in order to average up the retirement payout. I will admit that this exacerbates the problem, but I do not believe that it represents more than 10 percent in well-regulated schemes and perhaps 20 percent in more corrupt administrations.

The point is that, unless you are prepared to literally break the social contract made perhaps as long ago as 40 years and renege on pension promises, the only way to solve the problem is through some form of increased contribution and/or better management of the assets. The fact that so much more of the equation is determined by return streams than contributions makes me want to focus on the latter, but in the late stages of the retirement cycle when it is literally too late to use the power of compounding, contribution increases are often the only tool left.

If we all agree that this is the case, spending time in Chapters 4 through 8 on how to attack the asset side of the balance sheet in new and hopefully productive ways was time well spent. There are, however, other tools that are important to the solution as well. I call these "power tools" not because they are more powerful than compounding (perhaps the most powerful force other than the gravity that holds us all down to reality), but because they are not ordinary tools and may not even be at the full discretion of pension fund managers, but are often external though important (now or in the future) tools that impact pension funds.

PENSION BENEFIT GUARANTY CORPORATION

The Pension Benefit Guaranty Corporation (PBGC) is the hospital for sick U.S. pension plans, most often those of companies that have gone into bankruptcy. It is a federal corporation established under the ERISA, which established the PBGC to insure the benefits for participants in private defined benefit pension plans.

The PBGC currently guarantees payment of basic pension benefits earned by more than 44 million American workers and retirees in nearly 27,000 plans. It seeks to promote the use of private pension plans (in theory) by encouraging companies to keep their plans and paying benefits when they cannot. According to their own words:

> PBGC *was created by the Employee Retirement Income Security Act of 1974 to encourage the continuation and maintenance of private-sector defined benefit pension plans, provide timely and uninterrupted payment of pension benefits, and keep pension insurance premiums at a minimum.*[1]

This is a somewhat contradictory mission (as laudable as it is) since the imposition of ever-increasing premiums and more and more stringent rules governing funding in particular do anything but encourage the perpetuation of private defined benefit pension plans. Since 1974, PBGC has taken responsibility for almost 1.5 million people in 4,300 failed plans. It has about $26 billion in underfunded obligations, and the plans it guarantees have an additional $227 billion in underfunded obligations. As an institution, it has quite a continuous challenge on its hands.

The PBGC has three overarching strategic goals:

1. To preserve plans and protect pensioners
2. To pay pension benefits on time and accurately
3. To maintain high standards of stewardship and accountability

---

[1] www.pbgc.gov/about/who-we-are.html.

The PBGC is *not* a "full faith and credit of the United States Government" institution and is decidedly not a part of the government budget process. Its operations are financed by insurance premiums paid by covered companies that sponsor defined benefit pension plans and, of course, investment income on the assets from plans trusteed by PBGC. Occasionally, they supplement their coffers with recoveries from companies formerly responsible for the plans and, in some instances, from companies seeking the permission of the PBGC to initiate a corporate action like a divestiture or acquisition. Given that the PBGC receives no funds from general tax revenues, it is interesting that the PBGC's premiums are set by Congress. If I were advising the U.S. government on how to insulate itself from the risk of claim that the PBGC is indeed not an agency of the government, I might suggest that there be a change in that approach. However, the safety and soundness of private pension plans is simply too central to the mission of the Department of Labor and therefore to the federal government that it is likely that this "independent" entity called the PBGC is no more independent than Fannie Mae or Freddie Mac were when the chickens came home to roost, as they say.

Yet again another connection to the government is that the PBGC is administered by its director, who is appointed by the president, and confirmed by the United States Senate. Policy oversight is provided by a board of directors, but given that this board consists of the Secretaries of Labor (chair), Treasury, and Commerce, it's pretty safe to say that this quasi-governmental entity is short on quasi and long on governmental.

FACTORS AFFECTING THE PBGC INSURANCE PROGRAMS[2]

According to the PBGC's own Strategic Plan, these are the four factors that affect its programs the most:

1. **Demographics:** The average life span of Americans continues to increase, and the workforce is aging rapidly. Over the next five years, retirement ranks will grow as more than 76 million Americans born between 1946 and 1964—the Baby Boomers—reach their next life phase.

   This is a rather gross understatement.
2. **Economy:** The economic downturn and slow recovery have a direct impact on PBGC's financial status.

   Another gross understatement.

---

[2] Pension Benefit Guaranty Corporation Strategic Plan FY 2012–2016, www.pbgc .gov/Documents/2012-2016strategicplan.pdf.

3. **Defined benefit plans:** Fewer employers are participating in defined pension programs. Terminations of large plans, freezing of plans, closing plans to new entrants, deaths outstripping new entrants in mature plans, and an increase in the number of workers eligible for lump-sum distributions will all cause the number of covered participants to decline.

   This pretty much tells the tale of defined benefit pension plans globally.

4. **Long-term exposure:** Our 10- and 20-year forecasts indicate additional plan failures and higher deficits. Projections show a nearly 30 percent chance that the multiemployer program will run out of money entirely within 20 years.

This reminds me of the old joke of the dinosaur convention where the speaker says, "Ladies and gentlemen, the outlook is not good; the world climate is changing, vegetation is disappearing, meteor strikes are increasing . . . and we all have a brain the size of a walnut."

News Flash—The PBGC reported a $34 billion deficit for fiscal year 2012, a significant jump from the agency's $26 billion deficit the previous year. As we can see in Exhibit 9.1, the last decade has not been kind to the PBGC with the deficits mounting another 30 percent to $34 billion,

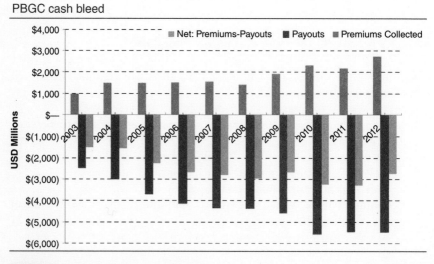

EXHIBIT 9.1   PBGC Deficit and Statistics
Source: PBGC.

and the number of plans and participants thrust into their care is growing significantly.

PLAN TERMINATIONS

The PBGC controls pension plan terminations and transfers under Title IV of ERISA and, increasingly, this may become its most significant function to corporate America. According to the PBGC "handbook,"[3] an employer can voluntarily ask to close its pension plan in either a standard or distress termination. In a standard termination, the plan must have enough money to pay all accrued benefits, whether vested or not, before the plan can end. Workers are paid their promised benefits in the form of a lump sum payment or an insurance company annuity (from a qualified insurer), whereupon the PBGC's guarantee is removed. In a distress termination, where the plan does not have enough money to pay all benefits, the employer must prove severe financial hardship—for instance the likelihood that continuing the plan would force the company to shut down or go into bankruptcy. In that instance, the PBGC steps in to pay the guaranteed benefits and then goes on to seek recovery of those funds from the employer and/or the courts.

The Pension Protection Act of 2006 has a number of provisions in it that affect the PBGC. These include such things as provision for a "termination premium" of $1,250 per participant per year for three years for any plans seeking to terminate, a provision to "stop the accrual music" on terminated plans as of the date of a plan sponsor's bankruptcy filing with special provisions for plant shutdowns within five years of that date, increases in the insurance premium charges, and reconfirmation that the PBGC only insures defined benefit plans and NOT defined contribution plans. There is also the issue that the determination of liabilities for calculating the termination costs is based on an all-important discount rate. Prior to the PPA, companies were allowed to use a blend of corporate and treasury yields. Now they must use the corporate yield exclusively, and this has the net effect of lowering the liability nut that must be covered since corporate yields are generally higher than treasury yields (this may not always be the case if the U.S. ratings continue to fall!).

The PBGC and like institutions in other countries (the Pension Protection Fund in the United Kingdom) are an important part of the pension fabric that provides retirement income security. As long as there are private pensions and private companies, there will be underfunding situations (by design or accident) and there will be company failures that leave "orphaned" participants without a plan sponsor to meet the

---

[3] www.pbgc.gov/about/how-pbgc-operates.html.

promised obligations. While this is an important and quite fundamental purpose of the PBGC, I want to point out that perhaps the more significant role in the future will be that of gatekeeper for corporate America. What I mean by that is that the existing companies that have defined benefit pension plans are very much at the mercy of the PBGC for their maneuverability in the future. Without approval from the PBGC, these companies cannot merge, divest, or acquire, and they are even prevented in some manner from liquidating or dissolving before meeting the obligations imposed by the PBGC. As more and more companies seek to cauterize their pension exposure, an exposure that we have shown has often grown to outsize the primary company altogether, their ability to freeze, transfer risk, and eventually fully terminate a pension plan and its concomitant obligations is very much dependent on approval from the PBGC. This will be less the case once all companies are using defined contribution plans rather than defined benefit plans (at least as it currently stands), but for now, a vast array of companies (over 27,500 representing 44 million participants) are literally at the mercy of the PBGC. As I have said, and as you will see further in the next section, the ability to transfer risk is becoming an increasingly important issue to pension fund managers given the fairly limited tools they have to manipulate liabilities and grow assets.

PENSION RISK TRANSFER

The following pages offer details on types of pension risk transfer techniques.

Risk Mitigation

The ability for plan managers to manipulate liabilities is very limited. Many firms will therefore choose increasingly to transfer their liabilities to a third-party firm. However, before plan sponsors take this somewhat draconian and expensive step, they will first determine the cost to maintain their pension liabilities, incorporating every possible form of risk mitigation strategies. Essentially, firms will need to mitigate the effects that pension obligations and investments have on their respective balance sheets, operations, expense levels, and liquidity. In order to do so, firms will implement the strategies we explained in Chapter 8, known as liability-driven investing (LDI), which focus on using fixed income investments to match pension assets with pension liabilities. As security durations coincide with corresponding liability tranches, LDI reduces volatility, makes requisite annual employer contributions more predictable, and limits impact on financial statements. Plans can supplement the more modest return profile of a fixed income allocation with cheap-beta, high-alpha strategies.

Exhibit 9.2 offers a little "cheat sheet" I use in my pension course to make it easier for students to understand pension economic forces.

Exhibit 9.2 should drive home the notion that private pensions and the underlying companies that sponsor them are inextricably linked to one another in a financial and economic scenario sense. Using growth and inflation as the two common central axes, you see that there are four quadrant outcomes that more or less match the reality that a fund and/or companies face. Everybody wins in a high-growth inflationary situation and the opposite is true in low-growth / low-inflation situations. While I would tend to say that pensions prosper in high-inflationary environments based often on the liability discounting dimension, it is worth noting that growth at the underlying sponsoring company can override this because funding is so very driven by the financial resources available to the firm. Equally, in the new "perfect storm" environment of FASB and PPA, a sponsoring company can easily get dragged down by its pension fund despite good growth prospects as those liabilities grow inordinately in a low-rate environment. I imagine corporate strategic planners are forced to spend more time than ever considering how their vestigial pension plans alter the company reality and future.

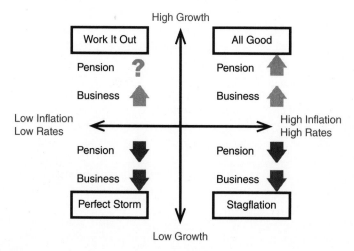

EXHIBIT 9.2 Pension Economic Scenario Matrix

The Freeze

As we started discussing in Chapter 5, before a pension plan can terminate, it has to freeze its plan. In fact, to determine the universe of likely plan termination candidates, you should start by looking at plans that have recently been frozen. There are many elements that go into plan freezing decisions. The overall probability that a company will consider a freeze has everything to do with its competitive position and what others in the industry are doing. Even though defined benefit (DB) plans are far less the recruiting and retention tool they used to be, this is not absent from consideration, especially in a competitive market. The second issue of very high import is the cost of the freezing action and the potential damage that a plan freeze will have on the company's cash position.

The hard financial issues that are looked at in a freeze scenario are the level or degree of underfunding (this determines the size of the hole that will need to be filled), the actuarial liability versus the current liability of the plan as a percentage of the market capitalization of the firm overall, the existing credit balance of the plan as a percentage of net income of the firm, the impact on loan covenants, and eventually the credit risk of potential counterparties in any anticipated termination actions.

The degree of difficulty of freezing goes beyond the purely financial considerations as well. One needs to look at the ratio of active to retired or departed employees that are plan participants. One needs to look at the status in union situations of the collective bargaining arrangements that exist and the repercussions that may be felt in the business.

Once one decides to freeze, the exact nature of the freeze can vary widely. As described by The Groom Law Group, experts in ERISA matters, a plan can:

- Be closed to new entrants while those participants already in the plan continue to accrue benefits (commonly called a soft freeze).
- Stop benefit accruals for all active participants, but allow benefits to increase with the growth in participants' wages (also sometimes called a soft freeze).
- Stop benefit accruals for some, but not all participants based on age, tenure, job classification, or plant location (commonly called a partial freeze).
- Stop service accruals for all active participants and all participants stop earning benefits. Assets remain in the plan and are paid out when

participants retire or leave, but the participants' benefits do not grow with additional years of service (commonly called a hard freeze)[4].

Termination Nation

For many firms, defined benefit plans are simply too difficult to maintain, and, for others, defined contribution (DC) plans are more attractive and useful. However, if a sponsor has an existing DB plan, it must initiate a plan termination prior to adopting a DC scheme for the same population in its stead. As explained in the previous section, there are two main types of termination: standard termination and distress termination.[5]

In a *standard termination*, the plan sponsor must have enough assets to meet all the vested obligations of its pension plan. The sponsor will either pay retirees and current vested beneficiaries a lump sum of money, or the plan will be transferred to an insurance company—which will provide the monthly payments in place of the sponsor. Basically, a termination discontinues all future benefits (though it maintains current and vested benefits) and typically offers new and nonvested employees access to defined contribution plans.

In a *distressed termination*, the plan sponsor cannot afford to pay beneficiaries and is severely financially distressed. In fact, it must be determined in a bankruptcy court that the sponsor cannot meet its pension liabilities.[6] After a distressed termination, the corporate pension liability is taken over by the Pension Benefit Guarantee Corporation (PBGC), and beneficiaries receive benefits, though not from the plan sponsor. However, it should be noted that the PBGC has maximum distribution limits, so highly compensated employees may take significant cuts.[7] Essentially, the *full* pension guarantee is only truly backed by the full faith and credit of the plan sponsor.

In addition to these two terminations, there is also an *involuntary termination*, which is basically where the PBGC simply steps in and takes action on its own accord, usually to cauterize its own liability in adverse situations.

---

[4] David N. Levine and Lars C. Golumbic, "Freezing Defined Benefit Plans," Groom Law Group, Chartered, www.groom.com/media/publication/733_Freezing%20Defined%20Benefit%20Plans.pdf.

[5] www.pbgc.gov/prac/terminations.html.

[6] www.pbgc.gov/prac/terminations/distress-terminations.html.

[7] For a detailed explanation of maximums, visit: www.pbgc.gov/wr/benefits/guaranteed-benefits/maximum-guarantee.html.

Recently, Moody's targeted Lockheed Martin, The Boeing Company, Northrop, and Exelis as likely targets for plan terminations.[8] The firms have not confirmed intent to terminate, but Moody's suggests these as appropriate candidates because of the ratio of pension obligations to market cap.[9] Intuitively, this makes sense. If a given pension obligation is very large compared to the market value of the company—it has to begin to detract from focus on the core business.

Now let us consider some empirical evidence about what key financial executives are most concerned about regarding defined benefit plans. Exhibit 9.3 illustrates results from a recent Mercer report that incorporates input from 192 senior finance executives—88 percent of whom work at firms with annual revenues in excess of $1 billion and 60 percent with defined benefit assets of over $1 billion.[10]

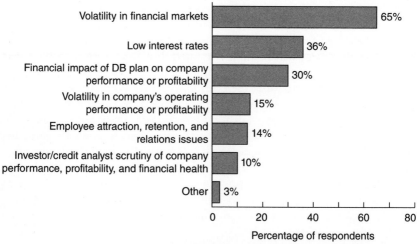

In your opinion, which of the following factors will have the greatest effect on your company's DB-plan decision making over the next two years?

Percentage of respondents
Note: Respondents were asked to select up to two.
Percentages will not total 100% due to multiple responses.

EXHIBIT 9.3 Mercer Survey on Pension Manager Concerns

Source: Mercer, "Redefining Pension Risk Management in a Volatile Economy," 2011.

[8] www.bizjournals.com/washington/blog/fedbiz_daily/2012/08/moodys-predicts-termination-of.html?page=all.

[9] www.bizjournals.com/washington/blog/fedbiz_daily/2012/08/moodys-predicts-termination-of.html?page=all.

[10]Mercer, "Redefining Pension Risk Management in a Volatile Economy," 2011.

The most important factor influencing these executives' DB deliberation is volatility in the financial markets. As we explained in Chapter 5, volatility is becoming the driving decision force in the management of defined benefit pension plans. This is largely consistent with trending toward further DB termination. The second most important variable is the effect of low interest rates on DB plans. The implications of this second area of sensitivity are a bit more subtle. When interest rates are low, pension liabilities are very high (inverse relationship between rates and liabilities). For some plans, this makes termination prohibitively expensive, as termination would necessitate paying for all vested pension liabilities in a lump sum payout or purchase of an annuity. With rates teetering around zero, there is nowhere to go but up. So, some of these plans are merely waiting for rates to rise. As rates rise, the rates by which pension liabilities are discounted will also rise—and in turn reduce the outstanding liability. Likewise, as the liability shrinks, it will be easier and cheaper for plan sponsors to settle the obligations to their employees and retirees, and transfer to more flexible defined contribution plans.

Firms are either unable to induce plan termination because of cost, or they are waiting for rates to make termination more attractive. Either way, this shows that rates will be highly impactful in DB decision making, particularly as rates rise.

An additional point of interest from Exhibit 9.3 is that only 14 percent of these executives cited employee attraction and retention as the most important factor dictating defined benefit decision making. This is a radical shift from the postwar era, when targeting loyal lifetime employees was crucial to the core strategies of so many great American firms—and consistent with our analysis.

Pension Buy-Ins

Pension buy-ins have the fundamentally same characteristics as an LDI solution except that they are contractualized, and provided by an insurance provider most often. They have the advantage of being an overlay of sorts and need not disrupt existing asset allocation. On a guaranteed basis, they get rid of almost every class of risk borne by a pension fund including mortality/longevity risk (the primary reason why one looks to insurance providers for this tool). This is often the next step on the ladder of eliminating pension obligations altogether. Because it is a revocable contract, it does not qualify for final settlement of a pension plan yet is still an interim step, and it does leave the door open to added obligations in the final settlement.

Pension Buyouts

Pension buyouts have been front and center with some of the most prominent U.S. companies, including General Motors (GM), Verizon Communications, Inc. (VZ), Ford Motor Company (F), and the New York Times Company (NYT).

In pension buyouts, the plan sponsor either pays qualified beneficiaries a lump sum, provides them with an annuity typically issued by an insurance company, or a combination of the two. The plan sponsors want to reduce the impact of defined benefit plans on their financial statements and transfer the risk inherent in retirement planning to either a third-party insurer, or the beneficiaries/retirees.

If the sponsor chooses to provide an annuity, they contact an insurance company to whom a portion of, or the entire outstanding and vested pension liability will be transferred. In this type of transaction, the insurance company will take over the pension obligations in question and be the new provider of pension payments to the beneficiaries. However, annuitants now deal solely with the insurance company, and the plan sponsor no longer has an obligation to the employees/retirees. The plan is backed by the full faith and credit of the issuing insurer, and is no longer backed by the PBGC. On October 17th, 2012, Verizon initiated a partial plan buyout by purchasing a group annuity contract from Prudential Insurance Company.[11] Final approval of this transaction is still pending, but this contract is expected to relieve Verizon of $7.5 billion of its roughly $30 billion pension obligation.[12]

This transaction enables Verizon to cauterize some of the pension wound and derisk a portion of its immediate liability. Pension risk transfer should incorporate all aspects of strategic corporate planning. For instance, partial plan buyouts may also be appropriate for firms that do still depend on defined benefit plans to attract and retain new talent. Similar to bond defeasance, where a bond issue is prefunded to take advantage of lower rates, partial plan buyouts can be used to derisk a particular tranche of pension liabilities, while modifying new defined benefit offerings to be more affordable.

Another buyout option is for plan sponsors to offer one-time lump-sum payments to plan beneficiaries. Plan participants usually have a choice of whether to accept the lump sum offer or not. The amount offered to each participant is estimated by final salary, life expectancy projections, and interest rates. There are several considerations one must analyze when contemplating

---

[11]www.pionline.com/article/20121017/REG/121019896.

[12]http://www22.verizon.com/investor/news_verizon_to_transfer_75_billion_in_management_pension_plan_obligations_to_prudential_10172012.htm.

a lump-sum offer. First off, one of the key advantages of defined benefit schemes is that plan participants do not have to take on investment risk—as they are promised a stream of benefits. However, inherent in the calculation of lump sum payouts is an assumed rate of return. That is, it is the modified present value of the stream of benefits a participant would receive if maintained under the plan. So, a plan sponsor invests to meet the obligations of its beneficiaries. However, if a participant takes a lump-sum payout, investment risk is directly attributed to the actions of each participant. The onus of investing and managing that lump-sum payment such that it provides an asset base sufficient to meet the needs of the participant in retirement now lies on the individual—not the plan sponsor. The New York Times Corporation offered lump sums to approximately 5,200 retirees to help derisk a portion of its pension liability.[13]

As rates rise, the cost of purchasing insurance annuities falls, and the costs of adhering to the increasingly complex regulatory environment becomes larger; plan sponsors will likely use a mix of these options to achieve pension risk transfer. GM set the stage for this in its landmark hybrid lump sum and annuity offer. GM has presented a transaction where it will purchase a group annuity contract for up to 118,000 retirees, but also offered roughly 42,000 of those retirees an option to choose between the new annuity and a lump-sum payout.[14] Basically, if retirees choose the annuity, they will receive monthly pension payments directly from Prudential. The PBGC insurance will be stripped and the monthly payments will be backed by the full faith and credit of Prudential. However, if the pensioners choose to take the lump sum, they will receive a check for a participant-specific calculated amount and receive no monthly pension payments in retirement.

The GM deal highlights two critical points:

1. A growing number of firms will embrace pension risk transfer and will use new offerings and insurance structures to attack their pension liabilities in substantial size.
2. Plan participants need to become better informed about the personal benefits and risks of pension risk transfer—especially for those who will be offered multiple payout options.

Let's go through one example to illustrate the issues an individual influenced by pension risk transfer may have to consider. On July 18, 2012, the

---

[13]www.businessinsurance.com/article/20120914/NEWS03/120919917.
[14]http://ljpr.com/files/GMLumpSumOfferWhitePaperLeonLaBrecque.pdf.

New York Times ran a story titled, "Retirees Wrestle with Pension Buyout from General Motors."[15] This article described the situation of a specific retiree, John Matthews, who was a GM salaried worker for the majority of his career. Matthews was offered a lump-sum payment of $818,000, or a lifetime perpetual annuity of $4,854 per month. Now we'll make three simplifying assumptions:

1. John is a healthy guy and he expects to live until he is 83 years old.
2. This means that on a pure raw numbers basis, John is deliberating over taking $818,000 payment today to spread over 240 months, and taking a $4,854 payment each month. *Just for reference: $818,000/240 = $3,408.*
3. There are many variables that are used to calculate both one's monthly pension payment and the lump sum offered to each beneficiary in a buyout. Just a few of these include: tenure at the firm, final salary, life expectancy, and so on. However, for the purpose of understanding an individual's decision, we are going to use an *implied growth rate* to describe the difference between money today and money 20 years from now. Again, these calculations differ from the exact calculations used in the GM plan, but it is more important to understand the issues conceptually than to memorize which mortality index and corporate bond benchmark was used.

If you simply take the $4,854 and multiply it by 240 months (12 months per year for the 20 years between 63 and 83)—John will receive $1,164,960 of cumulative nominal payments over the course of his retirement. If John accepted the $818,000 lump-sum payout and kept the cash in a non-interest bearing checking account, he could withdraw only $3,408 per month over the course of his 20-year retirement—leaving a completely depleted account upon passing. If this would be the extent of your analysis, you probably aren't reading this book closely. Rather, we would need to make certain return assumptions.

Let's assume John takes the $818,000 lump-sum payment, withdraws $4,854/month (to mimic the annuity option) for each of the 240 months in the 20-year period. He invests the whole amount to achieve a 5 percent return per year. John lives exactly 20 years as predicted, but at the end of his life he has $214,575 left in his investment account. If he had taken the annuity, he and/or his estate would be entitled to no further payments.

---

[15]www.nytimes.com/2012/07/19/business/retirees-wrestle-with-pension-buyout-from-general-motors.html?pagewanted=all&_r=0.

So, in this case, he was better off. Likewise, if his investment account made 6 percent per year, his final account balance would be $451,529. However, if he'd only achieved a 3 percent return each year, John would have run out of money after 218 months, leaving him with no monthly payments for the final 1.83 years of his retirement. If he had only generated 2.5 percent annual return over the period, he would have run out of money after 207 months—thereby offering no income stream for the final 2.75 years of his retirement. Obviously, many of the fixed assumptions in this example are unrealistic, but it provides a framework for asking the right questions.

Variations on the Issues

The following pages review brief explanations of just a few variations of the issues of the John Matthews/GM example just introduced.

Implications of Living Longer or Dying Sooner Than Expected

If John had tragically passed away after only 15, 10, or even 2 years of retirement, he would stop receiving annuity payments, and he and his family essentially lose a lot of the potential benefits he would be entitled to—had he lived longer. Conversely, if John eats his Wheaties, and lives to the ripe old age of 98 or 100, what decisions should John make about the annuity versus the lump sum? Are there family members that will depend on John's monthly income? Does John want to transfer wealth accrued from his defined benefit plan to future generations? Now reconsider the prior dilemma. Should John take the $818,000 or the annuity if he would only receive monthly payments for 5 or 10 years?

Risk of the Issuer

In the GM example, if John chooses the lump sum, he receives a check with near certain probability. Prudential happens to be a very stable company with significant expertise in pension risk transfer. However, if Prudential were to go belly-up, John's monthly annuity payments would be in jeopardy. Remember, when pension liabilities are sold to an insurer, the PBGC guarantee is stripped from the plan, and the annuity payments are backed by the full faith and credit of the insurer.

Additional Risk of Investment—Prepare for the Unexpected

Aside from the general summary of the aforementioned investment risk, one must always plan for the unexpected. Particularly as people age, unforeseen costs occur more and more frequently. Let's say that after five years, John needs a $40,000 surgery not covered by his current health-care provider.

It is true that the balance in his account is reduced, but over the course of the 20-year retirement time horizon, he also loses significant investment returns on that principal and returns on accrued returns. Small increases in planned expenditures can drastically alter the overall earnings potential, the effects of which are typically most salient in the later years of payout. When planning one's retirement, there must be a cushion to accommodate for the unexpected. We are all Monday morning quarterbacks, and it is easy to pontificate as to the appropriate choice given a certain set of conditions. However, the reality is that there are myriad numbers of questions participants must ask themselves, and with each new variable, one must readdress this iterative analysis.

One group that I work with on various pension risk transfer solutions is called Penbridge Advisors, and it is headed by Steve Keating, who cut his pension teeth at both Hewitt Associates (a major pension consulting firm) and Lazard Freres (the storied investment bank). He came up with Exhibits 9.4 and 9.5 to characterize the trade-offs in the various risk transfer solutions.

Pension De-Risking Strategies

Risk Management   Risk Transfer

LDI	Buy-In	Lump Sum	Buy-Out
• Controls interest rate and credit spread risk	• Transfers liability and investment risk to insurer	• Transfers investment and longevity risk to participants	• Irrevocably transfers benefit obligations from a plan sponsor to an insurance company
• Precision of duration and cash flow matching often increases with plan funded status	• Contract is an asset of the plan	• Corporate bond yields fully phased-in in 2012 for minimum lump sum calculations	• Triggers settlement accounting
• Strategy can be managed against plan maintenance or plan termination liabilities	• Does not trigger settlement accounting	• Can be offered to selected groups	• Only method to terminate plan and remove from balance sheet
	• Convertible to a buy-out at plan sponsor's election	• May trigger settlement accounting	

EXHIBIT 9.4   Defined Benefit Plan Risk Transfer
Source: Penbridge Advisors.

Pension De-Risking Strategies

		LDI	Buy-In	Lump Sum	Buy-Out
Risk Factors Addressed	Interest Rate / Credit Spread Risk	Y	Y	Y	Y
	Bond Default Risk	N	Y	Y	Y
	Longevity Risk	N	Y	Y	Y
	Benefit Option Risk	N	Y	Y	Y
Other Factors	Settles Liability	N	N	Y	Y
	Participants Assume Risk	N	N	Y	N
	Insurer Profit Spread	N	Y	N	Y

Positive	Negative	Y = Yes	N = No

EXHIBIT 9.5   Defined Benefit Plan Risk Mitigation Comparisons
Source: Penbridge Advisors.

SYNTHETIC MUTUAL FUND NOTES

Synthetic mutual funds are a fascinating concept invented by my most creative Wall Street friend, Peter Freund, while working for BankOne. On behalf of the bank, he filed a patent application in 2002, which was granted in 2009 (U.S. Patent 7,606,756). Peter is currently in the process of implementing his invention. This may still take some time since it is very earth shaking and so disruptive on many levels that it must be delicately executed. Imbedded in this concept is the shock and awe of what may well be the greatest and most persistent arbitrage in the history of mankind. Now that's a pretty bold assertion, so pay attention to what may one day get characterized as the monetizing of the alpha of alphas.

The Issue

The most important fact about asset management is virtually a secret. Over the past 29 years (since 1984), the dollar-weighted compound returns of domestic, actively managed, equity mutual funds lagged the S&P by at least an estimated 6 percent per annum. Today that market inefficiency amounts to almost $260 billion/annum (6% × $4.4 trillion). This presents an unparalleled opportunity to create tremendous risk adjusted returns.

Meanwhile, retail asset management is changing, much like institutional management, with indexation gaining penetration. Exchange-traded funds (ETFs) are mostly index tools that are traded like stocks on the public markets and they are growing rapidly. Mutual fund distributors are increasingly forced to be what is called "open architecture" oriented, which means that they offer a variety of products from multiple managers and not just proprietary product. Defined contribution sponsors are again seeking cost efficiency in their offering for participants, and this is once again taking precedence over branding. This is having a big impact on mutual fund flows. Nevertheless, mutual fund companies remain very profitable and valuable with operating margins of 30 to 40 percent and valuations of 3 to 4 percent of assets under management (AUM) . . . at least until this opportunity gets played out.

U.S. investors still own \$4.4 trillion of actively managed equity mutual funds. Retail investors are actually not well served by most mutual fund companies (at least not in *this* area). Frictional costs and tracking error against the benchmark index average 1.5 to 2 percent, as John Bogle and others have regularly pointed out (including fees, expenses, custody, etc.). Dollar-weighted, investors' returns for actively managed equity mutual funds lag the S&P by an additional 4.32 percent or more due to bad market timing according to experts like Dalbar, Zweig/Morningstar, and others.

The Concept

Launch a "synthetic funds" (SFs) business through a major fund platform owned by a well-rated corporate sponsor. This business will be positioned to attack all market sectors including retail—replacement of mutual funds, "instividual"—commingled funds for defined contribution plans, and institutional and high net worth—high alpha-generating transport mechanisms. It will simultaneously make the issuer the low-cost retail funds provider and the high value-added institutional alpha generator. It will provide the sponsoring company with a highly stable and saleable funding source based on the funding scheme that underlies this concept (shown in Exhibit 9.6).

The Solution

Synthetic funds—top-rated structured notes linked to mutual fund performance—offer investors the same choices they currently have with better and more certain performance. Investors will choose (potentially among all actively managed mutual funds) to take the market exposure for specific mutual funds while earning ½ percent per annum higher returns than the

Over decades, the dollar-weighted average returns for actively managed equity mutual funds ("MF") have lagged the general market by 600 bps/annum.

Parties	Returns
Note Investors	Investment MF+50bps
Pension Funds	Hedged basis trade: S&P-MF—300bps (expected profit: 300 bps)
Issuer	50 bps for expenses
Sponsor	Funding cost: LIBOR—200 bps

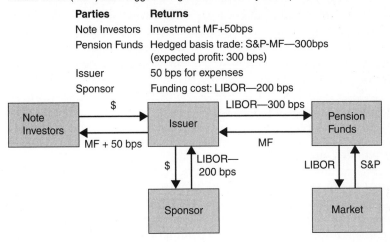

EXHIBIT 9.6 Synthetic Funds Flow

corresponding mutual fund shares, while enjoying the same liquidity and avoiding fees for changing exposures.

The issuer takes principal risk by selling, hedging, and managing the aggregated exposure, effectively "book-running" the aggregated exposure much like in a derivatives business, taking advantage of all netting and correlations. At virtually no marginal cost, the issuer can offer investors a market exposure to all mutual funds, and by hedging its market exposures synthetically will generate a large and very stable amount of funds, approximately equal to its virtual AUM, available for other purposes.

How the Product Works

A key aspect of the concept is minimizing behavioral changes of investors and their brokers. Investors can simply replace their existing mutual fund holdings with the issuer's top-rated notes to earn ½ percent more returns than their existing (active equity) mutual fund holding. For investors this will provide one-stop shopping with the issuer offering to mimic almost any actively managed equity mutual fund (and later branch beyond equity). The convenience to investors cannot be underestimated. All positions can be managed and reported in a single statement or be integrated into broker reporting systems. The issuer will be able to track and report in monthly statements the accretion of extra returns earned by investors.

There is also less regulatory paperwork with only a single prospectus required and the same broker/advisor incentives as mutual funds. With liquidity and fees identical to the reference mutual funds, plus higher returns and zero-cost fund switching, synthetic funds will offer the best mutual fund investor value proposition in the market.

A Compelling and Unique Opportunity

This opportunity is large and global. It encompasses investors from retail, institutional, and everything in between.

$4.4 trillion is currently invested in domestic, actively managed equity mutual funds. If SF issuers capture just 10 percent of the market, the basis trade will be enormous and the P&L volatility lethal for virtually all corporations. On the other hand, because pension funds have long-term investment horizons, it is much less painful for them to absorb the volatility of a very large basis position, especially if the expected return is high and their risk of loss is very low over any multiyear period.

Institutional investors recently have come to understand that uncorrelated assets allow them to earn incremental returns without increasing risk. The promise of uncorrelated assets explains the rapid growth in institutional hedge fund assets. The long-short position just described, then:

1. Is uncorrelated to other assets.
2. Is a strategy easily understood by investors, that does not rely on a "black box" or a trader's "hot hand."
3. Can be completely transparent to investors, with no need for complicated model pricing.
4. Will, unlike most other hedge fund strategies, remain profitable for a long time.
5. Is hugely scalable.
6. Permits pension funds to take big positions without spending much of their precious capital. (Pension Funds cumulatively will get the first 150 bps from an arbitrage that historically has produced >300 bps.)

There is the need to create a retail distribution channel that must leverage existing distribution systems, which may be conflicted or face hostility (funds are sold, not bought). This new channel adoption risk (particularly from defined contribution sponsors) will require work on changing market perception and positioning the product. This is fundamentally the same product in a different format. The mutual fund industry will put up resistance and perhaps seek to punish those who distribute and facilitate SFs.

SynFunds Summary

This patented synthetic mutual fund (SynFund, for short) technology I have described can give its sponsoring balance sheet company two new competitive advantages, both of which have the potential to "move the needle" and become strategically important:

- An enormous, persistent, source of alpha that will enable development of:
  - A de novo corporate asset management franchise with big profit margins and extraordinary competitive advantage
  - A comprehensive, simplified, streamlined, and much more cost-effective service to support corporate retirement services
  - A proprietary source of highly stable, long-term, low-cost funding, with virtually limitless capacity
- The two primary issuer benefits are the arbitrage spread (a.k.a. alpha) which comes from two market inefficiencies:
  - Seventy-five percent from bad market timing by mutual fund investors, caused by genetic imprinting of behavior that was adaptive long ago
  - Twenty-five percent mutual fund frictional costs

The trade has effectively unlimited capacity without spread compression because the AUM of Active Equity Funds is $4.4 trillion. It has a very attractive risk/return, 6 percent compound return for the past 29 years, with:

- No negative convexity
- No risk of catastrophic loss
- Never a period with negative three-year rolling average returns
- Returns that are weakly correlated with financial assets

As a funding source, because SynFunds can be hedged synthetically, the issuer does not need to own securities and is thereby insulated against most liquidity events.

Generally, managed assets are "sticky," and SynFund assets will be the "stickiest" because they offer the best investor value proposition for all active equity funds, and even the worst liquidity crises have not caused big redemptions of active equity fund assets.

THE ROLE FOR PENSION FUNDS

There are several ways pension funds will be able to take advantage of SynFunds. They will probably offer the most unique opportunity to act directly or through hedge funds as the risk counterparty to the swaps that the issuer will need to execute. In addition, SynFunds will be particularly attractive investment vehicles for both defined benefit and defined contribution pension accounts.

To capture the trading inefficiency of mutual fund investors, the issuer must maintain long/short positions that carry big basis risk (long S&P versus short SynFund investor returns). If the issuer captures even a small percentage of active equity fund assets, no corporate balance sheet in the world will be large enough to absorb its P&L volatility.

To eliminate P&L volatility, the issuer will share a portion of its alpha with pension funds and other long-term investors. The issuer will pay a preferred return to pension fund swap counterparties who will receive the S&P and pay actual SynFund investor returns. Pension funds will compare their alpha alternatives to the issuer swap, which is based on an arbitrage (long S&P versus short SynFund returns) that targets a market inefficiency which is well understood and easily explained, can be fully transparent, is not exposed to model risk or subjective asset values, has no gate, and no risk of side-pockets, does not rely on any special asset management skills or "black boxes," and can grow capacity enormously without spread compression.

In addition, the structure facilitates changes to the long position (e.g., the S&P), permitting the counterparties to add value by dynamically adjusting their long exposure.

As mentioned, it has returns weakly correlated with other financial assets, has no negative convexity, has no risk of catastrophic loss, and, since 1983 (first available data), three-year rolling returns have never been negative. This means that it pays a preferred return of 1.5 percent/annum on an arbitrage that since 1983 produced annual compound unlevered returns of more than 6 percent/annum, and should continue to produce similar returns for the foreseeable future. The pension fund counterparties will be able to terminate swaps on 30 days' notice without penalty and to extend swaps if their maximum return has not been realized. Unlike hedge fund investments, this requires very little capital (i.e., just margin) and deducts no expenses and charges no fees. Though the structure's goal is not tax avoidance, IRS Section 1260 may prevent SF swap counterparties from earning more LT capital gains than the underlying virtual trades would have generated.

The $5 trillion of U.S. defined contribution assets [401(k), 403(b), 457, etc.] are probably the best initial target for SynFund distribution and thus they have value for both DB and DC Plans. (SynFunds are particularly advantageous for investors in such accounts who change market exposures, because there is no fee for changing positions and no tax due until funds are redeemed.) SynFunds can help address a number of acute corporate problem areas:

- Employee irritation/anger at high fees and frictional cost (especially painful when investment returns are low)

- Limited trading opportunities
- Limited investment choices

SynFunds could be the critical enabling technology for wholesale reengineering of the infrastructure supporting many aspects of retail investments including: 401(k) plans, securities trading, and infrastructure to support corporate retirement investments. Standardization and synthetic asset exposures would significantly reduce administrative and transaction costs, as well as simplifying systems and consumer interfaces.

THE YALE MODEL (THE ILLIQUIDITY PREMIUM) VERSUS THE ALL-WEATHER MODEL

In my "Search for Alpha" class, I occasionally get a student not in the MBA program, but from another area of the university. Usually this would be a graduate engineer or an undergraduate from the business school. But recently I had the pleasure of having Scott Molnar, a principal investment analyst from the Cornell Investment Office. Scott was as knowledgeable about investments and hedge funds as anyone ever in my course. This was a great opportunity to pick his brain about the practical implementation of what has come to be called the Yale Model due to the allocation style popularized by David Swensen in his 2000 book, *Pioneering Portfolio Management,* that combines MPT diversification and correlation theories with generally aggressive asset class allocations in less liquid classes, presumably seeking to pick up the illiquidity premium. Scott chose to write his term paper on the Yale Model and defend its use. Since many pension funds have followed Yale into the deep end of the asset allocation pool, I find it instructive to see how the endowment practitioners are feeling after the breakdown of correlations and the combination of dramatically reduced valuations and extreme illiquidity. As such, I have asked and Scott has agreed to let me reprint it here:

Has the Yale Model Seen Its Day?[16]

In the height of the 2008–2009 financial meltdown, market liquidity evaporated and traditional diversification offered no protection for institutional investors. Increasing illiquidity and rising asset correlations challenged the assumptions behind Swensenites and the relatively conservative investment policies at the top U.S. university endowments. Until the crisis, schools like Yale, Harvard,

---

[16]Scott A. Molnar, Principal Investment Analyst, Cornell University Investment Office, "Has the Yale Model Seen Its Day?" November 2012.

and Cornell had consistently returned more than 15 percent per year, but things changed drastically in fiscal year 2008–2009. At June 30, 2008, Ivy League endowments plummeted by 25 to 30 percent, causing schools to slash spending and delay campus expansions. People began to question the Yale Model made famous by Yale's chief investment officer, David Swensen, who had gone 20 years without a down year and generated an extra $14 billion for the university versus a standard 60–40 passive portfolio. Has the magic of the Yale Model disappeared? Should universities abandon the model and look for another way to invest?

The Yale Model reduces all investment performance into one of three factors: asset allocation, market timing, and security selection. According to Swensenites, asset allocation is by far the most important. As long as correlation with traditional stock and bond portfolios remains low, adding unconventional assets would help reduce risk and increase return . . . the basic underpinning of the modern portfolio theory.

Unfortunately, this basic assumption led university endowments to emphasize higher returning and less liquid areas like private equity, real estate, and hedge funds. In normal times, the lower liquidity worked well for universities, as cash flows were sufficient to offset capital calls. The problem faced in the financial crisis was not from modern portfolio theory, asset allocation, or the Yale Model, but from the endowment policy of holding shockingly small amounts of cash relative to future funding needs. In essence, the portfolio was positioned on the wrong place on the efficient frontier and had invested far too little in cash and liquid assets rather than investing too much in alternatives.

While rising illiquidity hampered schools' spending in the short run, the Yale Model is still viable over the long run, which is the framework for which the model was developed. Relying heavily on modern portfolio theory, the Yale Model contains five key principles:

1. *Invest in equities.*
2. *Hold a diversified portfolio and avoid market timing.*
3. *Invest in areas that have incomplete information and illiquidity to increase long-term returns.*
4. *Use outside managers.*
5. *Allocate to investment firms owned and managed by the investment principals to avoid conflicts of interest.*

Based on asset classes, expected returns, risks, liquidity, and correlations, institutions determine their optimal portfolio on the efficient frontier subject to the risk the trustees are willing to take and other constraints (liquidity, concentration . . .).

While it is impossible to precisely match the optimal portfolio, the process of creating the efficient frontier and determining the desired allocation offers tremendous value for understanding risk tolerances of the investors and differences between asset classes.

Every step of the model is a widely accepted and well understood investment principal that has worked throughout time and is expected to continue to work over the long run. The issue faced by larger institutions was the fact that endowments have ongoing short-term liabilities in the form of unfunded capital commitments and school operating expenses. Historically, these expenses are financed with current income, distributions from existing funds, and new donations into the endowment. During the crisis, endowments were hit by the perfect storm: current income declined as yields fell and stocks cut dividends; distributions stopped as managers could not sell positions for a profit; donations slowed as people cut back on charitable giving; and the decline in liquid securities caused endowments to become overallocated to illiquid assets before accounting for increases from capital calls. In essence, large endowments broke the cardinal rule of investing by financing long-term assets with short-term liabilities. Smaller schools that did not follow the Yale Model, because of limited resources and higher demands from the endowment, outperformed due to their smaller exposure to alternatives and higher allocation to traditional fixed income.

Universities were not without options when the short-term assets began to dwindle and they faced liquidity issues. Like bloated corporations, schools often have more overhead than they effectively need to run operations. To solve the short-term funding issues, they could cut expenses and reduce payouts from the endowment to the university. Additionally, the greatest asset of the university is often the most underutilized—the school's high credit rating and balance sheet. Universities have tremendous amounts of real estate and other assets that are undercapitalized and schools like Cornell have an Aa credit rating, allowing them to tap the credit markets. To solve the asset/liability mismatch, universities issued debt including $1.5 billion at Harvard, $1 billion at Princeton, $800 million at Yale, and $500 million at Cornell. Though outsiders might view the bond issue as an act of desperation after the Yale Model "broke," the bond issuance was just a prudent asset management *tool similar to when for-profit corporations extend duration and push out liabilities. With the extended liabilities and the elimination of short-term liquidity needs, the Yale Model was allowed to work as intended for patient, long-term investors.*

In the bull market years, endowments boomed due to the overweight to riskier equity-like asset classes. While risk securities declined drastically during the financial crisis, the worst thing an investor can do is avoid risky assets after a market crash. The Yale Model focuses on equity securities and avoids market timing, but does not prevent investors from overweighting or underweighting asset classes when they are trading at dramatically different levels than underlying valuations. The emphasis on equity explained the enormous allocations to illiquid private equity and alternative securities, but allowed universities to increase exposure to equities after they declined significantly. When valuations normalized, university endowments reduced overweight exposures and redefined asset allocations to better balance the duration of assets with those of the liabilities (capital calls, spending . . .). In essence, the Yale Model was tweaked not eliminated to represent the new demands on assets and the new realities of the capital markets. Higher correlation makes diversification more difficult but more important. Furthermore, high correlation is not a perpetual state but exists during periods of extreme events when the return of an asset class becomes inversely related to its expected risk. Such periods are common after a shock in one asset class but short-lived as heightened correlation dissipates with market normalization. Rather than eliminate the base assumptions of the Yale Model, universities are going further in finding new alternative strategies to exploit since they offer differentiated exposures, lower correlations, and higher levels of expected alpha.

Finally, large institutions model and manage for risks associated with extreme "Black Swan" events but cannot invest as if one was to occur frequently. Fearing constant extreme events would force investors into only high-quality and low-returning Treasury securities, which would cause significant declines in the real value of portfolios overtime. Keeping in mind the risks, large endowments continue to allocate to the illiquid and higher returning asset class which offer better results in the long run; however, they adjusted their assumptions in line with modern portfolio theory and the Yale Model to increase allocations to highly liquid, short-term securities to meet funding needs. Despite the higher allocation to short-term securities, alternative investments continue to play an important role in well-constructed and well-diversified institutional portfolios. Regardless of short-term performance, the Yale Model is not going away for larger institutions and will continue to generate higher returns over the long run.

The Yale Model of investing is, in many ways, the culmination of 50 years of investment research and represents sort of "turbocharged" modern portfolio theory. Strangely enough, one of the most successful hedge fund managers, Ray Dalio, who currently runs the largest hedge fund in the world, the global macro fund Bridgewater, has proposed an alternative allocation methodology that he calls the All-Weather style. It is so contrary to MPT that he calls it Post-Modern Portfolio Theory. While the Yale Model has served its proponents well for many years, Dalio's PMPT approach has the great advantage of having performed extremely well during the recent financial crisis and the years directly following. This did not go unnoticed in the Pension Fund market as fund managers licked their wounds from 2008 to 2009.

Why the All-Weather Risk Balancing Approach Withstood the Stress-Test of 2008[17]

The All-Weather approach to asset allocation leverages up low-risk assets and deleverages high-risk assets so that the expected returns and risks of all the assets in the portfolio are roughly the same. This approach to asset allocation produced a better return to risk ratio than the conventional portfolio mix for a simple reason: Risk decreased more from better diversification than increased from the use of leverage.

Leverage was not a problem for a few reasons. First, leverage is used to create volatility in lower-risk assets which creates better diversification than would be possible without leverage. For example, if I put 50 percent of my money in an unleveraged Treasury bond and 50 percent of my money in stocks, my portfolio would have been dominated by stocks because stocks are more volatile; however, if I leveraged my bonds to have the same volatility as stocks, I would have had much better diversification and would have had much lower risks during the financial crisis. Second, All-Weather doesn't use very much leverage; the strategy is around two times leveraged, which is less than the amount of leverage an

---

[17]Ray Dalio, "Engineering Targeted Returns & Risks, a.k.a. Risk Parity," Bridgewater Associates, 2004.

*average large company in the S&P 500 employs and about 1/10th
the leverage the average U.S. bank employs (which we think is too
much). Third, leverage is employed in a range of highly liquid forms
that can be rebalanced and liquidated if asset prices fall. Finally, in
those areas where counterparties are the source of leverage, we actively limit exposure to lenders and actively select which lenders are
most reliable funding sources. As a result, the leverage itself was not
a problem in affecting the performance of the All-Weather strategy
throughout the crisis period.*

*Incorrect correlation assumptions were also not a problem
because we don't use them in the weighting process because they
aren't stable. Instead, our weighting of assets is based on understanding the ways that discounted economic conditions are reflected in asset pricing, and by ensuring the asset mix holds exposures
that are equally balanced across environments, and most importantly balanced with respect to rising and falling growth and inflation rates. This framework held up in the crisis period. In the crisis,
those assets that do badly when growth falls relative to expectations
(e.g. equities) did poorly, but were significantly offset by those assets
that do well when growth is weaker than expected (e.g. Treasury
bonds). By leveraging the bonds up so that our bond exposure was
comparable to our equity exposure, these positions could balance
each other; whereas if leverage couldn't be used, they could not. In
comparison, the conventional portfolio performance is more concentrated toward equities so it does worse when growth disappoints
and did worse in the crisis.*

*While I am not surprised, I am very pleased to see that this
approach to strategic asset allocation, which has been proven out
since we developed it 14 years ago and in 85 years of back-testing,
is now gaining in popularity. I believe that, as this approach is increasingly adopted, it will have a radical beneficial impact on asset
allocation that will be of a similar magnitude to that of traditional
portfolio theory as it gained acceptance.*

I am personally conflicted by each of these two arguments in favor
of MPT and PMPT. On the one hand, I believe in the illiquidity premium
and feel it offers pension funds a very important investment edge they
sorely need. I believe that with proper assessment of transactional cash
needs (to apply our Keynesian distinction), pension funds should be able
to invest in less liquid classes and expect a premium. I am not pleased by
learning that in the real estate markets (one of the three big illiquid classes
used by pension funds), research comparing REITs and private RE Funds

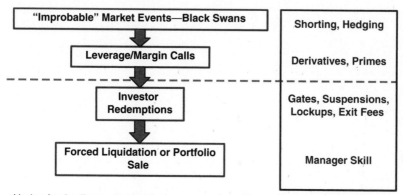

Hedge fund collapses begin when an unusual market event causes the portfolio to quickly fall in value. As margin calls and investor redemptions increase, the hedge fund is forced to either liquidate the portfolio or be acquired by another firm.

EXHIBIT 9.7   Hedge Fund Collapse

would indicate a negative illiquidity premium of almost 42 percent—hard to ignore![18]

On the other hand, it is hard to ignore that MPT and the underlying correlations failed miserably in 2008, just when they were most needed. What good is a fire extinguisher if it won't function properly in a fire? It is simply not rational to suggest that these were extreme, Black Swan events that are not reasonable tests of a diversification methodology. I would posit that fire extinguishers must function in a fire, and should probably do so without fail. Dalio's PMPT has the advantage of being fire-tested and thus gets a big benefit of the doubt on that account alone. I am perhaps more worried by the leveraging methodology on the basis of personal experience. I worry that what appears to be highly available financing can get skittish in adverse markets, particularly when the chosen asset class suddenly and unexpectedly gets illiquid, which happens more often than I care to remember. As explained in Chapter 7, Exhibit 9.7 shows how I explain this to my students.

Next up, we take a look at what is going on from a global perspective and review a case study I have from my past experience with Bankers Trust that may offer some hope.

---

[18]Brad Case, "The Illiquidity Premium Myth," April 1, 2010. http://wealthmanagement .com/review-deletion/illiquidity-premium-myth.

CHAPTER 10

The Poverty of Nations (Apologies to Adam Smith)

We spent a lot of time in Chapter 2 reviewing the impact that demographics and pension funding levels have on the prospects for countries filling their pension gaps in the next 40 years. The math that drives our crystal ball should not be mysterious to anyone. There is, first and foremost, an assessment of need based on how many retirees you will have in the next 40 years. The combination of population's statistics and longevity standards in each country give us that number fairly easily. Calculating pension need is done simply here by taking 60 percent of the final earnings level in that country. That may or may not suffice, but it is a fair estimate. We then discount those requirements back to present value of the need in assets today, assuming we will do a decent, but not herculean effort in compounding those assets over the retirement cycle. We compare that number to what is already saved and that gives us the gross funding gap.

The next step is important because the productive economy of these countries going forward is a key determinant of whether the gap is manageable or a serious problem. The old age dependency ratio estimates we have used incorporate the United Nations population growth forecasts and give us the approximate expected size of the population that must support the funding of that gap as we roll forward. The degree of this burden is clearly a function of economic growth, and we know that economic growth is very much correlated to population growth. Therefore, it is likely that in low population growth countries, where the burden is heaviest, growth will not likely provide a solution and, indeed, the pension funding burden will likely further impede growth.

IS THERE A PATH TO SALVATION?

I am repeating myself from Chapter 2 because this concept is so very important to comprehend: Population drives growth and population reduces the pension funding burden. It is late in the retirement cycle for this bulge we call the Baby Boom, as we have used up two-thirds of the valuable time value for compounding pension savings and we are now faced with starting to decumulate rather than accumulate assets. There is another bad economic impact of this that should not be missed. These pension assets that exist now are the corpus of the long-term capital that feeds economic growth in all nations. As this long-term capital gets used to fund the growing pension payment needs of this growing Baby Boom population, there will simply be less long-term investment capital around to drive growth. Ouch! That one really hurts. It's like adding insult to injury. Low growth leads to more low growth leads to even lower growth.

Warning: I am about to sound populist in my thinking. Pension assets are the assets of the masses. They are generally not the assets of the wealthy. The wealthy don't need pensions because they are . . . wealthy. So it is fair to say that while pension assets are depleting and long-term capital stock is also getting depleted, the value of private high net worth capital grows, based on scarcity alone. This is the argument for the circumstances of pension funding adding to the disparity of wealth in the world. Now to a certain extent, the wealthy are bound to get taxed more out of simple necessity. As Willie Sutton said when asked why he robbed banks: "That's where the money is." We hear this rhetoric daily in the United States, in France, and in a growing list of countries. This is why this is not a problem of all the grasshoppers who have failed to sufficiently save for retirement. This is a problem for everyone. As I've said, you can't build your walls high enough to protect you against this problem.

However, I do believe different countries will fare better than others and, as we have shown, different countries have differing degrees of problem to tackle because of their demographics, their national policies (most notably immigration), their current funding status, their ability to take on more debt, and the economic engine which fuels their future growth. It is also important to understand the amount of inherent national wealth (particularly natural resources) at the disposal of these countries. Use Norway as a perfect example. With the North Sea oil wealth that Norway has garnered and continues to harvest, this small, relatively obscure country has built its sovereign wealth fund into the largest on the planet, surpassing even the oil rich Gulf countries that have flaunted their SWF wallets for years. What is different about Norway is that they actually characterize their SWF as a pension fund for their people. There you have it; the model for solving the problem of the moment. Find oil (or something else of great value) and put the revenues into a pot to fill the pension gap that looms. It sounds like I'm making fun, since not every country has a North Sea at their disposal. But I am simply saying that the privatization or monetization of national wealth (in whatever form it is available) will now be a necessary step for almost every country to take.

When we look across the globe and see where the problems are greatest, we notice that the puritanical ways of the Anglo countries (the United Kingdom, the United States, Canada, and Australia) have generally served them well and put them in fairly good shape. The small, parsimonious countries like the Netherlands, Sweden, and Switzerland are equally or more so in fine shape. It is primarily the rest of Europe and Japan that are in a bad way. Of the BRICs, Brazil comes out the best with a result that has them more or less as well prepared as the United States and greatly helped by their population trend line that will give them a much lower old age dependency ratio. India and China look to be numerically equivalent in terms of adequacy, but the population shift that will see India roll forward in growth while China slows and reverses will occur just as the demographic bulge caused by the one child policy takes hold and drives the old age dependency ratio way up to almost 40 percent while India hovers lower at just over 20 percent as shown in Exhibit 10.1. Russia will find itself worse off than the United States and looking more like a developed country than the emerging market member it is (this is clearly the wrong time to be in the varsity versus the junior varsity).

Of course, the real problems in Japan and Europe will manifest themselves in many ways. Japan is a significant world economy and will undoubtedly realize that its situation is exacerbated by its xenophobia. This is unlikely to change a small island people's mentality about immigration, and the current population and opportunities there do not make it a candidate for that fix anyway. (For instance, I note that Japan is rebuilding its navy in anticipation of more hostilities with China.)

As for Europe, I have generally been outspoken about the fate of the Euro, if not the European Union altogether. Clearly, I have been wrong about its fate so far, but I see nothing in terms of a relaxation of sovereignty or a likely ability for the disparity of the members to suffer the stringency of the bans that are needed to keep the Euro on track. The only salvation would have come from the pillars of Germany and France providing the wherewithal to fill the debt holes on the balance sheets of Southern Europe, but I suggest every day to my students that the pension crisis alone negates that route. What Frenchman or German will stand by and allow his pension benefits to be significantly curtailed for the benefit of supporting the profligate ways of his Grecian, Italian, Spanish, or Portuguese brethren. Economic unity without federalism is an unlikely path.

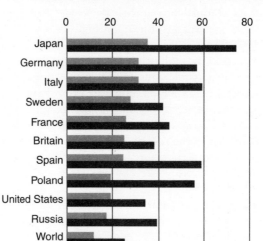

Number of people aged 65 and over
As percentage of labor force (aged 15–64), forecasts

EXHIBIT 10.1   Old Age Dependency Ratios
Source: www.economist.com/node/13611235.

It barely worked in the United States, as we saw during the Civil War; I doubt all the great rhetoric from the European Parliament in Strasberg will paper over the economic reality in a time of great economic strain like we have facing us for the next 40 years.

What then becomes of Europe? I grew up in Europe in my high school years. I have a great fondness for it and especially for the laid-back if somewhat casual ways of Italy (I lived in Rome). There is nowhere more pleasant to vacation than Europe in my opinion. Therein lies the future of Europe I believe. Europe seems destined to be the playground of the world. More and more non-Europeans will buy property, whether chateaus in the Loire Valley, castles on the Rhine, or great villas in Tuscany and Umbria. Europe has no significant military component and is simply too centrally located and natural resource–poor to do anything other than hunker down and become a somewhat servile service economy.

Is there any other path to salvation for countries, states, or even families other than to grin and bear it? I believe there is, and I like to use the example of Chile as a small microcosm example of how this problem can be tackled.

THE CHILEAN TERRARIUM

I began tuning into the importance of the pension market 25 years ago when I was handed the responsibility for $4 billion of bad debt to Latin America and was told to "find a way out of this mess." I was working at Bankers Trust, one of the leading pension trust banks in the world, but that had nothing to do with the commercial lending mess we (and every other major bank in the world) found ourselves in with our LDC (less developed country) loan exposure in 1986. While that whole episode in the world's history of financial crises is noteworthy, that's a different story except for the fact that our quickly deteriorating portfolio of sovereign debt caused us to think more radically about solutions and exits, and that led us to the small but interesting country of Chile.

Chile is that long narrow country that hugs the spine of the Andes mountains. It is less than 1/10 the land mass of Brazil and is perhaps best known for the plane crash that caused one of the more sensational cases of cannibalism in our modern era. But for such an obscure country, it also had a rather high-profile political and economic history in the past 40 years. After duly electing a Marxist to the office of President (Salvador Allende), the military, led by General Augusto Pinochet, overthrew and killed Allende, and assumed what would become long-term control of the country.

While I was a student of modern revolutions during my long-haired days at Cornell, and while there are many social and human rights issues that encompass this era in Chilean history, I am interested here in only one economic aspect of this era. Pinochet, an ultraconservative, empowered a group of highly educated technocrats (most trained at The University of Chicago under Milton Friedman, the great monetarist) to fix the broken Chilean economy. The general picture was that under Allende the country had "partied" its way into bankruptcy with the proliferation of consumer debt and all the bad financial repercussions that entails. This all happened in a post–oil shock world that had petrodollars flowing freely enough to induce worldwide banks to lend way too much to Latin America to subsidize these bad spending habits. So there was Chile, overleveraged in a crumbling worldwide recession with a need to clean house.

Enter the Chicago Boys led by an earth-shoe-wearing, Prince Valiant lookalike named Hernan Buchi. When I met Minister of Finance Buchi in the ornate Ministry Building on Constitution Square, he came in with a bicycle clip on his pant leg, since he rode his bike to work to be ecologically prudent. His solution for Chile at this moment of overextension and desired fiscal conservatism was to privatize major intervened companies and allow for the controlled use of foreign (dollar denominated) debt to be used to buy those companies. The first such asset to go on the chopping block was the country's largest pension fund company, Provida, and insurance company, Consorcio. These two companies had the distinction of leading the charge in Chile of providing pensions (of a "defined contribution" nature, as we will discuss later) for the first time for all workers in Chile. They also were the largest providers of long-term capital to the Chilean economy—a not inconsequential element in the rebuilding of the Chilean economy.

So let's pause and reflect on this fact pattern for a moment:

- Chile was in the hands of a right-wing dictator.
- Chile was bankrupt.
- Chile had just started a modern pension scheme following best practices from the United States.
- Chile decided that selling national patrimony (the assets of the people) was the best way to resolve its foreign debt burden and set the economy on a stable path.

I trust everyone senses the foreshadowing imbedded in this example. When we have overspent and overextended, we need to do what it takes to stabilize the situation. Having a dictator at the helm means there is little debate to slow down the process of taking necessary action. The engine of economic growth is long-term capital. Capital generally hates being committed long term, but the best place to find such patient capital is in the long-term savings pools, which tend to be retirement pools. Institutionalized retirement savings simply perform better (as we have discussed, by 2 to 10 percent, which is an enormous edge over the long horizon of retirement planning), and thus the discipline of mandatory retirement savings organized into pension funds may well be *the* most important element in creating a sustainable and prosperous economy. And please remember (for the libertarians in the audience) that mandatory retirement savings is the best means of avoiding the ultimate fiscal deadweight of nationally supported retirement, especially in an aging population.

So there you have it, a virtual tabletop terrarium of how to solve a fiscal and pension crisis. Sell assets to plug the hole. Force savings to stop the bleed and prepare for the future. Institutionalize the process to insure organized long-term capital supply. Add water and wait patiently for 20 years.

What I learned from this early exposure to Chile was that the pension system is the tree of life in this ecosystem. Without it there is just dirt and water. With it come all good things. But the tree needs tending, regularly. The system loves to underfeed the tree, thinking it big and strong enough to do with less. The tree needs pruning, as it can and does grow to dominate and unbalance the terrarium. And very often we overestimate the fruit-bearing capacity of the tree and expect it to feed twice what it was designed to feed.

If we look at Chile today, we see the benefits that resulted from this intelligent and holistic approach to their issues of the day. The national patrimony has been retrieved and Provida and Consorcio are more Chilean owned than not. And perhaps even more important, that did not occur through some administrative decree; it happened via open market processes. The fact is that local capital is often far better able to appreciate inherent value and is certainly prepared to be patient. It also bears mentioning that compared to many Latin American or other emerging market countries, Chile has had the good fortune to have a national business approach which truly believes in Chile and does not tend to overly hedge their bets by keeping the majority of their capital in offshore havens. This is far more the case in places like Argentina, where the inherent lack of long-term confidence has tended to breed a lack of long-term confidence in the country. The Chilean economy is more egalitarian with a larger middle-class population than any in Latin America. A visit by an average American to the suburbs of Santiago would leave him or her feeling like Chileans live as well or better than we do in the United States. And if you look at the fiscal status of Chile from the specific perspective of how healthy the pension system is and how much future fiscal burden is likely, you would wish that the rest of the world had done what Chile managed to do 25 years ago.

It is always easier to succeed in a microcosm than in the broader world we live in. Decision making in dictatorships is also easy, at least for a while. So I am not suggesting that all the world needs to do to solve the impending pension crisis is follow the Chilean game plan. There certainly are lessons there and many of the elements used are useful tools, but what I really want to point out from this opening example is two fundamental and perhaps obvious observations:

1. Pension plans and their critical role in providing retirement income and support are perhaps the single most important variable in the fiscal stability of the world economies, so understanding their status—country-by-country or entity-by-entity—is the key to assessing and/or running those economies.
2. Pension plans are the most important source of long-term capital in almost all economies and as such are the true engines of growth and must be tended to accordingly.

So Bankers Trust decided to bid to buy Provida and Consorcio in 1986 when they were put up for auction by the Chilean Ministry of Finance. We would be the first to use the newly authorized debt-for-equity exchange mechanism (called a Chapter 18 transaction), which would allow us to use Chilean sovereign debt we owned in the bid with the mechanical understanding that we would submit the debt for redemption into local currency to specifically make the acquisition if we won. I should pause at this point and remind you that doing a transaction like this has the double-edged effect of both reducing the foreign-dominated debt burden (clearly the biggest problem faced by Chile and almost all LDCs at that time) and boosting local currency monetary supply. Thus, in a strange turn of events, a problem exacerbated by an inflationary economy was being attacked with an inflationary tool. This may seem a nominal concern, but I can assure you it was not. Luckily, the pragmatic Chicago Boys of Chile saw the much greater benefit of dollar debt reduction and figured they could, as monetarists, find other ways to handle the inflation issues that came with it.

So we would bid the nominal value of the debt even though this debt was trading on the open market (a very, very small market in those days) for 60 cents on the dollar. This aspect is relevant because using this debt-for-equity mechanism, with its inherently inflationary impact, meant that this process was likely to be controlled and the value of the debt would be significantly impacted in a technical sense by these supply and demand factors. It was also not missed on us that inflation, while generally viewed as deleterious to the economy and the long-term investment climate, was also helpful to a pension business in ways we will discuss later. Oh, those sneaky Wall Street bankers, right?

On the day of the auction, we sent our man in with two sealed bids (one in each inside jacket pocket) for bids of $41 million and $43 million in sovereign debt. The idea was to give him some room to call an "audible" based on what went on in the auction room. So there he is sitting there while BAT (a global player in the pension market) put in its bid. Then, in walked Citibank (at the time, the largest financial institution in Chile, not to mention many other countries of the world) with what our man characterized as the largest envelope he had ever seen. Naturally, this prompted him to reach for the $43 million bid letter, which was what we officially tendered.

When the administrator opened the sealed bids, our $43 million bid was countered by BAT's bid of $26 million in new money and a small note from Citibank's huge envelope, which said that Citibank declined to bid. Such is the nonsense of business. Bankers Trust was declared the winner. The next day, the local newspaper, *Il Mercurio*, published a cartoon showing a store window with two gems called Provida and Consorcio and a skinny Brit in a bowler with a moth-infested purse that said $26M, while a big cowboy held two moneybags that said $43M. Our chairman loved that cartoon until I pointed out that $43M of debt was equivalent in market value to $26M of cash.

After buying these two gems for $26M in value, we proceeded to find professional management and built these businesses over the ensuing

10 years into approximately $1 billion in value and all the while making more money in our investment banking activities in Chile than we had ever done before, all courtesy of our central position in the long-term capital flows of the country.

Now, I do not want to imply that we at Bankers Trust either invented the pension solution for Chile or even set it on the right track. That was accomplished first and foremost by General Pinochet, who had the power and wisdom to put in place professional technocrats with very long-term visions of how best to solve Chile's pension and other economic issues. These people, like Pepe Pinero, the architect of the Chilean AFP defined contribution system, and Hernan Buchi, the minister of finance who had the wisdom and shrewdness to put in place the Debt-for-Equity conversion programs and privatization program, deserve the credit. We may have had the good sense to seek an early and profitable exit from our sovereign debt woes, but we had little sense or reason to focus on the pension system of a country like Chile.

The benefit to me was that it all started me thinking about the power of long-term capital in the constructs of pension funds and insurance companies. I directly saw how these financial services companies worked, how they intersected with local capital markets, and even macroeconomic trends like inflation; it got me thinking about defined benefit versus contribution pension plans and how best they are deployed. And perhaps the best thing was that it has allowed me to follow the progress of the changes enacted lo these 25 years ago (almost the length of a full retirement cycle). I have borne witness to the positive economic impact this and all the other prudent economic policies put in place have had on the country. It is particularly gratifying and instructive to see that the retirement system of little old Chile is now a model for the rest of the world.

I am sure that the exact formula in this example of Chile would not work for every country in the world, but there are several key elements that I do believe are needed somewhat universally:

Step #1: The first step is to fill the gap. This is a temporal problem and it's late in the cycle so countries need to find assets to fill the gap. Find some spare assets, give them to those with the wealth, and use the wealth to plug the hole.

Step # 2: I have mentioned the need to insure that the wealth does not leak out to those in the middle. Corruption is rampant when it comes to this scale of monetization.

Step #3: Determine where the funds are needed in a prioritized manner, and be sure that it goes to the most immediate needs first.

Provide sufficiently for health-care needs in addition to life-sustaining payments.

Step #4: Put in place a mandatory retirement system that can adequately provide for the next generations.

Let's take a last look at the fundamental elements of the Chilean system and hear what the Congressional Research Service of the United States had to say about the Chilean system in a report issued in March 2012. This may be the most objective perspective we can take:

Chile's public pension system consists of three tiers: a poverty prevention tier, an individual account tier, and a voluntary savings tier. The poverty prevention tier provides a minimum benefit to aged persons who did not participate in the public pension system and to retired workers whose monthly pensions financed by individual account assets (the second tier) do not reach certain thresholds. Workers contribute 10 percent of wage or salary income to an individual account in the second tier and choose a private-sector Administradora de Fondos de Pensiones (AFP) with which to invest their pension contributions. Employers are not required to contribute to employees' AFPs, although since 2008 employers have been required to pay the premiums for workers' survivor and disability insurance, which are provided by private insurance companies. Upon retirement, the worker may withdraw assets that have accumulated in the individual account as an immediate or deferred annuity or through programmed withdrawals. The third tier allows workers to supplement retirement income with voluntary, tax-favored savings.

Lessons from Chile's introduction of individual accounts may be helpful to other countries considering a similar transition, although not all of Chile's experiences are directly comparable to major Organisation for Economic Co-operation and Development (OECD) countries, such as the United States. For example, Chile's experience with high administrative costs may or may not be relevant to a second country, depending on whether the second country's public or private sector would manage account investments and the extent of financial-sector competition in the second country. Another difference between Chile and other countries may be the degree of public acceptance for the first, welfare tier of the system, which creates fiscal pressures similar to those of a pay-as-you-go system. Another political consideration is that Chile in the early 1980s, under General Pinochet, had considerable latitude to impose top-down reform of the pension system. Transition costs are another issue facing a country considering a move to a Chilean-type model. When Chile transitioned to a private account system in 1981, the earlier pay-as-you-go system was chaotic, insolvent, and unfair.[1] At the same time, Chile's non-pension budget in the early 1980s was in surplus and available for financing transition costs, and high growth rates of economic growth in Chile during the 1980s reduced the burden of transition on the economy. The 2008 reforms to the poverty prevention tier (the Solidarity tier) are generally acknowledged as the most important component of the 2008 reform package.[2]

Chile's public pension system continues to face challenges after the 2008 reforms, however. Although the 2008 reforms will bring many self-employed workers into the public pension system, much of the informal sector remains outside the pension system. It remains to be seen whether reforms to AFPs will increase competition and lower costs."[3]

Here is what I know: The world is headed for a turbulent 40 years with developed countries struggling more than emerging countries do, mostly due to the demographic monsters that they face. There is need for means to fill the gaps and set a course for the future for most of these countries. Chile is not one of the countries we need to worry about. They have implemented the changes and mostly filled the gaps. More importantly, they show us that future adjustments are always necessary to keep this sort of system relevant to the population's needs. Having participated in the early days of the Chilean system, I feel that if other countries had troubled to focus on their pension needs in the 1980s, we might not be facing the crisis we are.

---

[1] Mauricio Soto, "Chilean Pension Reform: The Good, The Bad, and The In Between," Center for Retirement Research at Boston College, no. 31, June 2005, at http://crr.bc.edu/briefs/chilean-pension-reform-the-good-the-bad-and-the-inbetween.

[2] The World Bank, "Reforming the Pension Reforms: The Recent Initiatives and Actions on Pensions in Argentina and Chile," SP Discussion Paper No. 0831, May 2008, p. 57.

[3] Alison M. Shelton, Analyst in Income Security, Congressional Research Service 7-5700, "Chile's Pension System: Background in Brief," www.crs.gov, R42449.

CHAPTER 11

The Ultimate Solution

I am not entirely sure who I should be addressing this chapter to and who is supposed to address the problems I have outlined with solutions. I can see the problem and I can assess the extent of the needs, but public policy is a world unto itself. I am far more interested in making sure people (first and foremost my students) gain awareness of the situation and begin to understand the extreme importance of the problem. It is my belief that this issue will pervade almost every area of modern life in the next 40 years and will have great impact on careers, fortunes, and lives. If handled badly, there will be great conflict as there always seems to be when resource allocation comes down to haves and have-nots. Those who are losing power are the ones who currently have the power, both economic and militarily. Those who are positioned to benefit are many of the up-and-coming people of the world. I can expound on the circle of life, but that is little solace to the expected losers.

Initially, I wanted to call this book, *You Can't Build Your Walls High Enough,* because that is the overwhelming sentiment that screams at me for this problem. I am struck by the belief that hiding from the problem is impossible, no matter how high you think you can build your walls. This problem will affect us all. So the question remains, how do we solve it? I will state with great confidence that many will find my solution either naïve or unrealistic, but better to start by being logical and then make compromises for expediency as we go.

THE NATION, STATE, MUNICIPALITY, AND COMPANY

So here is 10-step action-oriented list of what I feel needs to happen at the country, state, county, municipal, private plan, and, perhaps, personal levels.

1. A realistic analysis of need must be generated based not on optimism, but objective estimates of population trends, economic growth, and

longevity. It is necessary to determine and dimension the pension funding gap that must be filled. Need is somewhat subjective and likely to get underestimated in difficult times, but if we are rational, we will use something close to 60 percent of current preretirement income as a guide.

2. Take stock of the assets dedicated and available to solve the problem and the realistic level of burden that the economy of your country can afford to bear (this must take into account current indebtedness). It is not altogether clear that the estimates by pension consultants like Towers Watson or Mercer are completely accurate (in fact, they differ so much in some places that they cannot both be accurate). Everyone needs to take an inventory of assets that are or can be dedicated to retirement funding of the Baby Boomers. Be sure to exclude the retirement assets of the next generations. This will give us a net gap between liability and assets.

3. Do an inventory of other, perhaps nonmonetary assets of value that the country owns. Be creative here. Think outside the box. The Federal Reserve and others have taken a stab at this for the United States, and it is certainly something every entity with pension obligations that greatly exceeds their pension assets needs to do. Oil and copper are not the only things of value and do not take into account what will be valued over the next 40 years. Drop the concerns about national patrimony; this is a temporal problem that must be solved. Holding your national breath for 40 years won't work.

4. Find a way to monetize what needs to be monetized to plug the hole and defease that obligation once and for all. If the United States has a GDP of $70 trillion and dedicated pension assets of $16.5 trillion (107 percent of GDP in 2012) and we use the rough estimate of 6.2× GDP that the Federal Reserve Bank makes of what the nation's net worth is likely to be (I'm not even sure that included intellectual capital), that means we have a block of unallocated assets of $83 trillion ($99T − $16T = $83T) from which to fill the gaps we have. With the national debt at $16T and the pension gap at $7.5 trillion, this still leaves a 3.5× coverage so it does not seem totally unmanageable. Nevertheless, you still must find a proper balance (scraping out as much corruption as possible) between sufficiency and generosity. These are the builders of your country and they deserve a long and healthy life and a decent retirement. They are, indeed, your parents.

5. Simultaneously, revamp your pension system so that this remains a temporal problem, and the next generation is not left short or with the same problem to solve for themselves. The plan of choice is clearly defined contribution, but we must find a solution for several aspects.

- There must be sufficient participant contribution. Mandatory contributions are not a breach of civil liberties; they are a necessity of a thoughtful and forward-looking society.
- There should be a mandatory employer contribution. Yes, this is a tax, but it will work itself out as "total compensation" and certainly be less offensive than more direct taxation of the wealthy.
- A sufficiency test should be done conservatively and regularly to ensure that the contribution levels get everyone to the right place at retirement.
- Something needs to be done about the self-directed nature of the plans. I imagine that 80 percent or so needs to be somewhat more mandatory in lifecycle funds that are professionally managed. Leave 20 percent for self-directed discretion and have the sufficiency testing clearly show how the 20 percent performs relative to the 80 percent. Perhaps this will allow the percentage of self-discretion to fluctuate so as not to penalize those who manage their money well.
- Create a requirement for benefit provisioning at the various stages of the retirement cycle. Allow some degree of discretion at these points, but make sure that the mechanics no longer leave a lump sum in the hands of retirees at the exact moment when they want benefits more than cash and when the benefits are actuarially the most expensive to acquire.

6. Gradually increase the retirement age to keep pace with longevity. This is as much for the benefit of retirees as it is for the system. Retirement is not a panacea or an end unto itself. Some occupations are tiring to the point of a full retirement being desirable. But many occupations these days are not so grueling that they could not be scaled back or lead to part-time similar employment with an outcome of a more fulfilling and financially viable retiree who has improved health prospects due to remaining active into older age. I do not know what the optimal ratio of work life to retirement life should be, but let's explore some simple math.

   If the biblical life span of "three-score 10" (70 years) was connected to a working life of 50 years (65 – 15) that represents a productivity quotient of 71.4 percent. If our life span has risen to 80 years now, and we do not get productive until age 25 and retire at 65 for a 40-year working life, that quotient has fallen to 50 percent. If we extended working life to just 70, that takes it up to 56.3 percent, which is still low, but justifiable under the circumstances. Thus, we must consider extending retirement ages such that if a person can live on less pension benefits (perhaps due to reduced expectations or perhaps other savings), he or she can retire earlier, but the financial equation otherwise obliges them to simply work longer in deference to a longer life.

7. Despite the many comments in this book about the negative impacts of declining population and the concomitant decline in growth, it would not be right to suggest that we need to reverse that trend. Let us not be fooled by the argument that India will be better able to fund its retirement needs with a larger working population (in absolute terms and relative to the retiree population) than China in 2050. This would be folly to suggest. National demographics should not be manipulated to address a temporal problem like the pension crisis. I would also say that while China's one-child policy may impact its pension funding risks, it may well have done much more to promote prosperity and drive a significant improvement in the economic growth of the country than it did to hurt. Furthermore, if we extend our perspective out to 2100, we might feel very differently about how population growth differences between China and India impact those countries' economic viability. The variables are simply too great to predict the outcome, and fewer mouths to feed at some point trumps more backs on which to carry retirees.

8. Coming down to the state or province level, many of the same things need to be done in terms of assessment of liabilities and assets (monetary and nonmonetary). The most advantageous thing states can do is to set their public policies (those that remain in their hands versus being federalized) to decide what sort of state they want to be. Depending on their natural resources and industrial base, they may remain an important productive center, organized to favor working populations and the infrastructure they need.

   On the other hand, if the state is more likely to prosper as a lifestyle state, which can reasonably expect more prosperity from attracting an aged retired population, the public policy needs are probably quite different. This goes to infrastructure and taxation as well as promoting the sort of retirement communities that will be in greatest demand. The good news is that work is increasingly able to be done from anywhere, so it is easier than ever to segregate lifestyle and urban productivity without necessarily segregating workers and retirees in a hard and fast manner.

9. Individual private entities have a slightly different challenge because, unlike public entities that are designed to last forever, it is unclear that companies can or should expect the same. For older "rust belt" companies with massive retiree rolls and defined benefit pension plans that outsize their productive business, the only solution is to freeze and eventually terminate these plans, and replace them with more flexible defined contribution plans. The old DB Plans are quite attractive to the money management and insurance industry, so that must be seized to the company's advantage and the managers must find ways to gradually improve the funding level (better, more aggressive returns, more

contributions, using liability-driven investing whenever possible) and gradually cauterize the gap and eventually defease the entire obligation through a formal termination. This is an expensive process, but we have shown how companies can play the market cycles to move in this direction.

10. As for the retirement "panacea" of defined contribution, we have already listed the things that need to be addressed to improve those plans. What we have not yet discussed is whether a defined contribution plan is the best method for funding individual retirement. I believe it came into being driven by the fears of sponsors about the obligations of the future that would haunt them under DB. It was assisted by the semblance of self-determination, which always seems like a good thing when we are young. This mechanism gave people without wealth the feeling that they had wealth to manage. But what people *really* want are benefits, as we have said.

    Without implying that there is a mandated solution for this need, I will suggest that there is a very fertile commercial opportunity staring us in the face here. Young people need optionality, and as they age, they want and need benefits, some of which are mutually exclusive from other benefits that may have been needed had the person gone down another life path. This clearly has the benefit of optimized compounding if benefits can be selected early enough (compounding compounded by actuarial attributes). This also smacks of the ability to offer benefits with a compound option feature that allows them to be offered more cheaply on a bundled basis because of the inverse correlation they enjoy. Maybe this is only viable on an individual-by-individual basis, but why not use the classic law of large numbers in the insurance world and design products that serve a broader population that can somehow be banded together. This is hardly novel, but it hasn't been applied to the DC world much.

YOU AS AN INDIVIDUAL

At the individual level, there are also very many suggestions and solutions. Here are six:

1. Let's start with the easiest from the book *The Millionaire Next Door* by Thomas Stanley: Keep your expense nut manageable. Lower needs and expectations mean a happier retiree, right? Well, I'm not sure that will work so well for my profligate Baby Boomer pals, who have been weaned on self-gratification.

2. The second lesson is to be the ant and save, save, save. Or maybe more accurately, save early and then manage well. That might actually be more manageable even for the "I want it now" generation, but the truth is that it's a great suggestion for Generation X and beyond, but does little for the Boomers at this stage.

3. Certainly a good idea is to stop fancying yourself a good money manager. The only thing worse is fancying yourself a good asset allocator or hedge fund selector. Either get professional money management at a reasonable price and let them have at it over the long haul, or just put it into index funds and let it stay there.

4. Think about lifecycle. Where are you and your spouse on the longevity curve? Should that affect your investment program? It probably should somewhat, but remember that life goes on and asset accumulation can also go on after retirement date. A good money manager can accommodate this if you have "the talk," otherwise just buy lifecycle funds and make sure you are realistic in picking the picture that truly resembles you; we don't all look like Bradley Cooper and Megan Fox at all stages of our lives. Make sure you look in the mirror and assess things realistically.

5. Think about location. Where you live and in what regime/exchange rate/tax jurisdiction/public policy locale you live will determine more and more about your prosperity than it probably should. Pay attention to the local pension situations. Is the state and municipal system badly underfunded? How about the key infrastructure groups like fire and police? This can impact not only quality of life outside your walls, but also the cost of how much tax you have to pay on your walls. People used to move to Florida and Arizona for the weather and the inheritance taxes. People moved to Costa Rica and Panama for the cost of living. We are graduating beyond all of that and the equation is simply getting more complex in determining what locale best suits your needs and your attitudes. Maybe you are an ex-patriot in the making, but maybe you just want a sensible state that has quietly prepared for the future and is populated by other ants and few grasshoppers.

6. Finally, since I believe that the pace of change in business no longer favors the large corporation and that entrepreneurialism is the way of the future, I believe that the most important things that young people can do are the following:
   - Educate yourself about the impact of the global pension crisis, and get smart enough not to get caught by surprise by the twists and turns it takes.
   - Understand the specific impact that the pension issue has on your company, your municipality, your state, and your country. Know

where you and your institutional and locational choices place you in the line of fire. Think about your future choices in the context of the pension funding issue because now you better understand how important it is, no matter how high your walls are.

- Think about the opportunities that arise for you and the companies, municipalities, states, and countries that you know in the context of this earth-shaking set of changes. The old expression that "troubled waters make for good fishing" is your guide. Think about who wins in the new order based on the gyrations of the pension crisis. There will certainly be winners and losers and whole new fortunes will be made on the back of solutions to the problems people face due to this crisis. The real estate, natural resource/commodity, and foreign exchange dislocations alone are enough to create viable investment themes and arbitrages for years to come. If you are a natural trader, get smarter about the pension dynamics and find angles on which to trade.

Next up, a recap and a look at what the family described at the beginning of the book looks like, now that we know what we know, and can prepare for the future.

CHAPTER 12

A Peaceful Night's Sleep

L et's review the state of affairs. There is a nightmarish scenario awaiting us just around the corner. The Baby Boom generation is just graduating into retirement at its leading edge (those who can afford to). The situation looks bleak in terms of how much money the world (especially the developed world) has set aside for the retirement of this bulge population in the demographic continuum. It looks worse for some countries than others with a key differentiator being both the amount already saved and the general demographic trends of how many retirees there are going to be in the next 40 years versus the working population in those countries. Unfortunately, these demographics hold two disadvantages:

1. The sheer number of retirees versus workers.
2. The one potential saving grace for the budgets of these economies would be economic growth, but that is likely to be significantly curtailed by declining population. The correlation between the two is unavoidable.

But wait; at least we now understand the issue and the underlying math. And the world has wised up since the postwar era when all these defined benefit plan promises were made. Between the creation of ERISA and similar protective legislation promulgated in the United States and around the world, we are fairly protected now (reducing the fraudulent and even non-prudent leakage has great value). We have spent a great deal of time promoting defined contribution plans as a logical replacement for defined benefit plans. As we have seen, we are already at 43 percent of all retirement assets in DC plans and that belies the marginal reality that the corpus of DB overwhelms gross allocation numbers, but marginal dollars contributed are far greater and likely in excess of 60 percent. If we can work on the reinvestment rate of DC plans, they, or some hybrid version of them that offers more benefit selection rather than pure dollar accumulation, can probably allow future generations to avoid this type of pension crisis.

But as we all know, the thing about a bright future is that it depends heavily on getting beyond the bleak near-term problems that face us. And those problems are vast and globally transformational. A social psychologist would see clear indicators of potential conflict on a grand survival scale, both among demographically weak but asset- and weapons-rich countries and demographically and natural resource strong but asset- and weapons-weak countries. The same dynamic exists between the generations. You remember the old parking story where the young woman in the compact sneaks into a parking space, while a slower and more patient old man gets left in the street? She says, "See what a young person with a small car can do?," whereupon the old man smashes into the compact and wryly says, "See what an old man with money can do?"

It's a bit easier to imagine the ways that countries might work their way through this dilemma than it is to imagine how intergenerational conflict gets resolved. They are both very primordial, and are both functions of the Privilege Gap that exists in the world on both dimensions

There was a wonderful editorial in *AARP The Magazine* recently called "The Magic of the Fountain of Youth." It is particularly poignant and topical when thinking about the Privilege Gap and our pension crisis. It tells the tale of the author's grandfather, who retired at 70 from an academic position and immediately took a job as a college custodian, "trading his cap and gown for a mop"[1] for the next 15 years. The author believes his grandfather found the fountain of youth some 500 years after Ponce de Leon stopped looking for it on the coast of Florida. "Each day, nearly 9,400 people in America turn 65. And we are one day closer to 2014, when the last of the 77.5 million boomers turn 50."[2] I wish this was the story of a Baby Boomer, but it's actually the story of someone from the Greatest Generation. Someone who grew up in the Great Depression and stood strong during the Great World War. Someone who earned every penny of a peaceful retirement, but instead felt it important to be of service. I hope other Boomers like me are reading these inspiring AARP stories and choosing something other than the back nine and the Carnival Cruise Line on which to spend their last years. As my Welsh friend, Michael, always tells me, "You're a long time dead, boyo."

On the global scene, the issues are monstrous and vexing. I can see no easy way out for many developed countries that have simply spent themselves into oblivion to recapture their prior glory. All empires fall, but to

---

[1] Jim Toedtman, "The Magic of the Fountain of Youth," *AARP The Magazine*, January/February 2013.
[2] Ibid.

see this happen over one generation is extraordinarily difficult. The pace of change brought on by technology and always-on instant multidimensional communications is probably to blame for this accelerated pace. It is that same technology that gives the new world leaders their edge. I believe that those countries most open to technology and unafraid of the information and knowledge economy will prevail. We are also seeing some vindication of open borders and the embracing melting pot attitude espoused by the United States for 200 years. Imagine the visible advantage of a positive immigration policy versus the detrimental outcome of xenophobia and protectionism.

The world may not turn completely upside down. The lifecycle of communism served to show us the real value of capitalism and the prosperity it provides modern populations. In a similar way, the global pension crisis may serve to remind us that being inclusive and providing opportunity to all is truly better for us all, as we increasingly lean on growing populations and the entire base of the pyramid to support the rest of the pyramid.

There are a whole host of things that smart pension managers can do to kick-save their pensions and shield their aging operations from the liabilities that have drowned industrial America. There are more financial tools in the shed than ever before. Managers can laser focus on profitable risks and create asymmetrical return constructs and can chase unconstrained alpha while getting virtually costless beta. So much work has been done on modern portfolio theory, postmodern portfolio theory, factor analysis, global macro investing, and quantitative high volume trading that a pension manager can seek unconstrained alpha with some reasonable degree of transparency and combine that with low cost beta. He or she even has people coming up with creative new synthetic funds that capture human nature fallibility arbitrage . . . or at least have 0.5 percent of it handed back to participants via synthetic mutual funds in their defined contribution accounts. By doing all this, he or she might stand some hope of chasing his or her underfunded tail fast enough to have his or her returns exceed his galloping liabilities. If not, he or she has all manner of flash-freezing options followed by pension risk transfer options that can now be monitored continuously to be sure that he or she can terminate and cauterize his or her wayward plan at the optimal cost point. Individuals have this option with far less ERISA baggage to constrict them by simply using their lump sums to buy annuities, so long as they are smart about buying them from financially stable providers.

I would like to think that this book has laid a foundation of thinking about how to assess counties and even states in looking at what they have to offer residents in the coming years. Needless to say, there is much more to consider about both fiscal soundness as well as overall social policies.

But I believe we make a strong case as to why pension funding status and policy is quite critical for the fiscal soundness and the likely quality of life (taxed as a worker or simply as a retired person). I am not sure it will be so easy to make these assessments as time goes by, since history shows us that long-term problems like pension funding have ways of getting seriously obfuscated either by accident or design. And given that the problems will be floating to the surface very soon, great efforts to keep them from predefining a country or state's future is a likely political imperative. Nonetheless, as always, the more vigilant will be the best informed and most able to avoid problems and perhaps seize opportunities.

WHAT OUR FAMILY LOOKS LIKE NOW

Now let's look at what this means for our "family" that we outlined from the beginning of the book, so that we can rest more easily as we close our eyes on our wonderful 96-year-long lives.

Linda

God bless each and every person who gets to 98. May the worst thing she needs to worry about be the payout on her video poker machine.

Barbara

As life moves on for Linda, Barbara might think seriously of moving up to southern Utah. Nevada shows pretty badly in terms of its pension and health-care funding situation, where Utah is much better. Gambling is becoming more ubiquitous, and the Nevada tax protocols may come under duress causing the retiree population to become a greater target on the theory that it is simply less mobile and somewhat service-intensive.

Dave and Sharon

Rest in peace.

Michael

I consider young municipal workers to be one of the most "at-risk" populations. As we go through this retirement cycle for the Baby Boomers, there will be a growing sense of outrage (warranted or not) by those not entitled to a public pension. This may or may not impact the Baby Boomers fiscally speaking, but it is highly likely to impact younger workers as they see their plans frozen and/or curtailed as a knee-jerk reaction to the problems being recognized with the severe underfunding and future worker/taxpayer dependency burdens. Michael needs to do several things right away. He needs to get his investment program balanced and with a long-term view that he does not feel compelled to tweak and market-time. He also needs to seriously consider taking the time and bearing the expense to retool his skill set to be sure it is tuned to the new higher-tech economy.

Beth

Beth's pension is a ward of the state and she needs to be realistic about what her likely payout from the PBGC is going to be. If she were a professional receivables manager, she might take the time to assess the PBGC's obligations and the timing thereof relative to her pension payouts. In a perfect world, she would find a mechanism to take a lump sum payout sooner rather than later to get out ahead of the underfunding problem that the PBGC is undoubtedly going to face.

Kim

Since Kim is the love of my life, she will, by definition, be fine. We will move to a single-story home where the sun shines every day and all dogs go to heaven.

Pete and Geoffrey

They do not realize it, but Pete and Geoffrey have it better than most. They have realized early in life that retirement is not the goal, but a long and productive life should be. They do not view retirement as a likely outcome for them given their situation of starting their savings regime late. Nonetheless, increasing their savings rate is appropriate given the likely length of their life spans—strangely enough, probably made even longer by the fact that they are staying productively engaged in work. Clearly, they should not rely on social security or other public pensions, but should provide for themselves. They may be surprised to find that a serious savings regimen, even started this late, can accumulate and provide sufficient retirement income at a point given the relatively shorter duration needed in retirement.

Nancy and Anthony

I feel very bad for Nancy and Anthony, not on fiscal grounds, but on lifestyle grounds. They are prudent and smart enough to be reasonably well prepared for retirement and seem to have thought carefully about where they want to retire. North Carolina is one of the best-prepared states in terms of pension and retiree health-care funding. They have both the service mentality and the skills (in this case estate planning) to lead a long and productive life. But I cannot help reminding myself of that old joke about the bad Chinese restaurant where the food is lousy, but at least the portions are large. Who wants to live a long and miserable life? My guess is that financial sufficiency would be considerably less if Nancy and Anthony separated, so maybe this is a fiscal issue after all, but if so, then Nancy and Anthony had better solve their relationship issues so that a long and comfortable retirement is a desirable outcome. As for the kids, no need to worry about Jesse, let Valene sort out her own issues, and allow good estate planning to fill in the gaps, but only after Nancy and Anthony's own needs are met.

Jesse and Sofia

I like their prospects most of all for several obvious reasons. Jesse is a determined and well-educated man who is positioned in an industry that will prosper endlessly as long as people have to eat. He seems ready for life's needs both in terms of retirement and children's education. My guess is that Sofia's family connections in Brazil will cause them to move to Brazil and continue their prosperity there. Hopefully having Sofia's sense of social consciousness will contribute in helping Brazil's natural economic and resource strengths get supplemented by a social policy that creates greater income equality for the benefit of all. Sofia's father may not have chosen the path she will likely choose to help this situation, but he would likely be very proud of the outcome since it will likely improve the family prospects and wealth in the long run.

I do not worry about their son, Thomas, because, with responsible parents like Jesse and Sofia, he will get a proper education and be more or less prepared for life. My admonition in my nightmare is for his pension, which will be needed in the back half of the twenty-first century. My real point of interest here is that, just like the younger son who watches and avoids the mistakes of his older brother, our younger generations will grow up more like our parents' generation (The Greatest Generation) who grew up seeing the ravages of hardship and war and made conscious decisions to avoid those pitfalls. This, combined with a smoothing of the demographic bulge, should actually make life easier for Thomas's generation to prepare for and enjoy a more normal retirement. Who knows where longevity will take those generations. Some suggest it continues to march onward toward even longer lives. Others are beginning to hint at a reversal. The point of light here is that pension planning, as much or more so than most things in life, is a function of awareness and planning. Thomas and his generation will be prepared.

Valene and Zack

This is unfortunately the likely status of many of the young professionals now working their way through school or early career. Hopefully, the United States will see the wisdom of mandatory defined contribution payments by both employers and employees, and Valene and Zack and their employers will be forced to suck it up in the short run to solve the problem of the future. We cannot leave our young people—the very people who will support our overburdened pension obligations in the not-to-distant future—out in the cold. I could lecture them about being more parsimonious and saving more diligently, but they are where they are, and it is far more likely that a mandatory system is needed.

CONCLUDING THOUGHTS

I am an optimist at heart. I do, indeed, have a 96-year-old mother who lives in Las Vegas. I have children and siblings who are better or worse prepared for retirement. That all probably makes me pretty normal. But the more I studied and read about the global pension situation, the more my eyes have opened to the array of concerns and ironies embedded in the pension dynamics of my Baby Boom generation. It is not as though no one was thinking about this problem 60 years ago. But obviously there were miscalculations about a number of things. Probably the biggest miscalculations were around longevity and the spread between the earnings rate on assets and the discount rate on liabilities. These mistakes might have been swept under the rug if we had continued to use the defined benefit plan as our primary mechanism rather than switching over to defined contribution, but only if employer contributions (or a replacement with mandatory employee contributions) had kept pace with the changes. For those public funds that simply ignored the numbers (something that is bound to happen when the exigencies of politics enter into the equation), there was never any hope in the pay-as-you-go approach because some actuary should have showed the politicians the demographic charts that explained that the math simply did not work and never did.

As I have explained, when I teach my pension course I start by saying that nothing will affect the students during their lives more than the pension crisis. Their career choices, their lifestyle choices, and their very prosperity are on the line. It is imperative that they understand pensions and the looming crisis and how it affects not just their world, but the world around them. *This is the message that matters to me most.* If I can improve awareness and give my students the ability to know where to look more closely at the world and get out ahead of these issues to both avoid problems and seize opportunities, I will be very happy.

I have struggled with how a man of great optimism can write a book with such a pessimistic outlook. But wait, this is not pessimistic. Yes, we have a temporal problem and yes, it is a big problem. But the problem does, indeed, go away and the future beyond that does, indeed, look bright given the lessons we can reasonably expect our younger generations to have acquired.

Works Cited

Altoro, Jill. "Moody's Predicts End of Pension Plans at Lockheed, Boeing, Northrop, Exelis." *Washington Business Journal Online*, August 8, 2012. www.bizjournals .com/washington/blog/fedbiz_daily/2012/08/moodys-predicts-termination-of .html?page=all.

"Appendix F: pp. 139–141." *FAS Financial Accounting Series—Statement of Financial Accounting Standards No. 158, Employers' Accounting for Defined Benefit Pension and Other Postretirement Plans: An Amendment of FASB Statements Nos. 87, 88, 106, and 132(R)*. Financial Accounting Standards Board, September 2006. www.fasb.org/cs/BlobServer?blobkey=id&blobwhere=1175820923452 &blobheader=application%2Fpdf&blobcol=urldata&blobtable=MungoBlobs.

Baars, Jan, Kelly, Leah, Kocourek, Petr, and van der Lende, Epco. "Liability Driven Investing Hedging Inflation and Interest Rate Risk." *Global Asset Management: Multi-Asset Solution Research Papers*. November 5, 2012. www.cfsgam.com. au/uploadedFiles/CFSGAM/PdfResearch/121116_MAS_Research_Paper_5_ Liability_Driven_Investing.pdf.

Barry, Jonathan, and Nick Davies. "Redefining Pension Risk Management in a Volatile Economy." Mercer CFO Research Services, December 15, 2011. www. mercer.com/pensionrisk.

Bosse, Paul, and Vanguard Investment Strategy Group. "The Paradigm Shift in Liability-Driven Investing." Vanguard, 2009. https://institutional.vanguard .com/iam/pdf/Paul_transcript.pdf.

Burr, Barry B. "Mixed Opinions on GM's Plan to Transfer $29 Billion to Prudential." *Pionline: Pensions & Investments*. Crain Communications, August 22, 2012. www.pionline.com/article/20120822/REG/120819895.

Case, Brad. "The Illiquidity Premium Myth." *Wealth Management*, Penton Media Incorporated, April 1, 2010. http://wealthmanagement.com/review-deletion/ illiquidity-premium-myth.

Chapman, Mary M. "Retirees Wrestle with Pension Buyout." *New York Times*, July 18, 2012.

———. "Retirees Wrestle with Pension Buyout from General Motors." *New York Times*, July 18, 2012. www.nytimes.com/2012/07/19/business/retirees-wrestle- with-pension-buyout-from-general-motors.html?pagewanted=all&_r=0.

Citigroup. "Institutional Investment in Hedge Funds: Evolving Investor Portfolio Construction Drives Product Convergence." Citi Prime Finance, June 2012. http://citibank.com/transactionservices3/homepage/demo/tutorials41/IIHF_ June2012/files/assets/downloads/publication.pdf.

Davidson, Adam. "The Great Divergence." *New York Times Magazine*, January 15, 2013. www.nytimes.com/2013/01/20/magazine/income-inequality.html?ref=magazine.

Deloitte. "Financial Reporting Considerations for Pension and Other Postretirement Benefits: Financial Reporting Alert 09-5." Deloitte: United States Audit and Enterprise Risk Services, November 6, 2009. www.deloitte.com/assets/ Dcom-UnitedStates/Local%20Assets/Documents/AERS/us_assur_Financial_ Reporting_Alert_09-5.pdf.

Donovan, Shaun. "Mission." U.S. Department of Housing and Urban Development, n.d. Accessed December 12, 2012. http://portal.hud.gov/hudportal/HUD?src=/ about/mission.

Erlanger, Steven. "Young, Educated and Jobless in France." *New York Times*, December 2, 2012. www.nytimes.com/2012/12/03/world/europe/young-and-educated-in-france-find-employment-elusive.html?pagewanted=all&_r=0.

Food and Agriculture Organization of the United Nations. "Global Population & Food Supply (1961–2051)." UN Statistics Division, n.d. N. pag. *FAO STAT Statistics Database UN Sources*. Accessed January 9, 2013. http://faostat.fao. org/site/609/DesktopDefault.aspx?PageID=609#ancor.

Garcia, Monique. "Illinois' Credit Rating Downgraded after Pension Reform Failure, Standard & Poor's Took Action after Special Session Failed to Produce Deal on Issue." *Chicago Tribune*, August 30, 2012.

Hedge Fund Capital Group. "Tenth Annual Alternative Investment Survey Investor Insights on the Changing Hedge Fund Landscape." Deutsche Bank: Global Prime Finance, February 2012.

"Hedge Fund Growth in AUM, Growth in Number of Funds." Hedge Fund Research Institute, 2012. www.hedgefundresearch.com/index.php?fuse =products&1360444365.

Henderson, Peter, and Tim Reid. "UPDATE 5-Near-Bankrupt San Bernardino Votes to Default on Debt." *Reuters U.S. Edition*, July 25, 2012. www.reuters.com/ article/2012/07/25/sanbernardino-bankruptcy-idUSL2E8IOBZZ20120725.

HFRI. "HFR Global Hedge Fund Industry Report Second Quarter 2012." Hedge Fund Research Institute, n.d. Accessed 2012. www.hedgefundresearch.com/ index.php?fuse=products&1360444365.

"How OBGC Operates." The Pension Benefit Guaranty Corporation—A U.S. Government Agency, n.d. Accessed January 2013. www.pbgc.gov/about/how-pbgc-operates.html.

"Invest—Public." Ned Davis Research, n.d. Accessed January 2013. www.ndr.com/ invest/public/publichome.action.

Johnson, Steve, and David Ricketts. "US Pension Funds Sue BlackRock." *Financial Times*, February 3, 2013.

LaBreque, Leon C. "GM Retiree Lump Sum Buyout Owner's Manual." *LJPR, LLC*, 2012. http://ljpr.com/files/GMLumpSumOfferWhitePaperLeonLaBrecque .pdf.

Lack, Simon. *The Hedge Fund Mirage: The Illusion of Big Money and Why It's Too Good to Be True*. Hoboken, NJ: John Wiley & Sons, 2012.

Leonhardt, David. "Old vs. Young." *New York Times Sunday Review*, June 22, 2012. www.nytimes.com/2012/06/24/opinion/sunday/the-generation-gap-is-back .html?_r=0.

Levine, David N., Lars C. Golumbic, and Groom Law Group. "Freezing Defined Benefit Plans: This Practice Note Provides a Basic Overview of the Implications of Freezing a Defined Benefit Plan and Explains Some of the Issues That Can Arise After the Plan Is Frozen." Groom Law Group, Practical Law Limited and Practical Law Company, 2010. www.groom.com/media/publication/733_ Freezing%20Defined%20Benefit%20Plans.pdf.

Lezzera, Craig, and Fei Mei Chan. "S&P Indices: Market Attributes Securities Lending, Third Quarter 2011." *S&P Indices*, 2011. http://us.spindices.com/ documents/commentary/MarketAttributes_SecuritiesLending_Q3_2011Final .pdf.

Macey, Scott J. "An Emerging Assessment of the Pension Protection Act (June 2009)." AON Consulting, June 2009. Accessed 2013. www.aon.com/attachments/ pension_protection_act.pdf.

Marche, Stephen. "War Against Youth." *Esquire*, March 26, 2012. www.esquire .com/features/young-people-in-the-recession-0412.

Mauldin, John. "Somewhere Over the Rainbow." *Mauldin Economics: It's Time to Get Real about Your Investments*, December 31, 2012. www.mauldineconomics .com/frontlinethoughts/somewhere-over-the-rainbow.

McKinsey & Company. "The Coming Shakeout in Defined Benefit Market: McKinsey & Co." McKinsey Pension Research, 2007.

Mercer. "Melbourne Mercer Global Pension Index." Melbourne Mercer Global Pension Index, Australian Centre for Financial Studies, October 2011. www .globalpensionindex.com/pdf/melbourne-mercer-global-pension-index- report-2011.pdf.

Miller, Holly. "Operational Risk #10: Reading the Fine Print—Know Thy Legal Entities." Stonehouse Consulting, October 18, 2010. http://articles .stonehouseconsulting.com/2010/10/18/operational-risk-10-reading-the- fine-print—know-thy-legal-entities/.

"The Next Crisis: The Sponging Boomers." *The Economist*, September-October, 2012.

Nili, Matthew. "Capital Efficiency Matters: Multi-Asset Client Solutions Group." Black- Rock, 2013. https://www2.blackrock.com/webcore/litService/search/getDocument .seam?contentId=1111134370&Source=SEARCH&Venue=PUB_INS.

"Old-Age Dependency Ratios." *The Economist*, May 7, 2009. Accessed January 2013. www.economist.com/node/13611235.

Olsen, Kevin. "Verizon Transfers $7.5 Billion to Prudential in Partial Pension Buyout." *Pionline: Pensions & Investments*. Crain Communications Incorporated, October 17, 2012. www.pionline.com/article/20121017/REG/121019896.

"PBGC's Deficit Is over $34 Billion and Growing." *Zero Hedge*, ABC Media, November 16, 2012. Figure 6: PBGC Surplus/Deficit History 2003–2012 ($Million); Figure 7: PBGC Funded Ratio History 2003–2012. www.zerohedge .com/news/2012-12-26/will-rising-union-activism-expose-zombified-us-pensions.

Pension Benefit Guarantee Corporation. "Pension Benefit Guarantee Corporation: Strategic Plan FY 2012–2016." Pension Benefit Guarantee Corporation: A U.S. Government Agency. PBGC, n.d. Accessed January 2013. www.pbgc.gov/ Documents/2012-2016strategicplan.pdf.

———. "Who We Are: Mission Statement." Pension Benefit Guarantee Corporation: A U.S. Government Agency. PBGC, n.d. Accessed January 2013. www.pbgc .gov/about/who-we-are.html.

———. "Plan Terminations—Standard Terminations and Distress Terminations." Pension Benefit Guaranty Corporation: A U.S. Government Agency. PGBC, n.d. Accessed February 2013. www.pbgc.gov/prac/terminations.html.

"Pension Protection Act of 2006, Public Law 109–280 — August 16, 2006." *PLAW*. Congressional Record: Weekly Compilation of Presidential Documents: Legislative History — H.R. 4, August 17, 2006. Accessed 2013. www.gpo.gov/fdsys/ pkg/PLAW-109publ280/pdf/PLAW-109publ280.pdf.

"PPA Establishes New Rules for Multiemployer Plans." *Towers Watson Insider*, October 2006. Accessed 2013. www.watsonwyatt.com/us/pubs/insider/ showarticle.asp?ArticleID=16628.

A Prime Finance Business Advisory Services Publication. "Institutional Investment in Hedge Funds: Evolving Investor Portfolio Construction Drives Product Convergence." *Citi Prime Finance*. Citigroup, June 2012. Web. 2013. <http://citibank .com/transactionservices3/homepage/demo/tutorials41/IIHF_June2012/files/ assets/downloads/publication.pdf>.

"Projected Old-Age Dependency Ratio." *Eurostat Europa*, Europop bcv, November 5, 2012. http://epp.eurostat.ec.europa.eu/tgm/table.do?tab=table&init=1&plug in=1&language=en&pcode=tsdde511.

Purcell, Patrick, Specialist in Social Legislation and Domestic Social Policy Division. "CRS Report for Congress—CRS-3 RL33703." *World at Work*, Congressional Research Service: The Library of Congress, October 2006. www.worldatwork .org/waw/adimLink?id=15322.

Rofman, Rafael, Eduardo Fajnzylber, and German Herrera. "Reforming the Pension Reforms: The Recent Initiatives and Actions on Pensions in Argentina and Chile." World Bank: Social Protection and Labor, May 2008. http://siteresources .worldbank.org/SOCIALPROTECTION/Resources/SP-Discussion-papers/ Pensions-DP/0831.pdf.

Rowley, Emma. *Telegraph*. Telegraph Media Group, July 6, 2012. http://telegraph .co.uk/finance/French-President.

Shelton, Alison M. "Chile's Pension System: Background in Brief." Congressional Research Service, March 28, 2012. https://www.hsdl.org/?view&did=707798.

"Social Security." *Wordpress.com*, n.d. Accessed January 9, 2012. http://reavel.files .wordpress.com/2008/08/social_security_card2.gif.

Soto, Mauricio. "Chilean Pension Reform: The Good, the Bad, and the In Between." Center for Retirement Research at Boston College. Trustees of Boston College, June 2005. Accessed 2013. http://crr.bc.edu/briefs/chilean-pension-reform-the-good-the-bad-and-the-in-between/.

Stein, Charles. "Hedge Funds Lag behind a Generic Stock/Bond Mix—Smart Money Chart." *Businessweek*, July 19, 2012. www.businessweek.com/articles/2012-07-19/hedge-funds-lag-behind-a-generic-stock-bond-mix.

"Summary of Statement No. 158, Employers' Accounting for Defined Benefit Pension and Other Postretirement Plans—an Amendment of FASB Statements No. 87, 88, 106, and 132(R)." *Financial Accounting Standards Board*, n.d. Accessed 2012. www.fasb.org/summary/stsum158.shtml.

Tankersley, Jim. "Generational Warfare: The Case against Parasitic Baby Boomers." *National Journal Group*, n.d.

Toedtman, Jim. "Magic of the Fountain of Youth: The Aging of America Has Implications for the Nation." *AARP* The Magazine, January/February 2013. www.aarp.org/health/brain-health/info-12-2012/aging-america.html.

U.S. Department of Transportation. "Moving Ahead for Progress in the 21st Century Act (MAP-21)." United States: Department of Transportation, Washington, DC: DOT, October 26, 2012. www.dot.gov/map21.

Valley Vista Enterprises. "Mutual Fund Categorization." *Your Complete Guide to Investing in Mutual Funds*. Mutual Fund Bullet Tour Page 10: Expanded Stock Mutual Fund Style Box; Expanded Bond Mutual Fund Style Box; International. Valley Vista Enterprises, n.d. Accessed January 9, 2012. www.investing-in-mutual-funds.com/bullettour22.html.

"Verizon Buys Group Annuity and Sheds $75 Billion in Pension Liabilities." *Business Insurance*, October 21, 2012. www.businessinsurance.com/article/20121021/NEWS03/310219970.

Ward, Karen. "The World in 2050: From the Top 30 to Top 100." HSBC Global Research, January 2012. www.hsbc.com.mx/1/PA_esf-ca-app-content/content/home/empresas/archivos/world_2050.pdf.

Yin, Liang, and Jessica Gao. "Global Pension Assets Study: Page 34." *Towers Watson*, January 2012. www.towerswatson.com/assets/pdf/6267/Global-Pensions-Asset-Study-2012.pdf.

———. "Global Pension Assets Study 2012." *Towers Watson*, January 2012. www.towerswatson.com/assets/pdf/6267/Global-Pensions-Asset-Study-2012.pdf.

Index